Christian Faith and The Power of Thinking

A Collection of Essays, Marking the 800ᵗʰ Anniversary of the Founding of the Order of Preachers in 1216

Jay Harrington, O.P., Editor

NEW PRIORY PRESS
EXPLORING THE DOMINICAN VISION

Published by New Priory Press
1910 S. Ashland Avenue
Chicago, IL 60608
To order, call 312-243-0011
or visit us online at www.newpriorypress.com

Pre-print Editor: Albert Judy, O.P.
Production Editor: Terry L. Jarbe

Copyright © 2017 by the Dominican Province of St. Albert the Great (U.S.A.). All rights reserved. No part of this publication may be reproduced, stored in a retrieval system, or transmitted in any form or by any means—electronic, mechanical, photocopy, recording, or any other—except for brief quotations in printed reviews, without the prior written permission of the publisher.

Printed in the United States of America
Second edition. October 2017. The content of this anthology remains the same. Fonts and spacing have been adjusted for improved readability.

CONTRIBUTORS

Jay Harrington, O.P., Editor
    Foreword xi

Thomas F. O'Meara, O.P.
    "'The Astonishing Wonder.' Albert the Great (1200-1280). Scientist, Theologian, and Politician" 1

Richard Woods, O.P.,
    "Meister Eckhart and the Rhineland Mystics" 15

Jay Harrington, O.P.,
    "Augustine of Dacia, O.P., (+1285) and the Fourfold Sense of Scripture. The Bible in the Thirteenth Century" 39

Paul Philibert, O.P.,
    "Chenu's Vision of the Gospel and Church Institutions"75

Mark Wedig, O.P.,
    "Engaging Modernity through Art: The Dominicans and *L'Art Sacré*" 95

Charles Dahm, O.P.,
    "Conflicts and Ministries: The Dominicans in Bolivia in Recent Times" 113

Scott Steinkerchner, O.P.,
    "Channeling the Divine" 145

Benedict Thomas Viviano, O.P.,
"Democracy in the Bible and in the Dominican Order" 171

James V. Marchionda, O.P.,
"The Power of Preaching Through Music" 187

Contents

Foreword xi

"The Astonishing Wonder." Albert the Great (1200-1280) Scientist, Theologian, and Politician
    Thomas F. O'Meara, O.P. 1
      1. New Research.. 1
      2. Albert of Lauingen 3
      3. "Albert The Great," "Doctor Universalis," "Astonishing Wonder." 5
      4. Albert in Politics 8
      5. Bishop of Regensburg 10
      6. Albertus Magnus Today 12

Meister Eckhart and the Rhineland Mystics
    Richard Woods, O.P.. 15
      1. Eckhart of Hochheim: Prince of Mystics 17
      2. Dominican Influences: Albert and Thomas 20
      3. Eckhart and the Rhineland Mystics 22
      4. The Preacher 25
      5. Dominican Women Mystics in the Rhineland...........................27
      6. Elsbet Stagel, Margaret Ebner, and Their Sisters.......................29
      7. The Friends of God 30
      8. Later Influence 33
      9. The Inheritance..35
      10. Bibliography...35

Augustine of Dacia, O.P. (+1285) and the Fourfold Sense of Sacred Scripture. The Bible in the Thirteenth Century
    Jay Harrington, O.P.. 39
      1. Introduction 39
          Map of Dacia© Johnny Grandjean Gøgsig Jakobsen42

2. Augustine of Dacia: Dominican, Provincial, Excommunicate,
   Teacher 42
3. Augustine's *Rotulus pugillaris* 45
4. Study in the Priories of the Order 49
5. Augustine of Dacia and Albert the Great 53
6. The Reception of Augustine's Distich by Exegetes
   in the 20th Century 55
   a. The Catechism of the Catholic Church 55
   b. Joseph Ratzinger, Pope Benedict XVI 56
   c. Joseph Fitzmyer, S.J. and Peter Williamson 57
   d. Carolyn Osiek, RSCJ 59
   e. Further References to Augustine of Dacia's Distich 60
7. Conclusion 64
8. Bibliography 64

Chenu's Vision of the Gospel and Church Institutions
Paul Philibert, O.P. 75
1. Background and Influences 76
2. The Roman Crisis and Its Aftermath 81
3. Key Structures in Chenu's Thinking 86
   a. Dialectic between the Transcendent and the Provisional 86
   b. The Primacy of the Word of God 88
   c. Attending to the Signs of the Times 91
4. New, Successive Christendoms 93

Engaging Modernity Through Art: The Dominicans and *L'Art Sacré*
Mark E. Wedig, O.P. 95
1. Pie-Raymond Régamey (1900–1996) and Marie-Alain
   Couturier (1897-1954) 96
2. The Aesthetic Enemy: Kitsch 97
3. World War II and Couturier's Expatriate Resistance 98
4. The Dominicans in Paris after World War II 100

5. "Parier pour le genie:" Couturier's Inspiration for
   New Church Forms 102
6. The New Patronage: Plateau d'Assy; Vence, and Audincourt 104
   a. Assy 105
   b. Vence 106
   c. Audincourt 108
7. Posthumous Projects: Ronchamp and L'Arbresle 109
   a. Ronchamp 110
   b. La Tourette 111
8. Conclusion 111

Dominican Initiatives in Bolivia: 1956 to 1973
Charles W. Dahm, O.P. 113
1. The Reality of Bolivia in the Mid-Twentieth Century 113
2. Italian, German, and North American Dominicans in Bolivia
   in the 1950s 114
3. Conceptual and Pastoral Change in Latin America 116
4. A Dominican Pastoral Vision 118
5. Growth and crisis 121
6. Schools and Ministries 122
   a. Seminaries 122
   b. University Apostolates 124
   c. Ministry in the Catholic Normal School 128
   d. High School Apostolate 129
7. Instituto Boliviano de Estudio y Acción Social (IBEAS) 130
   a. The Rise of IBEAS 131
   b. The Decline and Fall of IBEAS 134
8. Change of Direction: Dominicans Initiate the
   Charismatic Movement 137
9. Further Ministries in the 1970s 140
Conclusion 142

Channeling the Divine: A Comparative Exploration of How Infinite Power Can Work Through Finite Human Persons within the Thought of Meister Eckhart, Tsongkhapa and Dolpopa
    Scott Steinkerchner, O.P. 145
        1. Introduction 145
        2. Method 146
        3. Tathagatagarbha: the Buddha Within 148
        4. Tsongkhapa's Rang-Stong View 149
        5. Dolpopa's Gzhan-Stong View 155
        6. Meister Eckhart in Comparison 159
        7. Conclusions 168
        8. Postscript: Questions for Buddhism 169
        9. Works Cited 170

Democracy in the Bible and in the Dominican Order
    Benedict Thomas Viviano, O.P. 171
        1. Some definitions and prerequisites of democracy. 171
        2. The Hebrew Bible. 172
        3. Athenian Democracy 175
        4. Paul 177
        5. Matthew. 178
        6. Luke-Acts. 179
        7. The Contribution of the Dominican Constitutions
            and Thomistic Theology 180
    Conclusion. 185

The Power of Preaching Through Music
    James V. Marchionda, OP 187
        1. Music in Support of Preaching 188
        2. Music Sometimes Saves Preaching 189
        3. Music to the Rescue 190
        4. Music Within the Homily 191
        5. Conclusion: Sermon and Song 192

Contents

Contributors 193

Acronyms and Abbreviations 196

Indexes 197

CHRISTIAN FAITH AND THE POWER OF THINKING

Foreword

The 800th anniversary of the foundation of the Order of Preachers (Dominicans) in 1216 helps us to realize there is much for which to be grateful and offers us the opportunity to look back in pride and to look forward in hope. The mystic Meister Eckhart said, "If the only prayer you ever pray is thank you, that would be enough." Each religious Order and congregation has some gift, some charism to offer to the Church. St. Dominic had a vision, a dream of a community focused on the sacred preaching. His vision was realized in part with preachers and confessors, mystics and scholars, missionaries and scientists, artists and saints. These essays by Dominican friars of the Central Province of St. Albert the Great and the Southern Province of St. Martin de Porres, who collaborate in the ministry of initial religious formation, give evidence of Dominic's wisdom that in order to be effective preachers, the Dominicans must also avail themselves of assiduous study as an essential element of the spirituality of the Order. St. Dominic insisted that "before all else, our study should aim principally and ardently at this that we might be able to be useful to the souls of our neighbors" (Primitive Constitutions, *Prologue*). And so our goal is to be helpful to our neighbors. It is the occasion of the 800th anniversary of the founding of the Order of Preachers which unifies the book, rather than any particular themes.

"Christianity is an intellectually demanding teaching. It makes you think. It pushes you beyond easy answers! Vincent McNabb used to say to the novices in the 1920s, 'Think! Think of anything, but for God's sake, think.'"[1] Inspired by the Spirit of the Risen Christ, St.

---

[1] T. Radcliffe, O.P., "Preaching: Conversation in Friendship", in M.E. Connors (ed.), *To All the World. Preaching and the New Evangelization*, Collegeville, MN: Liturgical Press, 2016, p. 4.

Dominic forged a new path of preaching and evangelization rooted in Christian faith, energized by the power of thinking, and anchored by assiduous and continual study. The study by the members of the Order has been characterized as evidence of "vast industry, varied learning, profound study and tireless research." [2] The essays in this volume witness to this characterization.

St. Albert, while he was alive, was given the title of "the Great." Who is this *doctor universalis*, this person whom the Middle Ages and centuries afterwards called "the Great," and should we be at all interested in him 750 years later? The article of Thomas F. O'Meara, O.P., *"The Astonishing Wonder." Albert the Great (1200-1280), Scientist, Theologian, and Politician*, describes and draws from the expansive research and publication on Albert that has appeared in the past thirty years, not only from the Albertus-Magnus-Institut in Bonn but from the work of many German scholars. These sources permit a look at Albert's broad and influential perspective behind all his writings, a thought-form linked to his role in advocating Aristotle's thinking. Aspects of his theology and some Christian topics he treated that are still challenging in theology are presented as well as his relationship to the politics of the times.

Guided by the genius of St. Albert the Great and drawing on the teachings of St. Thomas Aquinas, especially their rediscovery of the mystical works of Pseudo-Dionysius ("the Areopagite"), Eckhart of Hochheim became the most prominent mystical preacher and writer of the late 13th and early 14th centuries. Despite the condemnation of some of Eckhart's teachings, his disciples, the "Friends of God," preserved his memory and his teachings which have grown in importance and influence over the centuries. Richard Woods, O.P., *Meister*

---

[2] Very Rev. J.B. O'Connor, O.P. P.G., *Saint Dominic and the Order of Preachers*, New York: Holy Name Bureau, 1922 (Fourth Edition).

Eckhart and the Rhineland Mystics, explores Eckhart's spiritual and theological legacy within his historical context.

The interpretation of the Bible in the Church has been guided by various principles, methods, and approaches through the ages. Jay Harrington, O.P., *Augustine of Dacia, O.P. (+1285) and the Fourfold Sense of Scripture. The Bible in the Thirteenth Century*, focuses on the fourfold sense of Scripture which grew out of a twofold sense involving the literal and the spiritual, the latter being further delineated as the allegorical, moral or tropological, and anagogical, sometimes also referred to as the mystical, which is concerned with the life to come. The little known Dominican, Augustine of Dacia (or of Denmark), writing in the 13th Century, is considered the author of a distich which succinctly yet eloquently expressed the four senses of Sacred Scripture in a manner which made them easy to remember. Though oft-quoted, some scholars now critique the expression and question the enduring value of the couplet.

The late Paul Philibert, O.P. originally published *Chenu's Vision of the Gospel and Church Institutions* in a volume of the journal, *Cristianesimo nella storia*, which "focuses on the question of how true reform in the church is a work of building human solidarity, translating the Gospel into new life in emerging situations, and extending the ferment of grace into the fabric of culture." Marie-Dominique Chenu, O.P., arguably the most important ecclesiologist of modern times, and who was concerned about true reform, was a key figure in the renewal brought about by Vatican II. Though he was not an official expert (*peritus*) at the Council, he initially guided the bishops of Madagascar, then the larger body of bishops of Africa, and also the Latin American bishops. In addition, he helped Yves Congar, O.P., and other theological experts with research and writing. Three themes undergird his theological, historical, and pastoral vision: 1) the Dialectic between the Transcendental and the Provisional, 2) the

Primacy of the Word of God, and 3) Attending to the Signs of the Times. This vision enabled Chenu to "speak of his 'hope for a new Christendom' that will embody evangelical awakening, give primacy to the word of God, revive a missionary spirit, and show privileged concern for the poor."

By the early 1930's, a group of Catholic avant-gardes consciously moved away from the solutions of Catholic restoration in order to respond more openly to the culture of modernity. Artistic and architectural revival styles were rejected as overly romantic solutions to the modern world. Instead, the projects of a small but influential association of aesthetic reformers attempted to awaken the church to a completely new genre for church-building and image. Mark Wedig, O.P., *Engaging Modernity through Art: The Dominicans and L'Art Sacré*, traces the development brought about by the Dominicans Pie-Raymond Régamey and Marie-Alain Couturier in France with their journal *L'Art Sacré* that played a major role in this movement. The journal and the projects of the two Dominican friars were aligned with the larger social, political, ecclesial, and liturgical agenda of the Paris province of the Dominicans especially at the publishing house, *Les Éditions du Cerf.*

In *Dominican Initiatives in Bolivia*, Charles Dahm, O.P., describes the creative ministry developed by Dominicans from St. Albert the Great Province, U.S.A. in the late 1950s and 1960s in Bolivia. The Dominicans implemented the vision of Catholic Action as they responded to the unique realities of Bolivia and the directives of the Second Vatican Council. This progressive effort dissolved when many Dominicans in Bolivia embraced the Charismatic Renewal.

Scott Steinkerchner, O.P., *Channeling the Divine. A Comparative Exploration of How Infinite Power Can Work Though Finite Human Persons within the Thought of Meister Eckhart, Tsongkhapa and Dolpopa*, analyzes the medieval Dominican mystical theologian

Meister Eckhart's view that we are best fit for the Dominican work of "attaining our own salvation and the salvation of others" by being transformed through a wordless, imageless meditation of brilliant silence so that Christ might be reborn in us in a new and more powerful way. The analysis is pursued through a comparative reading with the medieval Tibetan Buddhist scholar Dolpopa Sherab Gyaltsen who taught how the power of the buddha-nature at core of every sentient being could be freed to act for attaining our own enlightenment and the enlightenment of others.

The essay of Benedict Viviano, O.P., *Democracy in the Bible and in the Dominican Order*, is an effort to develop a theology of democracy, based on the Bible and the resources of the Dominican Constitutions and Thomistic theology. The Hebrew Bible and Athenian democracy, Paul, Matthew, and Luke-Acts are briefly treated, and the influence of the Dominican Constitutions on other religious orders, the British parliament, and later political developments, especially Christian democracy in Europe, are also sketched.

James V. Marchionda, O.P., *The Power of Preaching through Music*, maintains that within music lies the potential to bring the message and meaning of God's Word directly to the hearts and souls of the faithful. Sacred Music is a powerful tool for preaching. Carried on the wings of a melody, a preacher's message can be recalled over and over again, long after the preaching event itself.

This volume is offered as a gift to the Order of Preachers, the Dominican family, and other interested readers as we celebrate and commemorate those who have gone before us, those who currently preach and serve, and those who will follow in the footsteps of St. Dominic. May he help us now with his prayers as he once inspired people with his preaching. The following is the Jubilee Prayer prayed by Dominicans throughout the world during this 800th anniversary year:

> God, Father of mercy,
> who called your servant Dominic de Guzman
> to set out in faith
> as an itinerant pilgrim and a preacher of grace,
> as we celebrate the Jubilee of the Order
> we ask you to pour again into us
> the Spirit of the Risen Christ,
> that we might faithfully and joyfully proclaim
> the Gospel of peace,
> through the same Christ our Lord. Amen.

Jay Harrington, O.P.
November 15, 2016
Feast of St. Albert the Great

"The Astonishing Wonder"
Albert the Great (1200-1280)
Scientist, Theologian, and Politician

Thomas F. O'Meara, O.P.

Albert the Great – or, to refer to him in an ordinary way, "Albert of Lauingen" – was already while he was alive given the title of "the Great."[1] One of his prominent students, Ulrich of Strassburg, wrote of him: "My teacher, Albert...was in every science an almost divine person, so much so that he can be described as the astonishing wonder of our time."[2] Dante, fifty years after Albert's death, introduced him in the *Divine Comedy* to give a poetical oration in the *"Paradiso."*[3] In Mary Shelley's *Frankenstein,* the subject of so many movies, Albert is listed as one of Baron Victor Frankenstein's preferred authors.

Who is this *doctor universalis*, this person whom the Middle Ages and centuries afterwards called "the Great"? And should we be at all interested in him 750 years later?

1. New Research

The expansive research and publication on Albert that has appeared in the past thirty years is unprecedented, and we know more

---

[1] Ingrid Craemer-Ruegenberg, *Albertus Magnus* [revised by Henryk Anzulewicz](Leipzig: Benno, 2005) 14. "He referred to himself as *Albertus de Lauing* in an early document, and later he was called *Albertus Coloniensis*" (Albertus-Magnus-Institut, "Einleitung," *Albertus Magnus und sein System der Wissenschaften* [Münster: Aschendorff, 2011] 9).

[2] Cited in Joachim R. Söder, "Albertus der Große. Ein Staunener-regendes Wunder," *Albertus Magnus (1200-2000), Wort und Antwort* 41 (2000): 145; see James Athanasius Weisheipl, O.P., "Albertus Magnus," Joseph Strayer, ed., *Dictionary of the Middle Ages* 1 (New York: Scribner, 1982) 129; Henryk Anzulewicz, "Albertus Magnus," Sebastian Cüppers, ed., *Kölner Theologen von Rupert von Deutz bis Wilhelm Nyssen* (Cologne: Marzellen, 2005) 30-68.

[3] Dante Alighieri, *The Divine Comedy*, Paradiso (New York: Bantam, 1989) canto X, 94-99.

than previous generations. The Albertus-Magnus-Institut in Bonn, sponsored by the Archdiocese of Cologne, has been editing for some years a critical text of Albert's writings – Alberti Magni, *Opera Omnia* (Editio Coloniensis) – of which thirty-one volumes out of a planned forty-one have appeared. Beyond work on the critical text, the Institute hosts visiting scholars and symposia. It aids the production of books and dissertations, sponsoring two series of monographs, and offers much on its websites.[4] The Director of the Institute, Henryk Anzulewicz, has written at least thirty articles on Albert.[5]

In the United States, Irven M. Resnick and Kenneth F. Kitchell, Jr. have published *Albert the Great: A Selectively Annotated Bibliography (1900 – 2000)*. This work has 2576 entries and an index of names and subjects occupying thirty pages. Books and articles are gathered into nineteen sections, ranging from "Albert's Life and Works" and "Iconography and Albert in Art" to "Theology – General" and "Albertism."[6] Resnick went on to edit the eight-hundred-page *Compendium to Albert the Great. Theology, Philosophy, and the Sciences*.[7] Recently, Prof Resnick established *The International Albertus Magnus Society*: it sponsors events, largely at the medieval

---

[4] www.albertus-magnus-institut.de; see Ludger Honnefelder, Mechthild Dreyer, *Albertus Magnus und die Editio Coloniensis, Lectio Albertina #1* (Münster: Aschendorff, 1999) and Bernd Göring, "Zur Überlieferung der Werke Alberts des Grossen – von der Handschrift bis zur modernen Überlieferung," *Wort und Antwort* 41 (2000): 186-89. One finds electronic resources under "Albert the Great – Links" or "Albertus-Magnus-Institut Bonn" and also in Irven M. Resnick & Kenneth F. Kitchell, Jr., "Introduction," *Albert the Great: A Selectively Annotated Bibliography (1900 – 2000)*, Tempe: *Arizona Center for Medieval and Renaissance Studies, 2004*, xi.

[5] For a selection of essays from publications in the last 20 years see Thomas O'Meara, ed., *Albert the Great. Theologian and Scientist. Bibliographic resources and translated essays* (Chicago: New Priory Press, 2013).

[6] (Tempe: Arizona Center for Medieval and Renaissance Studies, 2004).

[7] (Leiden: Brill, 2013).

conference at Kalamazoo, Michigan, while online it shares information and contacts among those interested in Albert.

2. Albert of Lauingen

Albert was born at the turn of the century, 1200, in Lauingen.[8] There, in southern German lands like Swabia, the Danube is beginning its long journey to the Black Sea. His early education likely took place in a monastic school, and he went south over the Alps to the University of Padua around 1221 (in Padua he had an uncle active in the Emperor's service). He entered the Preaching Friars there in 1223 – seven years after the Dominicans' foundation in 1216 and two years after Dominic's death. The Order of Preachers brings a new form of religious life: they are mobile, financially dependent on ministries and fundraising, and they work in the new worlds of the urban mercantile class and the university through preaching, teaching, and administering the sacrament of penance. Albert lived in a time of cultural change, of relative peace and commercial affluence, and of the exchange of ideas from South to North, from Muslim to Christian. Particularly important were the changes in education as the new universities expanded: more and more young men were drawn into their faculties, and the influence of knowledge, ideas, and skills spread into wider circles of an urban society.[9]

---

[8] Lauingen in the second half of the Twelfth Century became an urban dwelling with a wall...Albert belongs to a family involved with the military or, more likely, with the administrators of the nobility's estates" (Henryk Anzulewicz, "Albertus Magnus," S. Cüpers, ed., *Kölner Theologen* 31).

[9] Craemer-Anzulewicz, "Die geistegeschichtliche Situation in Europa des 13 Jahrhunderts," *Albertus Magnus* 24-35; see Ludger Honnefelder, *Albertus Magnus und die kulturelle Wende im 13. Jahrhundert - Perspektiven auf die epochale Bedeutung des großen Philosophen und Theologen* (Münster: Aschendorff, 2012).

After a novitiate and four or more years of basic studies in Cologne, Albert taught after 1233 in Hildesheim, Freiburg im Breisgau, Regensburg, and Strassburg in their Dominican priories. Then, he was sent to Paris for university studies in theology, became a *Magister Theologiae*, and was selected in 1245 to be a professor. By that time, at the University of Paris, Albert had developed his powers of research, memory, and synthesis. He had become an enthusiast for Aristotle and gained attention as a teacher. He became the first Master, that is, the first full professor or chair holder, of German origin, at one of the European universities.

At the end of 1245, Thomas Aquinas arrived in Paris as a Dominican novice and attended Albert's lectures.[10] A few years later, in 1248, the professor was sent to Cologne to expand the Dominican studium there, and the young Aquinas accompanied him to the Rhine. At Cologne, he helped to found the first University in Germanic and Slavic lands. Albert, and presumably Thomas were present at the laying of the cornerstone for the monumental Cologne cathedral.

Albert's mature years were busy and demanding. He traveled across Europe searching out new manuscripts in abbey libraries. He was a teacher with gifted students: the systematic personality of Thomas Aquinas and probably the mystical speculation of Meister Eckhart.[11] From 1254 to 1257, he was Provincial of the German Dominican Province. Then, he was bishop of Regensburg. After 1262, his life involved trips, papal missions, urban mediations, episcopal consecrations, and theological conferences. In 1277, when Bishop

---

[10] Jean-Pierre Torrell, "Disciple of Albertus Magnus (1245-1252)," *Saint Thomas Aquinas. Vol. I, The Person and His Work* (Washington, D.C., Catholic University of America Press, 1996) 18-35; for Albert's life see Albertus-Magnus-Institut, "Einleitung," *Albertus Magnus und sein System* 9-27.

[11] On Albert and Eckhart see Kurt Flasch, *Meister Eckhart. Die Geburt der "Deutschen Mystik" aus dem Geist der arabischen Philosophie* (Munich: Beck, 2006).

Étienne Tempier condemns certain positions in the writings of Thomas Aquinas, largely Aristotelian philosophy, Albert saw himself attacked along with his now dead student. Whether Albert at seventy-seven went to Paris to confront the Bishop is unclear – and unlikely. He died three years later on November 15th, 1280.

He is an extraordinary personality in a society that is changing dramatically.

3. "Albert The Great," "Doctor Universalis," "Astonishing Wonder."

Albert, some estimate, wrote 150 works. He wrote commentaries on books of the Bible (the Major and Minor Prophets, the four Gospels) and composed several theological *summae*, systems of Christian teaching around some pattern. He wrote commentaries on Greek philosophical works and essays on specific biological and botanical fields. His teaching and writings were a pioneering force in changing how Europeans thought. In France and Germany, Albert became the source of new ideas. He drew his many sources into a new systematic perspective arranging all that could be known – a kind of unified field theory being sought in the past century and now. Jens Peter Meincke sums up: "He was an inwardly independent man, serious in his ideas and his activity, an outstanding observer and a keen thinker. He worked towards laying a foundation for reality; he thought both in terms of what had been done and what should be done for today; he separated what lay hidden in dense areas and brought together disparate views."[12]

The majority of his writings and pages belong to philosophy; although, what we call "philosophy," he sees as basic scientific presentations of the structure of reality, the power of knowing, ethical

---

[12] Meincke, "Grüßwort," *Albert der Grosse in Köln*, (Cologne: Universität zu Published Köln: [Universität zu Köln], 1999. Köln, 1999) 5f.

activity, psychology, and the natural sciences. He was a pioneer of Aristotelian realism, a way of analyzing all of reality and each individual reality, a new framework for metaphysics, ethics, zoology, astrophysics. That realism could fashion for all fields ranging from botany to the Christian liturgy.[13] He wrote around forty commentaries on Aristotelian and other Greek works. "Aristotle" in the Thirteenth Century meant science and scientific method although later it becomes "philosophy." The Dominican wrote: "Our goal is to make all the parts (the various works) of Aristotle intelligible to the Latins (Westerners)."[14] A further remark from Albert shows his struggle and his personality: "Some, even Friars Preachers, criticize this philosophy. They are blaspheming, like dumb animals, something of which they have no real knowledge."[15]

Albert sought out new sources, not only from Aristotle and the neo-Platonists but from Avicenna, Augustine, Pseudo-Denys, and Rabbi Mosheh ben Maimon, who had died fifty years before.[16] Alain de Libera writes: "His knowledge is impressive: none of the Greek, Arab, and Hebrew sources translated in the Twelfth Century escape

---

[13] His work *De vegetalibus* described 350 kinds of plants and was influential for centuries (*Albertus Magnus, der grosse Neugieriger* [Regensburg: Stadt Regensburg, 2002] 46f.).

[14] Albert, *Physica* I, tract. 1, c. 4, Editio Coloniensis, IV, Pars 1, 1.

[15] Cited in Yves Congar, "*In dulcedine societatis quaerere veritatem*. Notes sur le travail en équipe chez s. Albert et chez les Prêcheurs au XIIIe siècle," C. Meyer, ed., *Albertus Magnus Doctor Universalis 1280/1980* (Mainz, 1980) 56. "Albert is the first and the only scholar of the Latin Middle Ages who from the writings of Aristotle...fashions a constructive dialogue with this philosophy *in toto* and adapts them into a system of the sciences" (Albertus-Magnus-Institut, "Einleitung," *Albertus Magnus und sein System...* 17).

[16] On Avicenna and Albert, De Libera, "Albert le Grand, 1200-1280," 26-69; on Aquinas and Jewish thinkers, Caterina Rigo, "Zur Rezeption des Moses Maimonides im Werk des Albertus Magnus," Walter Senner, ed., *Albertus Magnus...*, 29; see Elias Füllenbach, "Der frühe Dominikanerorden und die Jüden," *Dominikaner und Juden. Personen, Konflikte und Perspektiven vom 13. bis 20 Jahrhundert* (Berlin: De Gruyter, 2015) 275-79.

his study. In medicine he drew not only from writings by Aristotle and his commentators but from the texts of classic physicians like Galen, Hippocrates, and Constantinus Africanus.[17]

Drawing intellectual sources and principles into a living synthesis, he worked much like the master architect composing a medieval cathedral out of architectural and theological forms set in media ranging from ceramics to glass. Henryk Anzulewicz calls him "the thinker of totality." "His thinking wants to grasp all the reality of being and also to reach individual objects. Not only is the breadth of his broadly pursued research important but a totality-in-unity as the perspective of things."[18] He draws primal beginnings "through the process of self-realization with all the conditions of created contingency, on to ultimate goals. Through all of this runs the dynamic of life."[19] These writings of broad synthesis reaching through philosophy and science do not counter or replace revelation and religion. They provide a new context and realization for them. Albert sees God to be an artist creating things out of rich beginnings and for a complete goal.[20] His treatise *De bono* takes a theology of creation into moral theology; it opposes every dualism, drawing on a variety of sources joins moral life to creation and a salvation history for all humanity.

Today's experts observe the importance of Albert looking at the universe from its origins to its eschatology. No "creationism" and no "apocalyptic" final violence are present. The universe stands on its own. Albert researches natural things without expecting to find any

---

[17] Craemer-Ruegenberg 143.

[18] Anzulewicz, "Albertus Magnus – Der Denker des Ganzen," *Wort und Antwort* 41 (2000) 149.

[19] Anzulewicz, "Albertus Magnus – Der Denker des Ganzen," 150.

[20] Albert, *De causis et processu universitatis a prima causa*, Editio Coloniensis XVII, Pars 2 24f.

miraculous activities of an interfering God, and in the natural process of natural things there is no moralism or symbolism. He treats the goal and inner depth of the human person as happiness, and to reach that happiness God gives human beings a terrestrial life and one in the next life coming from his special presence. Human life and future happiness are the destiny of men and women.[21] Joachim Söder writes: "Albert's plan can be grasped as a monumental synthesis considering all things in light of the varied revelations of God: a revelation manifest in Scripture and incarnation and also in creation."[22] He was a synthetic thinker, and that was why he was called "Great."

The place in the Thirteenth Century for the new sciences and their scientific method is the new university, the faculty of arts and philosophy – and too the faculty of theology. Albert is one of the creators of the university.[23] Theology too should be a university discipline, employing an empirical and rational method. Albert's new model of the relationship between philosophy and theology emphasizes the proper life and reality of each thing. Because the two areas of creation and revelation are independent, each has its own way of knowing. Theology, he wrote, "is based on revelation and prophecy" and philosophy "is based on reason."[24]

4. Albert in Politics

Natural science, metaphysics, and the Bible are areas associated with Albert. Surprisingly politics, not just the presentation of

---

[21] Flasch, Albert der Grosse 373.

[22] Söder, "Albert der Grosse – ein staunenerregendes Wunder" 164; see Söder, "Der Mensch als Ganzheit. Alberts anthropologischer Entwurf," *Wort und Antwort* 41 (2000): 159-64; Georg Wieland, *Zwischen Natur und Vernunft. Alberts des Grossen Begriff vom Menschen* (Münster: Aschendorff, 1999).

[23] Thomas Marschler, *Praelati et praedicatores. Albertus Magnus über das kirchliche Leitungs- und Verkündigungsamt* (Münster: Aschendorff, 2015).

[24] Albert, *Metaphysics* Lib. II, tract. 3, ch. 7, Editio Coloniensis XVI, Pars 2, 532.

Aristotle's book on politics but political activism, was also part of the life of Albert of Lauingen. Thomas Aquinas' teacher was a well-known political activist.[25] Anzulewicz writes: "His significance in social and political as well as ecclesiastical spheres was considerable and important. He was given problems and asked to be present at the papal curias in Anagni, Viterbo, and Orvieto where popes gave him important missions to German-speaking areas and rulers like Ludwig IX of Bavaria, Wilhelm of Holland, and Rudolf von Hapsburg of Austria asked for his services."[26] More than twenty times he served as a political mediator in urban conflicts between nobles, bishop, and the rising mercantile class. Five of these concerned the city of Cologne, for that city called upon him repeatedly in times of crisis to join the commission set up for settling a dispute.

An important mediation was the *Great Decision* of June 28th, 1258, regulating constitutional questions, taxes, and the politics of the city. Prior to that in Cologne a devastating conflict broke out. A new Archbishop involved himself in deceptions and the breaking of agreements. Negotiations between the two parties were doomed and the city turned to violence. The Archbishop Konrad von Hochstaden was driven by egotism, extravagance, simony, and nepotism. In April of 1259, he took measures to make himself an autocratic ruler without the legitimate contributions of the noble families and commercial

---

[25] On the importance of Albert's writings and lectures in terms of the Aristotelian presentation of ethics and a new organization of moral theory for the Thirteenth Century see Stanley B. Cunningham, *Reclaiming Moral Agency. The Moral Philosophy of Albert the Great* (Washington, DC: The Catholic University of America, 2008); on the commentaries and treatments of Aristotle's writings on politics in Albert and Thomas Aquinas see Walter Senner, "Thomas von Aquin und die Politik – eine Nicht-Beziehung?" T. Eggensperger, ed., *Bewahren und Bewähren. Politische Theologie im Anschluss an Thomas von Aquin* (Mainz: Grünewald, 2015) 51-75.

[26] H. Anzulewicz, "Zum Priestertum und Ordenstand nach Albertus Magnus," *Kirchenbild und Spiritualität* (Paderborn: Schöningh, 2007) 63f.

interests. He entered Cologne on June 8, 1262 with an army and increased taxes. Citizens appealed to the Pope who sent a nuntius, largely sympathetic to the Archbishop, and an interdict was placed forbidding the celebration of the sacraments. Albert was contacted down the Rhine in Strassburg. At first convinced that there was no solution to this political situation he declined to go to Cologne, but then he changed his mind. Upon arrival, he spoke openly to the Archbishop about working for reconciliation within the city of Cologne. In the Reconciliation of April 17, 1271, the city prevailed in political and commercial areas; a proclamation stated that this was not simply the result of compromise and that the archbishop Engelbert had admitted that his entire style of ruling up to that point was a failure.

5. Bishop of Regensburg

Politics led to politics. Those mediations in Cologne gave the Pope in Italy the idea to nominate Albert as bishop in Regensburg, a diocese that had serious economic problems and whose leading clerics were often incompetent and corrupt.

Among the Dominicans and Franciscans, the new mendicants in the Thirteenth Century, however, there was the conviction that the social condition of being a bishop opposed a life of vowed poverty. The general chapters of the Dominicans stated several times between 1234 and 1255 that no friar could become a bishop without a special permission of the Master of the Order or the provincial. The Master of the Order, Humbert of Romans, the fourth successor to St. Dominic as the leader of the Friars Preachers, was personally acquainted with Albert. As soon as he heard the rumors circulating about the possible elevation of Albert, he explicitly told the Dominican friar to refuse. He calls the office of bishop a stain, "*maculam huiusmodi,*" meaning the feudal trappings, power, and wealth. Every layperson ("*secularis*") who hears about this will be shocked: they will think that we, mendicants, do not love poverty but only put up with it until we can get beyond it." Humbert's letter ends emotionally: "I would rather hear that my beloved son lies in his coffin than that he sits on the bishop's chair." [27] Albert, however, accepted the Pope's mandate.

Albert did not hesitate over his decision, for the letter of appointment by Pope Alexander IV issued on January 5, 1260 reached him in Cologne, and in March he is on the way to Regensburg to receive in July episcopal consecration. Albert, after some administrative decisions, left his see city and traveled to inspect the property of the Regensburg diocese in the Tyrol. In September, he is south of the Brenner Pass along with Duke Ludwig II of Bavaria and the Duke's brother-in-law, Count Meinhard II of Tyrol. A few weeks later, he took part with his brother bishops a synod presided over by Ulrich, Archbishop of Salzburg. After a trip to Vienna in 1261 he returned to Regensburg. As bishop he organized church finances and institutions, and looked for competent and moral leaders. This occupies Albert's time as a bishop – a short time.

To do justice to the daily demands of leading a diocese and its territory, a man needed administrative perdurance, diplomatic ingenuity along with political and (if necessary) military toughness. In short, a robust and smart intelligence with some experience of life counted for more than an intense spirituality, scholarly education, or caritative generosity. Contrary to later legends, Albert did not spend his time as bishop sneaking off to write a philosophical or theological work or visiting a church wearing old shoes. He was a traveling administrative reformer.

---

[27] Texts and narrative of this conflict can be found in Rudolf Schiefer, "Albertus Magnus. Mendicancy and Theology in Conflict with Episcopacy," T. O'Meara (ed.), *Albert the Great. Theologian and Scientist,* (Chicago: New Priory Press, 2013) 96f.

After not quite two years he saw that his appointments and reorganization had taken hold and resigned from being bishop. Letters of May 11, 1262 from Pope Urban IV to the cathedral chapter, the clergy, and the people in the city confirm the resignation of Albert and give papal approval to the election of his successor, the previous dean of the cathedral chapter, Leo. The activity of Albert of Lauingen as bishop in Regensburg was only a brief episode in the long life of the "*Doctor universalis*" – less than two years.

6. Albertus Magnus Today

Albertus Magnus, "Albert the Great." Are there ideas from his pen that are of interest to us today?

First, his philosophy and theology are a critique of every sectarianism and fundamentalism. Fundamentalisms are everywhere at this time: Protestant evangelical, political, Islamic, or Catholic reactionary. One characteristic essential to every fundamentalism is to replace creation with divinity. God is glorified by monopolizing all that is good and religious. Every good action is only God's action; every truth – mathematical, political – is a revealed truth. For Albert, nature and Gospel, cosmos and theology are independent realms of the one God. In this time of fundamentalisms, nature and faith need to be themselves, excluding any opposition or competition. Creation glorifies God by being itself; it does not need to be baptized into symbols or displayed as the miraculous. "I don't concern myself at all with God's miracles when I am studying nature."[28] Albert described the realism and the causality of the Holy Spirit in human life – in grace and in nature – but in different ways. The Incarnation, sacraments,

---

[28] Albert, *De generatione et corruptione* I, 1, 22, Editio Coloniensis, V, Pars 2. Albert warns theologians to show discipline and remain within the limits of faith and not to find easy enjoyment through what is only imagined; A. Fries, *Albertus Magnus. Ausgewälte Texte. Lateinisch-deutsch* (Darmstadt, Wissenschaftliche Buchgesellschaft, 1981) 20.

church offices, the inner life of the Spirit in their active presence resemble forms and forces in the world.

Second, in psychology and natural science he wrote works on topics like how the senses work, memory and sleep, youth and old age, and nourishment. Dreams, he concluded, come not from God or outside forces but from the physical condition of the brain during sleep. They usually focus on the present and have some relationship to the primary purpose of sleep, restoration of strength. He thought that they have little to do with the life of the intellect. People who claim supernatural powers from their dreams are often psychologically disturbed.[29]

Finally, his theology interests us who live in a time of religious pluralism, for it ponders how God's grace has existed outside of Judaism and Christianity. He sees religions before Abraham in a single long salvation-history. From the beginning of human illness there has also been the time of medicine, either in signifying or in causing, like moral rules, natural law, and rituals.[30] The beliefs (of other religions) may be limited but their mode of faith and their rituals are not evil. "The principle of religion is that God should be honored and worshiped; this nature teaches and not only faith. This or that form for religious cult is taught by reason and faith, arranged by natural law for a universal way but arranged in detail by positive law."[31] Those living long ago (for him, before the Jews) have a morality of natural law and a religious orientation to what will come: a mediator and kinds of sacramentals in religions nourishing an

---

[29] Albert, *De somno et vigilia* 157ff, 169ff. cited in Craemer-Ruegenberg 154–59.

[30] Albert, *De bono,* tr. 5 [*De Justitia*], q. 2, ad 9, Editio Coloniensis, XXVII, Pars 2, 286.

[31] Ibid. tr. 5, q.2, XXVII 289.

implicit faith.[32] They are "Christians in another time."[33] In short, "because God can bring salvation outside of the sacraments, it is said that he has not bound his power to the sacraments."[34]

Albert of Lauingen is a thinker of his times and a source for the future. There have been many wide-ranging human intellects, before and after the Dominican professor, but today, he is valuable for his insights and for being an advocate of a wide perspective and a cosmic variety. There individual life and the life of grace are in conversation about the plans and patterns in motion by God.

Albert wrote of the dignity of the human person in light of the dignity of the astrophysical universe. "The human intellect continuously extends itself, upwards, so that by studying the sky it is drawn to a contemplation of divine things, and by contemplating them fully in astronomical realms the mind appears like a sun."[35] Astronomy opens to theology. Both inspire the human person to think and to explore.

---

[32] Ibid., tr. 5, q. 2, a. 2, ad 7, Editio Coloniensis XXVII, Pars 2,285-89; see *De Incarnatione*, tr. 5, q. 2, a. 6, Editio Coloniensis XVI, 217. The headship of Christ is for some in baptism and for others in implicit faith. There is in the human race "a unity of the Spirit vivifying all before and after the Incarnation" (Ibid.)

[33] Albert, *Super III Sent.* d. 25, a. 6, ad 2. "We have seen laypeople being arrested and examined on the most obscure articles of the faith; and if they are found to err or to be ignorant they are released as heretics. So there is the impression that they are obliged to believe everything explicitly" (*Super III Sent.* d. 25, a. 4, ad 7). "If ordinary people not able to distinguish these things are to be burned then the inquisitors also should be burned for they do not know much more" (Ibid.).

[34] Albert, *De sacramentis,* tr. 1, q. 2, Editio Coloniensis XXVI 4.

[35] Albert, *Metaphysica* XI 1, 9 Editio Coloniensis, XVI, Pars 2 473. Edith Stein (who lived in a religious house in Cologne seven centuries after Albert did) said that the Dominican resembles Pseudo-Dionysius, for in both, streams of the material universe lead to what is spiritual (see Bernd Urban, *Edith Stein und die Literatur. Lektüren, Rezeptionen, Wirkungen* [Stuttgart: Kohlhammer, 2010] 73-76).

Meister Eckhart
and the Rhineland Mystics

Richard Woods, O.P.

In the late Thirteenth and early Fourteenth Century, western Europe experienced a seismic spiritual upheaval unprecedented in the history of Christianity. The epicenter was the German-speaking territories along the Rhine from Cologne to Switzerland, but ripples extended in all directions – beginning in the Lowlands, but affecting France, England, and Italy and, to a lesser degree, Spain. It was in many respects a mystical revolution which, in the Rhineland, began arguably with St. Albert the Great and reached a climax in the career of Meister Eckhart.

The rise of the spiritual movement known as the *Vita Apostolica* in the eleventh and twelfth centuries that led to the formation of the mendicant orders in France and Italy together with the lay-oriented beguine movement originating in the Netherlands had prepared the way for the great mystical awakening of the high Middle Ages. But it was clearly the towering genius of Albert of Lauingen, St. Albert the Great, that set in motion the theological engines that would power the later revolution. And it was a true revolution, for Albert, the most influential schoolman of his time, had discovered the mystical theology of the early Church in the newly translated writings of the mysterious early sixth-century figure known as "Dionysius the Areopagite."

The four brief "books" and ten letters of this pseudonymous figure, and particularly *The Divine Names* and the *Mystical Theology,* had long since profoundly impacted eastern theology, partly because of the spurious apostolic authority accorded to one who identified himself as the disciple of St. Paul (see Acts 17:34) and according to later tradition became the first bishop of Athens.[1] The Neoplatonic scaffolding on which the pseudo-Dionysius erected his theology had its own appeal, but the heart of the teaching was a masterful synthesis of scripture, the earlier theology and spiritual writing of the Cappadocian Fathers, Evagrius of Pontus, and other Greek writers, both Christian and pagan, such as the philosopher Proclus, and not least of all his own considerable genius.

First translated into Latin in the ninth and tenth centuries, the works were little known until in the next two centuries new and more accurate translations by John Scottus, John Sarracenus, and commentaries by Hugh of St. Victor and others prepared the way for a fresh translation of the whole by Robert Grosseteste in 1240-43. The "rediscovery" of the *Corpus Areopagiticum* deeply affected the theology and spirituality of the period, beginning in Paris and spreading widely and rapidly.

In the meantime, Albert the Great had developed a keen and lasting interest in the works of Dionysius. He composed paraphrastic translations of major works – *The Divine Names*, the *Mystical Theology*, the *Celestial Hierarchy*, and also the *Letters*.[2] Albert

---

[1] The attribution was not pointless, since the author had probably attended the Academy in Athens, long before it was closed by Justinian in 529. See *Pseudo-Dionysius: The Complete Works*, trans. by Colm Luibheid and Paul Rorem, New York: Paulist Press, 1987, Andrew Louth, *Denys the Areopagite*, London & New York: Continuum Press, 2001, Eric D. Perl, *Theophany: The Neoplatonic Philosophy of Dionysius the Areopagite*, Albany: SUNY Press, 2007, and Paul Rorem, Pseudo-Dionysius: A Commentary on the Texts and an Introduction to Their Influence, New York: Oxford University Press, 1993. For a recent commentary on "Dionysian" themes, including in the works of Meister Eckhart, see Denys Turner, *The Darkness of God: Negativity in Christian Mysticism*, Cambridge: Cambridge University Press, 1995.

[2] Collections of Albert's works include the *Opera omnia*, ed. E. Borgnet (38 volumes starting in 1890). The critical edition being published by the Institute of Albert the Great in Bonn will include 40 volumes: *Sancti Doctoris Ecclesiae Alberti Magni, Ordinis Fratrum Praedicatorum, Opera omnia*, ed. by Manuel Santos Noya, Ruth Meyer, et al. See also "Albert the Great, "Commentary on Dionysius'

passed along his enthusiasm for Dionysius to his students, especially Ulrich Englebert of Strassburg, Dietrich of Freiburg, Hugo Ripelin, and to a lesser degree, Thomas Aquinas. (Thomas cites Dionysius about 1,700 times in his writings.)[3] Albert's disciples passed that enthusiasm on to the next generation, preeminently Eckhart of Hochheim and through his preaching and writing, to Heinrich Seuse, Johannes Tauler, and a widening circle of mystics and theologians.

1. Eckhart of Hochheim: Prince of Mystics

Eckhart's place of birth and the date are unknown. The same is true of his death. Other details of his life and ministry are known with confidence and a substantial body of sermons and treatises, both in German and Latin, survived the last stormy days of his career. He was born around 1260 in Thuringia, a part of north central Germany, either in a small village called Hochheim, near the city of Erfurt, or in a village called Tambach not far from there.[4] He most likely died in Avignon on January 28, 1328 – a date only recently found in a late medieval calendar of the Order. Because that is also the date commemorating the Translation of the Relics of St. Thomas Aquinas, and now celebrated as his principal feast, Eckhart's death date was subsequently overlooked.[5]

Mystical Theology," Simon Tugwell, O.P. (trans.), in S. Tugwell, *Albert and Thomas: Selected Writings*, New York: Paulist Press, 1988.

[3] For a masterful study of the influence of Dionysius on Albert and Thomas, and their interpretations of his doctrine, see Bernhard Blankenhorn, O.P., *The Mystery of Union with God: Dionysian Mysticism in Albert the Great and Thomas Aquinas*, Washington: Catholic University of America Press, 2015.

[4] Eckhart's father, a knight of the same name, is recorded as bailiff in "Waldenfels" in 1265, presumably in the Thüringer Forest near Tambach.

[5] See McGinn, *McGinn: Mystical Theology of Meister Eckhart: The Man from Whom God Hid Nothing* (New York: Crossroad, 2001), p. 33, who notes that Fr. Walter Senner, O.P., discovered that a late seventeenth-century Dominican source indicated that Eckhart's anniversary was celebrated in German convents on that date. The place of his death and burial remains unknown.

Evidently, he was the son of a knight also named Eckhart von Hochheim, who died in the year 1305 according to an entry also recently discovered in a Dominican chronicle.[6] About the age of fifteen, Eckhart joined the Dominican Order at Erfurt. After his novitiate period, he was sent to the studium at Cologne in 1280 for his theological training. There he seems to have met and was certainly influenced by Albert, who was about 80 by then and died later that year.

A few years later Eckhart was sent on to the University of Paris for advanced studies in theology. In 1302, he was awarded the degree of Master of Sacred Theology and thus became known, and will be forever known, as Meister (Master) Eckhart, the only medieval figure still known by that title. In between times and immediately afterwards, he also held a series of important administrative positions in the German provinces of the Order, including those of prior, vicar provincial, provincial, and regent master. He was widely celebrated as a preacher as well as a teacher, and was assigned the care of the hundreds of Dominican nuns in the region surrounding the then-German city of Strassburg from 1311 to 1323, when he returned to Cologne perhaps as regent master of the studium where he began his career as a teacher and preacher.

But beginning sometime in 1326, by order of Henry of Virneburg, the prince-archbishop of Cologne, Eckhart was subjected to a series of investigations for preaching heresy. These culminated in his defensive appeal to the Holy See in 1327. At the age of 66, accompanied by his provincial, the papal delegate Nicholas of Strassburg, and several members of his priory, Eckhart walked 500 miles to Avignon in southern France to plead his case before the pope.

---

[6] See McGinn, ibid., p. 2, n. 8. Hochheim seems to have been the family name rather than a toponymic or place name.

He died sometime the following year. In March of 1329, fifteen propositions taken from his Latin and German works were condemned in a papal bull as heretical, and eleven more were censured as rash and leading to heresy. Two others were condemned as heretical, but it was said that Eckhart had not taught them. (He had in fact taught them, but they have been shown not to be heretical.)[7]

Eckhart was the first Dominican whose teachings were condemned for heresy. Most contemporary students consider the trial and condemnation to have been the outcome of a variety of political and ecclesiastical intrigues in a complex and turbulent era rather than because his teachings were truly erroneous. Careful scholarship has shown that the articles condemned as heretical were mainly Eckhart's forceful presentation of orthodox teachings of the great mystical theologians of the early Church, preeminently St. Augustine. Many were simply rhetorical flourishes. All were taken out of context. Despite the condemnation, Eckhart's influence continued to shape German, Dutch, Spanish, and even English spirituality for centuries to come.

In 1980, the Dominican Order began a decades-long process to exonerate Eckhart. The Chapter of Walberberg established a special investigative commission of leading European Eckhart scholars in response to a petition by English lay Dominicans later organized as the Eckhart Society by its founder, Mrs. Ursula Fleming. In 1986, the General Chapter of Avila asked the Congregation for the Doctrine of the Faith for "an official declaration acknowledging the exemplary character of Eckhart's activity and preaching and recommending his

---

[7] See, *inter alia*, Oliver Davies, "Why Were Eckhart's Propositions Condemned?" *New Blackfriars* 71 (1990): 433–444; Bernard McGinn, "Meister Eckhart's Condemnation Reconsidered," *The Thomist* 44 (1980): 390 – 414, and Richard Woods, "The Condemnation of Meister Eckhart," *Spirituality*, 33, 6 (Nov.-Dec. 2000), 342-47.

writings... as an expression of authentic Christian mysticism and as trustworthy guides to Christian life according to the Gospel."

In January, 1992, the panel's conclusions were published by the University of Fribourg.[8] And in March, 1992, the Master of the Order, Fr. Damian Byrne, formally requested Cardinal Joseph Ratzinger to abrogate the bull of condemnation. That did not happen and may never come to pass. But even more significant in some respects was the commendation given Eckhart by Pope John Paul II in an audience of September, 1985: "... I think of the marvelous history of Rheno-Flemish mysticism of the thirteenth and especially the fourteenth centuries... Did not Eckhart teach his disciples: 'All that God asks you most pressingly is to go out of yourself... and let God be God in you'?"[9]

Such an acknowledgment from the highest teaching authority in the Church surpasses any dictum of a congregation. And one way or another, Eckhart's influence is possibly greater now than at any time in history.

2. Dominican Influences: Albert and Thomas

In developing his rich and complex teaching, Eckhart drew on many resources – scripture, the doctors and fathers of the Church, and especially his "old teacher," Albert the Great, whose influence would have been profound at Cologne just at the time Eckhart arrived there to begin his advanced theological studies. Many of Albert's immediate disciples became celebrated teachers and preachers – principally among them Dietrich of Freiburg and Ulrich Englebert of Strassburg, Berthold of Moosberg, Henry of Halle, and the brothers

---

[8] Heinrich Stirnimann and Ruedi Imbach (eds.), *Eckardus Theutonicus, homo doctus et sanctus*, Fribourg: University of Fribourg, 1993.

[9] Quoted in *L'Osservatore Romano*, 28 October 1985. See also Édouard-Henri Wéber, O.P., "À propos de Maître Eckhart et de son procès," *Mémoire Dominicaine*, N. 2 (Printemps 1993): 135-37.

Johann and Gerard Korngin of Sterngassen.[10] Dietrich and Ulrich, Albert's favorite student, particularly inherited his Dionysian orientation and passed it on to the next generation, including, of course, Eckhart.[11]

Although Albert was Eckhart's major resource, especially in regard to the prominent Dionysian strand in his teaching,[12] the works of Thomas Aquinas would also influence him greatly. Thomas died three or four years before his younger contemporary entered the Order, but Eckhart may have been a student in the faculty of arts at Paris in 1277 when several of Thomas's propositions were condemned together with those of Siger of Brabant.[13]

---

[10] On Albert and the "Cologne School," see Alain de Libera, *Introduction a la Mystique Rhènane d'Albert le Grand à Maitre Eckhart* (Paris: O.E.I.L., 1984), pp. 10-13, 31-41. On Eckhart and Albert, see B. Geyer, "Albertus Magnus and Meister Eckhart," *Festschrift für Josef Quint anlässliche seines 65 Geburtstages überreicht* (Bonn: 1964), pp. 253-54.

[11] On Eckhart as a Christian Neoplatonist, see Edmund Colledge and Bernard McGinn, trans. and eds., *Meister Eckhart: The Essential Sermons, Commentaries, Treatises and Defense* (New York: Paulist Press, 1981), pp. 27, 34, 40-44; Andrew Louth, *The Origins of the Christian Mystical Tradition from Plato to Denys* (Oxford: Clarendon Press, 1981), pp. 110f.; *Pseudo-Dionysius: The Complete Works*, trans. by Colm Luibheid and Paul Rorem (New York: Paulist Press, 1987), p. 30; Bernard McGinn, "God as Absolute Unity," pp. 137-39; Reiner Schürmann, *Meister Eckhart, Mystic and Philosopher* (Bloomington, Ind.: Indiana University Press, 1978), pp. 140-43 and *passim*, and Frank Tobin, *Meister Eckhart: Thought and Language* (Philadelphia: University of Pennsylvania Press, 1986), p. 62, 210, n. 81. Cf. also Evelyn Underhill, *The Mystics of the Church* (London: James Clarke, n.d.), p. 134.

[12] Eckhart cites Dionysius at least a dozen times directly in his German sermons and several more times in his *Talks of Instruction* and the treatise "On Detachment." *German Sermons DW* 20B, 57, 58, 63, 71, 73, 77, 82, 83, and 101, and *DP* 58 (Walshe 2). He cites Dionysius indirectly in *DW* 72, 31, 37, and 72. The attribution in *DW* 19 (Walshe 35) is incorrect. He also cites the Areopgite in *Talks of Instruction*, No. 23 "Of Inward and Outward Works," and *Von Abegescheidenheit* (On Detachment).

[13] According to William Hinnebusch, O.P., a premier historian of the Dominican Order, "...Eckhart began his training at the University of Paris, where he studied philosophy under Siger of Brabant about 1277." William Hinnebusch, O.P., *The History of the Dominican Order*, Staten Island, NY: Alba House, 1973, Vol. II, p. 303.

There can be no doubt about Eckhart's loyalty to Thomas, even apart from the adherence to the basic tenets which had been enjoined upon members of the order at the Chapters of Montpellier and Paris in 1278 and 1279.[14] He names Thomas more frequently than he does Albert, and never mentions Albert's immediate disciples by name. That is not to say that Eckhart did not depart from Thomas in important respects. He remained fundamentally Neoplatonic in his approach to philosophy, theology, and spirituality, being deeply imbued with the Dionysian mysticism favored by Albert and his disciples. He nevertheless created an eclectic, highly original, and profoundly influential mystical theology that bears his own indelible stamp.

3. Eckhart and the Rhineland Mystics[15]

Heinrich Suso (or Seuse) has been called the lyric poet among the mystics, the last of the Minnesingers. Born in Constance in 1395, he was the son of Count Heinrich Von Berg, "a worldly-minded, perverse, difficult man."[16] When Heinrich entered the Dominicans, he retained his mother's family name, Sus (or Süs)[17], for she was

---

[14] The general chapter of 1309 and that at Metz in 1313 similarly legislated that Dominicans must conform to Thomas's doctrine. On Eckhart and Thomas, see See Hinnebusch, Vol. II, pp. 156f., Jeanne Ancelet-Hustache, *Master Eckhart and the Rhineland Mystics*, New York and London: Harper and Row/ Longmans, 1957, pp. 36f., and Benedict Ashley, OP, 'Three Strands in the Thought of Eckhart, the Scholastic Theologian', *The Thomist*, 42 (No. 2, April 1978), p. 227 n. 3. Dom David Knowles writes, "In 1880 Denifle discovered at Erfurt a string of Latin works which, when examined and analyzed, showed Eckhart as holding and using all the metaphysical framework that Aquinas had created out of Aristotelian materials, and using exactly the same authorities as the schoolmen – Augustine, William of Auvergne, Bonaventure and Aquinas." David Knowles, O.S.B., "Denifle and Errhle," *History* 54 (1969): 4.

[15] For a more detailed account, see "The Legacy," in Woods, *Eckhart's Way* (Dublin 2009), pp. 157-78, on which I have drawn for some of the following sections.

[16] Hinnebusch, II, p. 312.

[17] Variants include "Suess" and "Suso" in awkward English. The German "Seuse" seems to have been an invention of Heinrich Denifle, who preferred it to the

everything that his noble father was not – religious, sensitive, and tender-hearted.

When a student friar, Seuse first lived at Strassburg and it is possible that it was there he met both Eckhart and his younger confrere of that city, Johannes Tauler. Seuse and Tauler were also together at the studium in Cologne from 1323 to 1325, just as Eckhart himself arrived from Strassburg. Toward the end of Seuse's studies, the first accusations against his teaching master were pressed. At least partially as a defense, Heinrich composed his first book, *The Little Book of Truth*. Soon circulating widely, it soon brought unwelcome attention from higher authorities.

As the trial of Meister Eckhart dragged on in Avignon, Seuse finished his studies and returned to Constance as lector. He also began to preach and minister to the nuns of the region and found time to write *The Little Book of Eternal Wisdom*. But before it was published in 1330 he found himself summoned before the Dominican chapter at Maastricht which reprimanded him for publishing unsound doctrine and deprived him of his teaching position.

Seuse retained the confidence of his brethren, however, who elected him prior of the community a few years later. During the papal interdict against King Ludwig of Bavaria, the Dominicans of Constance were forced into exile because of their loyalty to the pope. In 1343, Seuse was elected prior of one such group which had taken refuge outside the city. Throughout this time he preached widely and gave spiritual instruction to the Dominican nuns and lay mystics who were already calling themselves the Friends of God. He became a close friend of Elsbet Stagel, the prioress of Töss in Switzerland. As the convent chronicler and a woman of uncommonly good sense as well as

---

homelier rendering of the German, which literally means "sweet." See Edmund Colledge, O.S.A., and J. C. Marler, "'Mystical' Pictures in the Suso 'Exemplar' MS Strasbourg 2929," *Archivum Fratrum Praedicatorum* 54 (1984), p. 326.

holiness, she preserved his letters and in effect served as his amanuensis. Many scholars consider the collection of letters of Seuse and Stagel to be the finest of its kind from the Middle Ages.

Sometime after 1334, Seuse composed his only Latin work, the *Horologium Sapientiae* (the Clock of Wisdom). By then he had earned the Order's benediction and was granted permission to publish *The Little Book of Eternal Wisdom*, which Denifle accounted "the finest fruit of German mysticism."[18] It became one of the most widely read spiritual books of the later Middle Ages.

At the age of forty, Seuse gave up writing and teaching, but towards the end of his life he consented to edit his earlier works together with a prologue and two books of letters into a single volume, the *Exemplar*. *The Life of the Servant*, a biography possibly begun by Stagel but edited by Seuse was included in that edition.[19]

Seuse died in Ulm on January 25, 1366. His contribution to German literature is possibly as great in many respects as that of Eckhart himself. His loyalty to his mentor was eventually rewarded by full exoneration within his lifetime. His name is mentioned with pride in the Chronicles of the Order along with that of Tauler. Four hundred and sixty-five years later, he was beatified and his cult approved by Pope Gregory XVI.

---

[18] Cited in Hinnebusch, II, p. 316.

[19] The standard reference is Karl Bihlmeyer, *Heinrich Seuse, Deutsche Schriften*, Stuttgart: Kohlhammer, 1907 and Frankfurt, 1961. The best English translation is that by Frank Tobin, trans., ed. and commentary, *Henry Suso: The Exemplar with Two German Sermons*, preface by Bernard McGinn, New York: Paulist Press, 1989. Cf. also James M. Clark, trans. and intro., *The Little Book of Eternal Wisdom* and *The Little Book of Truth*, London: Faber and Faber, 1953. The degree of collaboration between Seuse and Stagel has recently been disputed. See Frank Tobin, "Henry Suso and Elsbet Stagel: Was the *Vita* a Cooperative Effort?" *Gendered Voices: Medieval Saints and their Interpreters*, ed. Catherine M. Mooney, foreword by Caroline Walker Bynum, Philadelphia: University of Philadelphia Press, 1999, pp. 118-35.

4. The Preacher

Johannes Tauler, perhaps the most famous of Eckhart's disciples, was born in Strassburg about the year 1300. He entered the Dominicans when about sixteen. Eckhart would have been in Strassburg at that time as lector, preacher and spiritual director of the sisters of Alsace and Switzerland. Seuse was likely still a student there as well. In 1325, Tauler was sent for further studies to Cologne, where Eckhart may have been regent master and Seuse had preceded him. There he seems to have fallen even more under the sway of the Meister's mystical teaching.

The impact of Eckhart's accusations, trials, death and condemnation must have been a source of profound dismay for both young friars. Shortly afterwards, Tauler returned to Strassburg as lector and remained there until the community was forced to leave the city for Basel during the struggle between the pope and King Ludwig of Bavaria, now also the Holy Roman Emperor.

In 1338, as the tension resulted in excommunication of the Emperor, the Dominican priory elected to remain loyal to the pope. The following year, the community was expelled and went to Basel. Correspondence from this period between Tauler, the secular priest Heinrich of Nördlingen, who knew Seuse, and Margaret Ebner, the prioress of Maria Medigen, indicates that Tauler was there at Easter, 1339, and also testifies to the strong bond between the three friends.

In 1343 the Dominicans returned to Strassburg, but Tauler remained in Basel for three more years. There he seems to have cultivated the informal network of mystics known by the name he would popularize, "the Friends of God." He returned to Strassburg in 1347 and remained there until his death in 1361 at the age of sixty or sixty-one. Always a popular preacher, Tauler further endeared himself to the citizens of Strassburg during the outbreak of the Black Death in 1348 by devoting himself to the care of the sick and dying.

Like Eckhart and Seuse, Tauler taught, preached, and offered spiritual direction to the many convents of Dominican nuns in the region. Eighty-one of his sermons, transcribed from memory by his hearers, have been preserved.[20] He mentions Eckhart only once, but there are many allusions and his sermons strongly reflect the Meister's characteristic themes. His preaching was doctrinally profound, but unlike Eckhart, Tauler prudently avoided theological controversy. Like Eckhart, he also discouraged ascetical extremes. Around 1347 he became confessor to a wealthy merchant, Rulman Merswin, who was of some influence among the Friends of God. On learning of Merswin's austere penitential practices, Tauler typically ordered him to cease, although the headstrong merchant returned to them as soon as the time-limit had expired.

The influence of Tauler's sermons on subsequent German spirituality was enormous. But as was the case with Eckhart and Seuse, not only were spurious works attributed to him in later years, but fantastic accounts of his life were written and circulated, many of them surviving to the present. That and especially his mystical appeal earned Tauler the opprobrium of later censors such as the stern Jesuit general Everard Mercurian, who in the Sixteenth Century proscribed the writings of both Seuse and Tauler to members of the fledgling

---

[20] The standard reference is Ferdinand Vetter, *Die Predigten Taulers,* (Deutsche Texte des Mittelalters, 11) Berlin: 1910. Cf. also Georg Hofmann, trans., *Johannes Tauler: Predigten*, Freiburg, 1961 and Einsiedeln, 1979, and Louise Gnädinger, ed. and commentary, *Johannes Tauler: Gotteserfahrung und Weg in die Welt*, Olten und Freiburg-im-Breisgau: Walter Verlag, 1983. English translations include Maria Shrady, ed. and trans., *Johannes Tauler: Sermons*, New York: Paulist Press, 1987; *John Tauler, Spiritual Conferences*, trans. and ed. by Eric and Mary Jane Colledge, Rockford, IL: TAN Books, 1979; and *Signposts to Perfection: A Selection from the Sermons of Johann Tauler*, ed. and trans. by Elizabeth Strakosch, St. Louis and London, 1958. A short excerpt can be found in *The Varieties of Mystic Experience*, ed. by Elmer O'Brien, S.J., New York: New American Library, 1965, pp. 139 - 42.

Society of Jesus. But Tauler also became a favorite among Protestant reformers, especially Luther.[21]

Later, both Tauler and the "pseudo-Tauler" had some impact on the early German Romantics. His sermons were read by Brentano, Görres, Von Baader, and Hegel. Also like Eckhart, only in the Nineteenth Century were the authentic outlines of his story and teaching freed from legend and propaganda. Rhineland mysticism even reached American shores early in the Nineteenth Century when John Greenleaf Whittier, the Quaker and abolitionist, composed a poem in Tauler's honor which begins, grandly enough,

> Tauler, the preacher, walked, one autumn day,
> Without the walls of Strasburg, by the Rhine,
> Pondering the solemn Miracle of Life,
> As one who, wandering in a starless night,
> Feels momently the jar of unseen waves,
> And hears the thunder of an unknown sea,
> Breaking along an unimagined shore.[22]

5. Dominican Women Mystics in the Rhineland

Dominican nuns featured prominently among the Friends of God movement in the Rhineland. Eckhart, Seuse, and Tauler, as well as Heinrich of Nördlingen, all served as spiritual directors, guides, and friends to many nuns of the region who left accounts of their confreres as well as their own spiritual journeys in the convent chronicles

---

[21] Cf. ibid., pp. 48f. Also see Steven Ozment, *Homo spiritualis: A Comparative Study of the Anthropology of J. Tauler, J. Gerson and M. Luther (1509-16) in the Context of their Theological Thought*, Leiden: Studies in Medieval and Reformation Thought, Vol. 6, 1969, and "Eckhart and Luther: German Mysticism and Protestantism," The Thomist, 42 (1978), pp. 259.

[22] "Tauler," *The Complete Poetical Works of John Greenleaf Whittier*, Boston: Houghton, Mifflin & Company, 1884.

(*Schwesternbücher*) that were widely circulated among the various monasteries.

From the earliest period of its history, the Order of Preachers had established monasteries for religiously inspired women who wished to embrace the spirituality of the preachers, beginning with St. Dominic's foundations in Italy and Spain in 1221. The greatest period of expansion occurred between 1246 and 1358, when the number of monasteries grew from the three established by Dominic to 157. Seventy-seven of those were in the German provinces, where the Dominican Order particularly took root. By 1300, there were 90 monasteries in all of Europe, but most of them were in the province of Teutonia alone.[23] Jeanne Ancelet-Hustache writes,

> ...in Germany the houses of the Dominican nuns flourished particularly. They sprang up everywhere, in the Rhineland, Franconia, Bavaria, and in Switzerland. In 1277 Germany had forty convents of Dominican nuns as compared with eighteen in all other provinces of the Order combined. In 1287 there were seventy. When, in 1303, the German province was divided into Saxonia and Teutonia, Saxonia had nine women's monasteries against sixty-five in Teutonia, which comprised the Rhineland and the southern regions. About the same date Strasbourg had seven houses of Dominican nuns. Many of these had from eighty to a hundred religious, some even more.[24]

---

[23] See Hinnebusch, I, pp. 377-90, Herbert Grundmann, *Religious Movements in the Middle Ages*, Notre Dame and London: University of Notre Dame Press, 1995, pp. 250 - 51 and Clark, *Great German Mystics*, p. 4.

[24] Ancelet-Hustache, op. cit., pp. 19-20. Estimates of the numbers of women in these monasteries vary, but it seems evident that the average was over 50. So Hinnebusch (Vol. I, pp. 382- 83). Rufus Jones estimated 100 (*The Flowering of Mysticism: The Friends of God in the Fourteenth Century*, New York: Hafner Publishing Co., 1971, p. 158.).

The influence of Eckhart, Seuse, and Tauler among the nuns was pronounced. As Rufus Jones observed,

> Meister Eckhart, as we have seen, and also Tauler and Suso [sic], were appointed as preachers and father confessors in the Dominican convents for women, and all three of them carried on at various times a preaching mission in these convents. Many of their sermons and other writings were copied by the sisters and preserved for us through the zeal and interest of these women. These preaching mystics, all three of whom possessed contagious qualities of life, produced a profound effect upon their hearers and their confessants, and every glimpse we get into these sisterhoods of the period reveals a widespread and very intense mystical life in these groups, usually under the leadership of some signally devout woman mystic.[25]

What drew well-educated, often noble medieval women to a life of poverty and prayer has been attributed, especially in the Rhineland, to the combination of mystical spirituality and a zeal for study and learning, which was not encouraged in many more traditional women's houses of the period. Significant in this regard is the gift by Heinrich of Nördlingen of a complete set of Thomas Aquinas' *Summa Theologiae* to the nuns at Maria Medigen.

6. Elsbet Stagel, Margaret Ebner, and Their Sisters

A number of Dominican women stand out strikingly in the origin and development of Rhenish mysticism of the period, of whom Elsbet Stagel and Bl. Margaret Ebner are perhaps most representative of the accomplishments of the nuns but are probably not entirely exceptional.

---

[25] Jones, ibid. Also see Clark, *Great German Mystics*, p. 23.

Elsbet Stagel was the prioress and chronicler of the monastery of Töss in Switzerland, with whom Seuse corresponded for some time. Born to an aristocratic family in Zurich early in the Fourteenth Century, she died around 1360. Although an invalid most of her religious life, Elsbet "knew Latin, possessed considerable theological erudition, was thoroughly versed in Scripture, and displayed a fine literary style, simple, direct, witty [*drue*], and lively."[26]

Margaret Ebner was born in 1291 at Donauwörth in Bavaria and made profession in the Dominican monastery at Maria Medingen in 1306. By her own account, her true conversion began in 1311, when she was twenty years old. Shortly thereafter she fell seriously ill and remained bedridden for nearly thirteen years. Her continual suffering and life of prayer brought her to the heights of contemplative union with God. Prioress and chronicler of her monastery, she became one of the most prominent of the Rhineland mystics, known and admired by her Dominican brothers, Seuse and Tauler and the close friend of Heinrich of Nördlingen.

Renowned for her wisdom as well as sanctity, Ebner's advice was sought by church leaders and even the Emperor himself. Among her writings are her *Spiritual Journal*, or autobiography, written about 1344, and also a treatise on the Lord's Prayer.[27] She died on June 20, 1351, and she was beatified by Pope John Paul II on February 24, 1979. The case for her canonization is pending.

7. The Friends of God

In addition to the growing network of friars and nuns, lay people were also drawn to the movement known as the Friends of God.

---

[26] Jeanne Ancelet-Hustache, "Elizabeth Stagel," *Dictionnaire Spirituelle*, Paris: Éditions Beauchesne, Vol. 4, p. 589.

[27] Margaret Ebner, *Revelations and Pater Noster*, trans. and ed. by Leonard Hindsley, O.P., New York: Paulist Press, 1992.

Largely through Tauler's preaching and direction, Eckhart's doctrine influenced Rulwin Merswin at Grüner Wörth in Strassburg[28] and enjoyed a wide following in the Netherlands and beyond. His doctrine was known to Jan van Ruusbroec and Gerard Groote, at least indirectly to the author of *The Cloud of Unknowing*, to Margery Kempe in England,[29] probably through the Dominican nuns she encountered and even figured in Franciscan spirituality, especially the writings of the greatest of the late fourteenth-century mystics of that order, Marquart of Lindau.[30] As already noted, through the sermons of Tauler, Eckhart's spirituality affected even Luther himself.

James Clark characterized the Friends of God as an informal association of "persons with strong mystical tendencies and interests, and in particular those who had attained union with God, the highest stage of the contemplative life."[31] The leadership was strongly Dominican – Seuse's name is frequently mentioned in the literature, but more especially that of Tauler, along with Margaret Ebner, Christina Ebnerin, John of Tomback, Dietrich of Colmar, Johann and Gerard Korngin, and Nicholas of Strassburg.[32]

Not surprisingly, Eckhart's influence upon this loose-knit band was definitive, especially as channeled through the preaching and guidance of Seuse and Tauler. Already, however, the *Lebemeister* had

---

[28] See Thomas S. Kepler, ed. and interp., *Mystical Writings of Rulman Merswin*, Philadelphia: Westminster Press, 1960, p. 16.

[29] Cf. Sanford Brown Meech and Hope Emily Allen, *The Book of Margery Kempe*, Vol. I (EETS, No. 212), London: Oxford University Press, 1940, pp. 376-78.

[30] See Clark, ibid.

[31] Clark, Great German Mystics, p. 92.

[32] For a recent and very thorough commentary, see Bernard McGinn, *The Harvest of Mysticism in Medieval Germany (1300-1500)*, New York: Crossroad Publishing Co., 2005, pp. 414-431. Cf. Also Ancelet-Hustache, pp. 142-44, Clark, *Great German Mystics*, pp. 91-96, Hinnebusch, II, pp. 320-21, and Jones, op. cit., pp. 104-38.

acquired an umbra of legend, looming not only larger than life in the years following his death, but in an increasingly distorted form. This is particularly evident in the writings of Merswin (1307-1382), whose mysterious correspondent, the "Friend of God from the Oberland" was established as a pious (or not-so-pious) fraud by Heinrich Denifle in 1880.[33]

This is also true of the spirituality of the Low Countries, although Jan van Ruusbroec at Groenendael, his disciple Gerard Groote of Deventer, and Jan Van Leeuwen exercised critical caution with regard to spurious doctrine. It was in the Netherlands that the important distinction between "true" and "false" Friends of God was made and applied, for dissident partisans of the Free Spirit had also appropriated the spiritual authority not only of Eckhart but of his disciples. (Nicholas of Basel, Rulman Merswin's successor at Grüner Wörth, was burnt as a heretic at Vienna in 1409.)

Towards the end of the century, reflections of Eckhart's doctrine appeared in the anonymous *Book of Spiritual Poverty* (*Das Buch Von Geistlicher Armut*), for a while attributed to Tauler.[34] Another anonymous disciple, perhaps a member of the Teutonic Knights, interpreted Eckhart's doctrine in the *Theologia Germanica*, a book so highly valued by Luther that he published versions of it in 1516 and 1518.[35] Later in the Fifteenth Century, Cardinal Nicholas von Kues

---

[33] Cf. Clark, ibid., pp. 84-86. See also Thomas S. Kepler, ed., *Mystical Writings of Rulman Merswin*, Philadelphia: Westminster, 1960. Perhaps the best study of Merswin is chapter five of Clark's *Great German Mystics*.

[34] H. Denifle, ed., Munich, 1877. There is an English translation in archaic language by J. R. Morell, *The Following of Christ*, London, 1886, and a newer translation by C. F. Kelley, *The Book of the Poor in Spirit* by a Friend of God, London 1955.

[35] See The *Theologia Germanica* of Martin Luther, trans. by Bengt Hoffman, New York: Paulist Press, 1980. Cf. also Oliver Davies, "Ruysbroeck, á Kempis and the *Theologia Deutsch*," in Cheslyn Jones, Geoffrey Wainwright, Edward Yarnold, S.J., *The Study of Spirituality*, New York: Oxford University Press, 1986, pp. 321-24.

(Cusa) esteemed Eckhart greatly. A copy was discovered in his library of parts of Eckhart's proposed theological masterwork, the *Opus Tripartitum,* with cautionary marginal notations. His development of the doctrine of "learned ignorance," his fondness for paradox, his fascination with the reconciliation of opposites, and his Neoplatonic mysticism all hail back to the Rhineland tradition of Albert and Eckhart.[36]

8. Later Influence

Eckhart's impact on Luther and the early Reformers has been much debated over the past several years. Clearly, Luther had read and been deeply impressed by Tauler's sermons, some editions of which included excerpts from Eckhart's sermons. The Dominicans' resistance to ascetical practices and penances as unproductive exterior "works" naturally appealed to him. His dalliance with this aspect of Rhineland teaching may have delayed the emergence of his final theological position, however. And in other areas, as Steven Ozment has shown, Luther was either unaffected or even misunderstood the earlier doctrines. In any event, his use of the Rhineland mystics was highly selective and, in later centuries, generally overestimated by both Protestant and Catholic writers.[37]

Sebastian Franck, Valentin Weigel, Johann Arndt and other radical Lutherans were also indebted to Eckhart to varying degrees. The Meister's influence was also felt more indirectly by Spiritualists, Anabaptists, Hutterites and eventually the Pietists. It is present in works such as *The Temple of Souls* and the writings of Daniel Sudermann.

---

[36] See especially McGinn, *Harvest of Mysticism,* op. cit., pp. 432-83. Cf. also Clark, *Great German Mystics,* p. 24, McGinn, "Introduction," pp. 255 n. 85, and Ancelet-Hustache, pp. 167-70.

[37] Cf. Ozment, "Eckhart and Luther," art. cit., and *Homo spiritualis,* op. cit., passim.

In the Seventeenth Century the Rhineland tradition resurfaced in the mystical doctrine of Jacob Boehme (1575-1624).[38] But among the various interpreters of Eckhart's teaching during the post-Reformation period, pride of place should doubtless go to Johannes Scheffler (known as Angelus Silesius, "the Silesian Angel"), whose great poem, *Der cherubinischer Wändersmann* (*The Cherubic Wanderer*) remains a monument of German mystical theology as well as a surprisingly accurate rendering of the Meister's doctrine.[39]

Born in 1624, Scheffler was the son of an immigrant Lutheran Polish nobleman who had settled in Breslau, Silesia. After a successful career as court physician Scheffler was received into the Catholic Church in 1653. In 1661, he was ordained to the priesthood, and devoted his remaining years to disputation with other Christian groups. *The Cherubic Wanderer*, written shortly after his conversion when Scheffler was in his twenties, was first published in 1657 under another title. It consists of 302 verses composed during four days of ecstatic inspiration. While influenced by Boehme and especially by the thought of Meister Eckhart, the contents reflect Scheffler's own mystical experience. Scheffler died in 1677.

Rediscovered by poets in the Eighteenth Century, Eckhart's teaching touched philosophers in the nineteenth. And by the end of that era, scholars had begun the process of textual reconstruction that would make the authentic teachings known to the entire world in the Twentieth Century.

---

[38] Cf. Ozment, art. cit., pp. 272ff. Cf. also Henry L. Finch, "A Note on Two Traditions in Western Mysticism: Meister Eckhart and Jacob Boehme," *Centerpoint*, 3 (No. 1, 1978), pp. 41-50.

[39] The standard reference is the critical edition by J. Schwabe, Basel, 1955. Works: H. L. Held, ed., 3 vols. Munich: 1921, 1924; cf. also the edition of G. Ellinger, 2 vols., Berlin: 1924. English translations: Angelus Silesius, *The Cherubic Wanderer*, trans. by Maria Shrady, New York: Paulist Press, 1986; Angelus Silesius (Johannes Scheffler), *Cherubic Wanderer* (selections), tr. and intro. by J. E. Flitch, CT: Hyperion (Library of World Literature Series), 1978 (1932).

9. The Inheritance

The influence on the subsequent history of western spirituality of Eckhart, Seuse, Tauler, and the cohort known as the Friends of God – the great host of Rhineland Mystics of the Fourteenth Century – was widespread, profound, and remains indelible. After a period of decline in the theologically troubled eighteenth and nineteenth centuries, the recovery of manuscripts and more careful scholarship in the following decades produced a new wave of interest in the mystics generally and, beginning in Germany, the Rhineland tradition in particular. These remarkable men and women, so many of them Dominicans, are more widely known today than ever before and continue to enlighten and inspire generations of God-seekers. And no doubt will do so for many generations to come.

10. Bibliography

I. Texts:

The Complete Mystical Works of Meister Eckhart, translated by Maurice Walshe, ed. by Bernard McGinn (Herder and Herder / Crossroads 2009).

Margaret Ebner, Revelations and Pater Noster, trans. and ed. by Leonard Hindsley, O.P., New York: Paulist Press, 1992.

Meister Eckhart: Selected Writings, ed. and trans. by Oliver Davies, London: Penguin, 1994.

Meister Eckhart, The Essential Sermons, Commentaries, Treatises and Defense, ed. by Bernard McGinn and Edmund Colledge (New York: Paulist Press, 1981).

Meister Eckhart: Teacher and Preacher, ed. by Bernard McGinn and Frank Tobin (London: SPCK, 1987).

James Midgely Clark, *Meister Eckhart: An Introduction to the Study of His Works with an Anthology of His Sermons*, Edinburgh: Nelson, 1957.

James M. Clark and John V. Skinner, eds. and trans., *Treatises and Sermons of Meister Eckhart*, New York: Octagon Books, 1983. (Reprint of Harper and Row ed., 1958.)

Frank Tobin, trans., ed. and commentary, *Henry Suso: The Exemplar with Two German Sermons*, preface by Bernard McGinn, New York: Paulist Press, 1989.

II. COMMENTARY: BOOKS

Jeanne Ancelet-Hustache, *Master Eckhart and the Rhineland Mystics*, New York and London: Harper and Row/Longmans, 1957.

Bernhard Blankenhorn, O.P., *The Mystery of Union with God: Dionysian Mysticism in Albert the Great and Thomas Aquinas*, Washington: Catholic University of America Press, 2015.

James M. Clark, *The Great German Mystics*, New York: Russell and Russell, 1970 (reprint of Basil Blackwell edition, Oxford: 1949.)

Oliver Davies, *Meister Eckhart: Mystical Theologian*, London: SPCK, 1991.

Herbert Grundmann, *Religious Movements in the Middle Ages*, trans. by Steven Rowan, intro. by Robert E. Lerner, Notre Dame and London: University of Notre Dame Press, 1995.

William Hinnebusch, O.P., *The History of the Dominican Order*, 2 vols., Staten Island, NY: Alba House, 1966 and 1973.

Rufus Jones, *The Flowering of Mysticism: The Friends of God in the Fourteenth Century*, New York: Hafner Publishing Co., 1971 (facsimile of 1939 ed.).

Richard Kieckhefer, *Unquiet Souls: Fourteenth Century Saints and Their Religious Milieu*, Chicago and London: University of Chicago Press, 1987.

Bernard McGinn, *The Harvest of Mysticism in Medieval Germany (1300-1500)*, New York: Crossroad Publishing Co., 2005 (Volume 4 of *The Presence of God*), New York: Crossroad, 2005.

Bernard McGinn, *The Mystical Thought of Meister Eckhart: The Man from Whom God Hid Nothing*, New York: Crossroad, 2001.

Paul E. Szarmach, ed., *An Introduction to the Medieval Mystics of Europe*, Albany: State University of New York Press, 1984.

Maria Shrady, ed. and trans., *Johannes Tauler: Sermons*, New York: Paulist Press, 1987.

P. H. Stirnimann and Rudi Imbach, eds., *Eckardus Theutonicus, homo doctus et sanctus*, University of Fribourg, 1993.

Frank Tobin, trans., ed. and commentary, *Henry Suso: The Exemplar with Two German Sermons*, preface by Bernard McGinn, New York: Paulist Press, 1989.

Richard Woods, O.P., *Mysticism and Prophecy: The Dominican Tradition*, London and New York: Darton, Longman and Todd/Orbis Books, 1998.

Richard Woods, O.P., *Eckhart's Way*, Dublin: Veritas Publications, rev. ed., 2009.

Richard Woods, O.P., *Meister Eckhart: Master of Mystics*, London and New York: Bloomsbury, 2011.

III. COMMENTARY: ARTICLES

Jeanne Ancelet-Hustache, "Elizabeth Stagel," *Dictionnaire Spirituelle*, Paris: Éditions Beauchesne, 4, 588-89.

Benedict Ashley, OP, 'Three Strands in the Thought of Eckhart, the Scholastic Theologian', *The Thomist*, 42 (April 1978) 2: 226-239.

Edmund Colledge, O.S.A., and J. C. Marler, "'Mystical' Pictures in the Suso 'Exemplar' *MS Strasbourg 2929*," *Archivum Fratrum Praedicatorum* 54 (1984): 293-354.

Margaret B. Guenther, "The Spirituality of Eckhart's German Sermons," *Studies in Spirituality* 9 (1999): 93-108.

Richard Kieckhefer, "John Tauler," *An Introduction to the Medieval Mystics of Europe*, ed. cit., pp. 259 – 72.

Frans Maas, "Meister Eckhart: Man's Divine Life," *Studies in Spirituality*, 16 (2006): 71-109.

Bernard McGinn, "Meister Eckhart on God as Absolute Unity," *Neoplatonism and Christian Thought*, ed. by Dominic J. O'Meara, Albany: State University of New York Press, 1982, pp. 128 - 39.

Steven Ozment, "Eckhart and Luther: German Mysticism and Protestantism," *The Thomist*, 42 (1978) 2: 259 - 80.

Frank Tobin, "Henry Suso and Elsbet Stagel: Was the *Vita* a Cooperative Effort?" *Gendered Voices: Medieval Saints and their Interpreters*, ed. Catherine M. Mooney, foreword by Caroline Walker Bynum, Philadelphia: University of Philadelphia Press, 1999, pp. 118-35.

Frank Tobin, "Religious Life at Töss as reflected in Elisabeth Stagl's *Leben der Schwestern zu Töss*," paper delivered at the Medieval Congress, Kalamazoo, MI, Friday, May 6, 1988.

Richard Woods, O.P., "Women and Men in the Development of Late Medieval Mysticism," *Eckhart and the Beguine Mystics*, ed. by Bernard McGinn, New York: Crossroad, 1994, pp. 147-64.

Augustine of Dacia, O.P. (+1285) and the Fourfold Sense of Sacred Scripture
The Bible in the Thirteenth Century

Jay Harrington, O.P.

1. Introduction

The origin of the idea of a fourfold sense of Scripture can be traced back to John Cassian (ca. 360-435). It was a popular means of interpreting Sacred Scripture in the Middle Ages. Though surrounded by relative obscurity, at least in the English-speaking world,[1] the name of the 13th-century Dominican, Augustine of Dacia, occasionally appears in modern literature concerning biblical interpretation.[2] In their treatment of Hermeneutical Questions in the

---

[1] One notable exception is the published doctoral dissertation, completed at the Pontifical Institute of Medieval Studies, Toronto by M. Michèle Mulchahey, *"First the Bow is Bent in Study....:" Dominican Education before 1350* (*Studies and Texts* 132), Turnhout, Belgium: Brepols,1998, who treats Augustine of Dacia on pp. 204-207. The dissertation was directed by Fr. Leonard Boyle, O.P. who also published on Dominican education in the medieval priories.

[2] His name takes various forms depending on different languages and sources: Augustinus, Ako, Agus, Aki, Aage (A. Walz, "Der Aage von Dänemark '*Rotulus Pugillarus*' im Lichte der alten dominicanischen Konventstheologie," Classica et Mediaevalia 15 (1954) 198–252, p. 205. Other variants as listed in the Consortium of European Research Libraries' Thesaurus are: "Aage <de Danemark>, Aage <von Dänemark>, Augustin <Dacus>, Augustin <de Dacie>, Augustinus <Dacien>, Augustinus <Dacus>, Augustinus <von Dänemark>, Dacia, Augustinus de" (https://thesaurus.cerl.org/record/cnp00286924). De Lubac mentioned that F. Chatillon reminded readers that his real name was Aage of Denmark (*Typologie, Allegorie, Geistiger Sinn. Studien zur Geschichte der Christlichen Schriftauslegung*, Freiburg: Johannes Verlag Einsiedeln, 1999, 22007, p. 341), from a note in *Théologies d'occasion*, Paris: Desclée de Brouwer, 1984, referring to F. Chatillon, "Vocabulaire et prosodie du distique attribué a Augustin de Dacie sur les quatre sens de l'Écriture," in L'Homme devant Dieu. Mélanges offerts au Père Henri de Lubac (*Théologie* 57), Paris: Aubier, 1964, p. 136, Note [= *Typologie, Allegorie, Geistiger Sinn. Studien zur Geschichte der christlichen Schriftauslegung*, trans. R. Voderholzer, Freiburg: Johannes Verlag Einsiedeln, ²2007, p. 341, Anmerkung].

document, *The Interpretation of the Bible in the Church* (1993),[3] the Pontifical Biblical Commission recalled Augustine of Dacia's couplet and situated it in its historical context: "Ancient exegesis, which obviously could not take into account modern scientific requirements, attributed to every text of Scripture several levels of meaning. The most prevalent distinction was that between the literal sense and the spiritual sense. Medieval exegesis distinguished within the spiritual sense three different aspects, each relating, respectively, to the truth revealed, to the way of life commended and to the final goal to be achieved. From this came the famous couplet[4] of Augustine of Denmark (13th Century):

---

[3] The three Dominican friars who served on the Pontifical Biblical Commission in 1993 when the document was promulgated were José Loza Vera, O.P., who taught Old Testament in Mexico and at the École biblique for twenty four years, Adrian Schenker, O.P., Professor of Sacred Scripture and former Vice Rector at the University of Fribourg in Switzerland, and Jean-Luc Vesco, O.P., former Director of the École biblique and professor of Old Testament exegesis. Another Dominican, Jean-Dominique Barthélemy, O.P., a professor of Old Testament and Vice Rector at the University of Fribourg, had been a member of the PBC "who took part in the initial exploration of the topic in 1989 but did not continue when the membership was renewed in 1990..." (P. Williamson, *Catholic Principles for Interpreting Scripture. A Study of the Pontifical Biblical Commission's The Interpretation of the Bible in the Church Subsidia Biblica* 22, Rome: Editrice Pontificio Istituto Biblico, 2001, p. 16.)

[4] A distich is defined as "a self-contained couplet; two lines of rhyming verse that is separate unto itself or has meaning independent from the entire work; a type of closed couplet" (M.S. Mills, *Concise Handbook of Literary and Rhetorical Terms*, Lexington, KY: Estep-Nichols Publishing, 2010, p. 232). "As nouns the difference between couplet and distich is that couplet is (literature) a pair of lines with rhyming end words while distich is (prosody) a couplet, a two-line stanza making complete sense." (http://wikidiff.com/distich/couplet). One scholar even refers to it as a jingle (Frans van Liere, *An Introduction to the Medieval Bible*, Cambridge: University Press, March 2014, p. 121) while another calls it a ditty (K. Froehlich, *Sensing the Scriptures*, p. 9, n. 16). Still another terms it a "formule didactique" (J. Greisch, *Entendre d'une autre oreille. Les enjeux philosophiques de l'herméneutique biblique*, Paris, Bayard, coll. « Bible et philosophie », 2006, pp. 144-152, p. 145: "L'autre Quadriparti: le quadruple sense de l'Ecriture:" It is also referred to as a medieval "quadriga." Richard A. Muller, *Dictionary of Latin and Greek Theological Terms*, Grand Rapids: Baker, 1985, s.v., "Quadriga."

*'Littera gesta docet, quid credas allegoria,
moralis quid agas, quid speres anagogia'"*

The literal teaches the facts;
 the allegorical, what you are to believe;
the moral what you are to do,
  the anagogical, what you are to hope.[5]

This essay will briefly discuss important aspects of the life of Augustine of Dacia. Next, consideration will be given to Augustine's compendium of theology, the *Rotulus pugillaris*, and its contribution to the intellectual formation of friars, preparing them to preach and to hear confessions and the education as prescribed in the Dominican priories of the 13th Century, followed by an evaluation of the distich. The question, whether Augustine was dependent upon Albert the Great for this distich, will then be considered. The final section examines the reception and use of the distich by modern authors, including Pope Benedict XVI, finally drawing a conclusion to our research. A few biographical details of the life of Augustine of Dacia provide an entrée to this study.

---

[5] J.A. Fitzmyer, *The Biblical Commission's Document "The Interpretation of the Bible in the Church. Text and Commentary*," Rome: Editrice Pontificio Istituto Biblico, 1995, p. 117. J. Brož, "From Allegory to the Four Senses of Scripture. Hermeneutics of the Church Fathers and of the Christian Middle Ages," in P. Pokorný and J. Roskov, (eds.), *Philosophical Hermeneutics and Biblical Exegesis*, Tübingen: Mohr Siebeck, 2001, pp. 301-09, p. 301. Augustine's distich is positively described: "The description of the fourfold division of senses was epitomized by the Dominican Augustine of Dacia" (W. Cizewski, "Biblical Interpretation," in J.R. Strayer, (ed.), *Dictionary of the Middle Ages*, Vol. 2, NY; Scribner, 1982-; p. 224); Augustine "fast die Lehre handlich zusammen" (handily, conveniently) (C. v. Bormann, "Hermeneutik I," in *Theologische Realenzyklopädie* Bd. 15, 117-118).

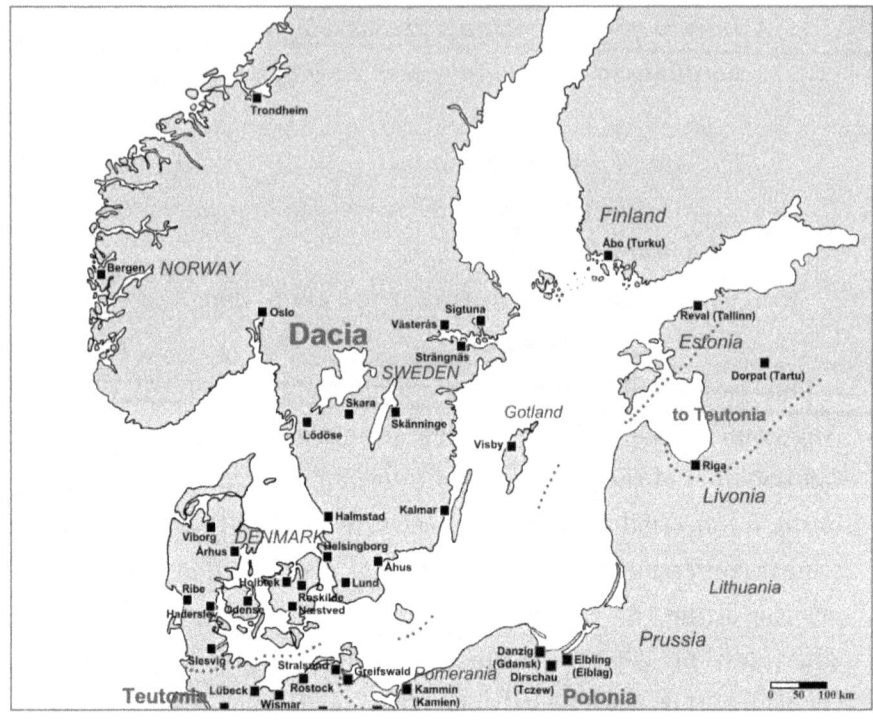

©Johnny Grandjean Gøgsig Jakobsen

2. Augustine of Dacia: Dominican, Provincial, Excommunicate, Teacher

There is no available information as to the date of Augustine of Dacia's birth. He served as the fourth provincial of the province of Dacia, where he served two terms.[6] The Dominican province of Dacia

---

[6] See A. Walz, *Augustini de Dacia, O.P. "Rotullus Pugillaris. Examinatus atque Editus*, Rome; Pontifical Institute Angelicum, 1929, pp. 2-7, concerning the life of Augustine of Dacia. (W. Senner, "Augustinus (Aage) v. Dänemark, OP," in W. Kasper (ed.), *Lexikon für Theologie und Kirche*, Freiburg: Herder, 1993, Vol. 1, col. 1247; p. 1102; His date of death is sometimes given as 1282, e.g. de Lubac, *Medieval Exegesis*, Vol. 1, p. 1 [=*Exégèse médiévale*, pp. 23]; also J. Brož, "From Allegory," pp. 301, n. 1. However, de Lubac listed the date of death as 1285 in *Typologie, Allegorie, Geistiger Sinn. Studien zur Geschichte der Christlichen Schriftauslegung*, trans. Rudolf Voderholzer, Freiburg: Johannes Verlag Einsiedeln, 1999, ²2007, p. 426. Here in his bibliography de Lubac stated that Aage, who died in 1285, was Provincial in Scandinavia 1261-1266 and

was constituted of the three Scandinavian kingdoms: Denmark, Norway, and Sweden.⁷ He had previously served as Prior of the community in Oslo and Chancellor of the King.⁸ According to the Acts of the General Chapters, Augustine was excommunicated by the papal legate, the Cistercian, Guy of Bourogogne. Then he was relieved of his position as provincial during the Dominican General Chapter at Trier in 1266. ⁹ The exact reason for this deposing is unknown. V. De Wilde, O.P., suggested that it was perhaps due to Augustine of Dacia's involvement and support of the king of Denmark against the

---

1272-1285 (Jensen, https://wiki.uib.no/medieval/index.php/Augustinus_de _Dacia, s.v. Biography, Senner, "Augustinus (Aage) v. Dänemark, OP") making him a contemporary of Albert the Great (around 1200-1280) and Thomas Aquinas (1225-1274). A. Walz, "Des Aage," p. 205, maintained that Augustine served two terms as provincial: 1261-1266 and 1272-1285. So also J. Schütz, *Hüter der Wirklichkeit. Der Dominikanerordern in der Mittelalterlichen Gesellschaft Skandinaviens*, Göttingen: V&R unipress, 2014, p. 94. However, V. De Wilde, O.P., stated that his first term as provincial was around 1254 and then the General Chapter in 1266 relieved him of duties (col. 436-437). As provincial, he was particularly solicitous toward the nuns of the Order, and had encouraged Ingrid Elosskotter to found a monastery of the Dominican nuns in Skänninge in the diocese of Linköping, Sweden (De Wilde, col. 437; see also Walz, *Rotulus*, p. 7). According to De Wilde, around 1276 he received the religious profession of Agnes, daughter of the King of Denmark, who had founded a monastery of Dominican nuns at Roskilde, located 30 km west of Copenhagen on the Danish island of Zealand. Johnny Grandjean Gøgsig Jakobsen, *Prædikebrødrenes samfundsrolle i middelalderens Danmark*, p. IV: "The Order of Friars Preachers...arrived in Denmark in the early 1220s and remained here for the next 300 years until its friars were forced to leave due to the Lutheran Reformation. By that time, 15 Dominican convents existed in Denmark as part of the Nordic-Dominican province of Dacia with a total of 31 convents."

⁷ For the possible background to the name, see Jakobsen 2012 (http://jggj.dk/Dacia.htm).

⁸ De Wilde, "Augustin de Dacie," col. 437.

⁹ *Acta capitulorum generalium O.P.* Acts from the general chapters of the Order of Preachers. *Archivum Generalis Ordinis Praedicatorum*, Rome. Published in *Monumenta Ordinis Fratrum Praedicatorum Historica* vols. III-IV, VIII-XIV, Rome 1898 ff. "In nomine patris et filii et spiritus sancti. Amen. Acta capituli generalis apud Treverim celebrati anno Domini MCCLXVI. (...) Absolvimus priores provinciales provincie Provincie fratrem P. de Valencia, Theutonie, Dacie (...)." (http://www.jggj.dk/DiplOPdacie.htm#ACG).

Archbishop of Lund.[10] Kurt Villads Jensen concurs that it resulted from a disagreement between the king, Eric Glipping, and the Archbishop of Lund, Jacob Erlandsen, because Augustine violated an interdict.[11] According to Angelus Walz, O.P., the interdict first involved the kingdom of Dacia, and the papal legate extended the excommunication to the king, the king's mother, Margaret, and bishops devoted to the king.[12] Johnny Grandjean Gøgsig Jakobsen, whose dissertation concerned the role of Dominicans in medieval Danish society, asserted that Augustine was elected the first time in 1261 "and absolved by the General Chapter in May, 1266." Jakobsen questioned "to what extent that [excommunication] actually was ever implemented, as [Augustine of Dacia] was still referred to as 'provincial' when he was excommunicated in 1267. The idea that he was relieved from the provincial office due to his excommunication and/or what led up to it seems very unlikely" in Jakobsen's opinion, "as Guido's [Guy's] patience with the Danish Dominicans only started to wear out in the summer of 1267 – until then they were his biggest hope of solving the conflict between the king and the archbishop."[13] Nonetheless, with the ban lifted, in 1272 Augustine of Dacia became provincial for a second time and remained in office until his death in 1285.[14] It may be assumed that Augustine of Dacia was considered

---

[10] De Wilde, "Augustin de Dacia," col. 437.

[11] Jensen https://wiki.uib.no/medieval/index.php/Augustinus_de_Dacia, s.v. Biography. See Schütz, *Hüter*, p. 94.

[12] Walz, *Augustini de Dacia, O.P.*, p. 5.

[13] J.G.G. Jakobsen, email message to author, September 7, 2016.

[14] "Quintus fuit frater Nycholaus, vir bonus, (...) priorque fuit annis quinque aut sex, fuitque absolutus a provincialatu in generali capitulo Florencie anno domini MCCLXXII, et fuit factus penitentiarius in curia Romana, ubi obiit in officio penitentiarii. Frater Augustinus predictus secunda vice successit fratri Nycholao anno domini MCCLXXII (...)". The source of this detail is *Priores provinciales in provincia Dacie*. A list of Dominican priors provincial of Dacia c.1226-1308 included in Bernard Gui's *Tractatus de tribus gradibus Praelatorum in Ordine Praedicatorum* (c.1310), with an addition of the list in one transcript to 1328.

both competent and popular among his Dominican confreres because he served two terms as prior provincial, and especially for being re-elected after a period of excommunication.

3. Augustine's *Rotulus pugillaris*

The *Rotulus pugillaris*, a work he composed around 1260, is significant because it is the "sole extant work of education from a Scandinavian Dominican."[15] Jensen suggested that *Rotulus pugillaris* "might be a condensed version of his *Compendiosum breviarium theologiae*, to which Augustinus refers in *Rotulus* but which is now lost."[16]

Preserved in several manuscripts of which two are kept in Archivum Generalis Ordinis Praedicatorum, Rome, and one in the University Library of Barcelona. Several publications, e.g. by E.F. Wedel-Jarlsberg in *La Province de Dacia*, Rome - Tournai 1899, pp. 276-277; by K.H. Karlsson in *Handlingar rörande Dominikaner-Provincen Dacia*, Stockholm 1901, p. 6; in *Monumenta Ordinis Fratrum Praedicatorum Historica* vol. III; by S. Tugwell O.P. in *Archivum Fratrum Praedicatorum* vol. 70, Rome 2000, pp. 88-89; by P.B. Halvorsen O.P. in *Dominikus*, Oslo 2002, pp. 248-249; and (with a Danish translation) by J.G.G. Jakobsen on *Scriptores ordinis predicatorum de provincia Dacie* online. (http://www.jggj.dk/DiplOPdacie.htm#PPPD).

[15] The work may have been published just a year before he was elected to his first term as Provincial. "Augustinus de Dacia" *Wikipedia*, last modified March 17, 2012, https://wiki.uib.no/medieval/index.php/Augustinus_de_Dacia. See also J. Brož, "From Allegory," p. 301, n. 1. It does not seem that Augustine of Dacia was a Scripture scholar since C. Spicq, *Esquisse d'une Histoire de L'Exégèse Latine au Moyen Age*, Paris: Librairie Philosophique J. Vrin, 1944, pp. 318-330, did not include Augustine of Dacia among the principal exegetes of the 13th Century. Mulchahey noted the possibility that another Dominican, Simon of Hinton, of the English province, had also published a manual of popular theology while he was serving as provincial, of which Augustine made some use in his own work (*First*, pp. 206, 207). Christian Troelsgård has been preparing a new critical edition of the text based on the second edition of A. Walz (1955).

[16] https://wiki.uib.no/medieval/index.php/Augustinus_de_Dacia. Jensen indicates that Augustine refers to this work in the *Rotulus*, but that it is now lost. Also noted by G. Morin, "IX. Le *Rotulus Pugillaris* du Dominicain Augustin de Dacie (XIIIe s.)," in *Basler Zeitschrift für Geschichte und Altertumskunde* 26 (1927) 223. The text of the *Rotulus pugillaris* contains fifteen tracts, namely: an introduction to the science of theology; faith, the Creeds, the articles of faith; angels and souls; grace and its different types; the theological, cardinal, and others virtues; the gifts of the [Holy Spirit] and works of mercy; the Beatitudes and contemplation; prayer and especially the Lord's Prayer; precepts, which

The distich is found in the text of *Rotulus pugillaris*, which was intended as a handbook for young Dominicans containing instruction in preaching, the hearing of confessions, pastoral care, and theological knowledge. The title indicates that it was a roll of a manuscript, small enough to be held in one's hand. As M. Mulchahey observed, "The work's title, literally *A little roll that can be held in the hand* or, as we would say, *A handbook*, gives some sense of the modest dimensions in which the author felt he could fit the fundamentals."[17] The contents were intended to provide the friars who were studying with the basics needed for their ministry.

A consideration of the translation and phrasing of the distich is in order:

> *Littera gesta docet, quid credas allegoria,*
> *moralis quid agas, quid speres anagogia*

The couplet is in the subjunctive mood. The first clause is the main clause; the following three are the dependent clauses. "Docet" is being applied, then, to the three remaining dependent clauses.

Thus, a very literal translation (done to prove the point):

> *The letter (or the literal) teaches/shows deeds already done,*
> *allegory [teaches/shows] that which you might believe in,*
> *the moral [teaches/shows] what you might do,*
> *the anagogical [teaches/shows] what you might hope for*

---

include ceremonial, judicial, and moral and plagues or punishments; vows, oaths, and ignorance; sins and their types and differences in general; certain sins in particular; the sacraments, distinctions of time; on the anti-Christ and the final judgment. Cf. M. Mulchahey, *First*, p. 205.

[17] Mulchahey, p. 204, also described the work "as a synopsis of Dominican basic training." Walz "Des Aage," p. 204, 247, characterized the work as "das theologische Handbüchlein" and a "kleinen Handbuch."

The verbs in the dependent clauses are in the present tense, but they serve the main verb "docet." The dependent clauses are relative clauses, which must therefore be done in the subjunctive, suggesting obligation or possibility. Perhaps we should speak of potentiality, which deals with possibility, because the dependent clauses are based *on the possibilities* of what each of the four senses *might* do when taught/shown. It is definitely not obligational, which would usually require the gerundive.

Augustine of Dacia is not telling people what they *should* do; because that would be obligational; but because it is subjunctive, he is merely hypothesizing or pointing out possible meanings embedded in the text. In other words, Augustine is not being tendentious.[18]

The couplet is located toward the beginning of the document, in the first tract, as part of the introduction to the science of theology and "constitutes the summary of the first chapter."[19] The distich follows a discussion of the literal sense, in which Augustine of Dacia pointed out one literal sense and three spiritual senses (allegorical, tropological or moral, and anagogical) after which he proceeded to list the canonical books of the Bible. In his discussion of the four senses he used Jerusalem as an example.[20] Jerusalem, according to the literal

---

[18] I am indebted to Christian Troelsgård and Adrian McCaffery, O.P. for their insights on the manner of translation. Christian Troelsgård, e-mail message to author, September 5, 2016 and Adrian McCaffery, O.P. email message to the author, September 25, 2016. For an analysis of the vocabulary of the distich see F. Chantillon, "Vocabulaire et Prosodie du distique attribué a Augustin de Dacie sur les quatre sens de l'Écriture," in *L'Homme devant Dieu. Mélanges offerts au Père Henri de Lubac* (Théologie 57), Paris: Aubier, 1964, pp.17–28.

[19] De Lubac, *Medieval Exegesis*, Vol. 1, pp. 1-2 [=*Exégèse médiévale,* p. 24], refers to the first chapter of *Rotulus*: "This chapter expounds the teaching of Saint Thomas as contained in the first Question of the Summa."

[20] Schütz, *Hüter*, p. 99, n. 329, described Jerusalem as "das klassische Beispiel" [the classic example], having been used by the Benedictine Rabanus Maurus (d. 856), the Benedictine Guibert of Nogent (d. 1125), Pope Innocent III, and Stephen Langton (d. 1228).

sense, refers to the city in Judea; the allegorical sense signifies the church militant. The faithful soul and its operations are signified by the tropological or moral sense. Finally, the anagogical sense is the church triumphant.[21]

Christian Troelsgård, Associate Professor at the SAXO-Institute - Archaeology, Ethnology, Greek and Latin, and History at the University of Copenhagen, assessed the value of *Rotulus* in the following manner: "The section on the quadruple 'Allegoresis' has been quoted several times for the mnemonic verse (which is a recurrent feature of the work), but it is in fact not quite as central as it may have appeared to people, especially since Benedict XVI quoted it. The section on the interpretation of the Scripture is interesting, but elementary; it is not especially original and of quite limited extent. The primary merit of the work is something else: it witnesses to a systematic system of education in the province. The *Rotulus* thus describes what were the basic expectations for the theological training of any Dominican friar. With its many mnemonic verses, it testifies to the pedagogy of that time. It can be said to be the earliest 'certification' of any formal educational curriculum in Denmark, since the Scandinavian Universities were founded only much later. Thus, the selection of theological themes and their mutual 'ranking' gives an interesting picture of Dominican practice in the period." Now we turn our attention to a brief comparison of Augustine of Dacia's distich with similar documents of the Middle Ages.

---

[21] A. Walz, *Augustini de Dacia, O.P., 'Rotulus Pugillaris' Examinatus atque Editus,"* Rome: Pont. Institutum Angelicum, 1929, p. 30: "Verbi gratia Ierusalem secundum sensum litteralem est quaedam civitas in Iudaea. Et hoc signatum sive haec civitas secundem allegoricum significat ecclesiam militantem, secundum sensum tropologicum sive moralem signifcat animam fidelem et eius operationem, secundum sensum anagogicum significat ecclesiam triumphantem."

The Franciscan Nicholas of Lyra is credited with a couplet that varies slightly from that of Augustine of Dacia.[22] H. Brinkmann, maintaining that Augustine of Dacia was the author of the couplet, noted however, that Nicholas of Lyra had changed the anagogical reference to "*quo tendas anagogia*" from Augustine of Dacia's "*quid speres anagogia.*"[23] Nicholas had, according to de Lubac, quoted the distich in his commentary on St. Paul's Letter to the Galatians around the year 1330.[24] De Lubac asserted that the modification introduced by Nicholas "does not change the meaning."[25] Next let us consider theological education and pastoral formation in the Dominican communities.

4. Study in the Priories of the Order

St. Dominic prized education. James Weisheipl, O.P., considered the very nature of study: "What did St. Dominic and the early

---

[22] Joseph Cardinal Ratzinger observed that "the Scholastic maxim of Nicholas of Lyra: "Littera gesta docet, quid credas allegoria, Moralis quid agas, quo tendas anagogia" (quoted in the Quaracchi edition of Bonaventure's works, 5:205, n. 5" (*Principles of Catholic Theology: Building Stones for a Fundamental Theology*, trans. M.F. McCarthy, San Francisco: Ignatius Press, 1987, p. 181, n. 157).

[23] H. Brinkmann, *Mittelalterliche Hermeneutik*, Tübingen: Max Niemeyer Verlag, 1980, p. 244. Clearly this is the case since Augustine published the *Rotulus* around 1260 and Nicholas of Lyra was only born in 1270. This difference was also noted by Jean Greisch, *Entendre d'une autre Oreille. Les enjeaux philosophiques de l'herméneutique biblique*, Paris, Bayard, 2006, pp. 144-145. Brinkmann indicated that the statement was similar to that of Hugh of St. Victor (1096-1141), only he does not name anagogical, since he included that theme under allegorical. Mulchahey, *First*, p. 139 observed: "The purpose of reading the Bible '*cursorie*' is, of course, to read first and foremost for the historical sense, the *sensus historicus*; and, in medieval exegesis at least from the time of Hugh of St-Victor, to read Scripture for the *sensus historicus* meant to read in order to understand the narrative structure of the text as well as its literal meaning."

[24] De Lubac, *Medieval Exegesis*, Vol. 1, p. 1 [= *Exégèse médiévale* I, p. 1, p. 23].

[25] De Lubac, *Medieval Exegesis*, Vol. 1, p. 2 [= *Exégèse médiévale* I, p. 24]. So also J.A. Fitzmyer, *The Biblical Commission's Document "The Interpretation of the Bible in the Church." Text and Commentary*, Rome: Editrice Pontificio Istituto Biblico, 1995, p. 118, n. 158.

brethren mean by the word 'study'? Does study mean simply reading, as one would read a newspaper, a magazine, or a bestseller? The Latin verb *studere* means a pushing forward with effort, or a striving after something with zeal. The Latin word *studium* means not only 'study' or a place of study in the English sense, but very often it has its original sense of 'zeal'."[26]

Thus Dominican education in the priories was directed to the preparation of the young friars (*iuvenes fratres*) as preachers and confessors. The *Rotulus pugillaris* "became the standard textbook of the training of young friars in Dacia," which H. de Lubac understood was intended to benefit the "simple."[27] De Lubac further asserts that "its form was meant to act as an aid to memory and was at once popular and quasischolastic."[28] The *iuvenes fratres* were to know and understand these essentials, and then they would be examined and approved to preach and hear confessions.

Within the Dominican priories there were *fratres communes*,[29] "those, that is, who were not selected for special studies at a *Studium*

---

[26] J.A. Weisheipl, "The Place of Study in the Ideal of St. Dominic," River Forest, IL, 1960, II,1.

[27] H. de Lubac, *Medieval Exegesis. The Four Senses of Scripture*, Vol. 1, Grand Rapids: Eerdmans, 1998 & Edinburgh: T&T Clark p. 1 [= *Exégèse médiévale. Les quatre sens de l'Écriture*, Paris: Aubier, p. 23], quoting Augustine of Dacia. So also Mulchahey, *First*, p. 204, who explains further: Walz, "Des Aage," p. 204, described the work as "das theologische Handbuchlein." As a literary form it would be considered a compendium or a Summula (Walz, "Des Aage," p. 247). Johnny Gøgsig Grandjean Jakobsen: Review of: Johannes Schütz: *Hüter der Wirklichkeit. Der Dominikanerorden in der mittelalterlichen Gesellschaft Skandinaviens*, Göttingen: V&R unipress 2014, in: sehepunkte 15 (2015), Nr. 2 [15.02.2015], URL: http://www.sehepunkte.de/2015/02/25880.html. H. de Lubac, *Medieval Exegesis*, Vol. 1, p. 1 quoting Augustine of Dacia. So also Mulchahey, who explains further: "For 'simple' read not only the uneducated people, but the simple friars or *fratres communes* who will serve them" (*First*, p. 204).

[28] De Lubac, *Medieval Exegesis*, p. 1 [=*Exégèse médiévale*, pp. 23-24].

[29] Boyle, L. "Notes on the Education of the 'fratres communes' in the Dominican Order in the Thirteenth Century," in F. Creytens and P. Künzle (eds.), *Xenia medii Aevi Historiam illustrantia oblata T. Kaeppeli*, (Storia e letteratura

provinciale or a *Studium generale*."[30] It was for the *iuniores* explicitly that Augustine of Dacia, O.P., when serving as provincial of Scandinavia, wrote his *Rotulus pugillaris*. The General Chapter of 1259 insisted: "Let them not become (be made) lectors or preachers or confessors unless there are (should be) so (such) sufficient that they could exercise these offices without notable danger of this kind."[31] The first Constitutions of the Order in 1220 emphasized the importance of study and required that each house would have a superior (prior) and a teacher (lector).[32] "As a rule, all young Dominicans began their studies in a local priory under the local lector, and most never obtained any education other than that provided in these priories and by these lectors. When the lectors taught Scripture, they were advised to concentrate first on the literal sense.[33] Opportunities for higher studies were small."[34] Attendance at the lectures was considered mandatory and a dispensation was required to excuse them from the lector's classes. "No one, not even the prior, was to be absent from lectures."[35] Mulchahey, a student of the distinguished medieval scholar Leonard Boyle, O.P., observed that students "would be allowed to miss choir before they were allowed to

---

raccolta di Studi e Testi 141), Rome: Edizioni di Storia e Letteratura, 1978, p. 253. It seems to have been a 14th-century term. So also Mulchahey, *First*, p. 131, n. 4.

[30] Boyle, "Notes," p. 253.

[31] Ibid., p. 254, quoting from *Acta capitulorum generalium ordinis praedicatorum*, I (1898), p. 100. "Non fiant lectores vel praedicatores vel confessores nisi sint tam sufficientes quod possint sin periculo notabili huiusmodi officia exercere."

[32] Ibid., p. 255. Walz pointed out that Albert the Great was a lector in the Dominican communities in Strassbourg, Freiburg, Hildesheim, Regensburg, and Cologne (Walz, "Des Aage," p. 234).

[33] Ibid., p. 140: "Instructions to Dominican lectors that they 'expound the literal sense first' in their lectures on the Bible survive, in fact, from as late as the first quarter of the Fourteenth Century."

[34] Ibid., "Notes," p. 255.

[35] Ibid., "Notes," p. 255, 256.

skip class."³⁶ To clarify, superiors could grant dispensations from the communal choral office so that the friars could attend to study and preaching. Mulchahey highlighted the purpose of the lectures in the priory schools: "In a convent school, where the majority of the friars in attendance were either just beginning their theological education or were men destined to spend most of the lives as work-a-day preachers and confessors, the purpose of the lectures they heard was to give them a basic familiarity with Scripture and the fundamental arguments of Christian theology, the tools of the priest."³⁷

Those who were particularly gifted intellectually were given certain privileges. "Students of particular promise could be assigned private cells, in which they were allowed to sleep apart from their brothers in the dormitory, to read, write, pray, and to stay up late to study by candlelight."³⁸ Clearly these concessions point to the importance of study in the Order. "Although the original mission of the Dominican order was that of preaching, within four years of its foundation the order became an Order of Confessors as well as an Order of Preachers."³⁹

Dominic valued the university education available and sent friars to study at Bologna (1218), Palencia (1220), Montpellier (1221), and Oxford (1221) just before he died.⁴⁰ This would have been in accord with the Primitive Constitutions of the Order. "If the prior of a province or a kingdom has brethren capable of teaching and who can

---

³⁶ Mulchahey, *First*, p. 133.

³⁷ Ibid., p. 139.

³⁸ Ibid., p. 39. In n. 131 she cited *Constitutiones antiquae* II.29, p. 362. Cf. P. Mandonnet - M.H. Vicaire, *Saint Dominique*, II, p. 290.

³⁹ L. Boyle, "Notes," p. 249. He continued: "This change, it appears, was not wholly the doing of Dominic, but was largely due to the attempts of pope Honorius III to implement certain constitutions of the Fourth Lateran Council in 1215, under his predecessor Innocent III."

⁴⁰ Ibid., p. 250.

shortly learn to rule, he shall take care to send them to places where study is flourishing."[41] The training of those who would be Doctors of Theology consisted of a minimum of four years of study. The Scriptural interpretation of the saints was recommended as a guide to the literal sense, particularly of the Psalms and Prophets.[42]

Study needs books. They are treated under the theme of "Miscellany" in Chapter XXXVI of the Primitive Constitutions. "When a brother is sent from one province to another to assume authority, he shall take with him all his books, glosses, bible, and manuscripts. If he is not sent to rule, he shall take only his bible and writings. If he should die on the way, the house of destination shall say the Masses and psalters for him, and shall have right to the books he had."[43] Four friars chosen by the Provincial Chapter functioned as Visitators, to determine whether the friars were being faithful to their religious life. The Visitators were given the task of considering "whether the brethren are living in peace, are diligent in study and fervent in preaching; what their reputation is and what is the fruit of their labors"; Dominic spoke of the members of the Order being assiduous in study.

5. Augustine of Dacia and Albert the Great

A debate ensued whether the distich originated with Augustine of Dacia or with Albert the Great. A Jesuit Scripture scholar, Alberto Vaccari, a *peritus* (expert) at Vatican II, was of the opinion that

---

[41] *Primitive Constitutions*, Part II, XVI: The Power of the Prior Provincial. http://www.op.org/sites/www.op.org/files/public/documents/fichier/primitive_consti_en.pdf

[42] *Primitive Constitutions*, Part II, XXX: "No one shall become a public doctor unless he has studied and heard lectures in theology for at least four years. *Likewise, none of our brethren shall read into the Psalms or Prophets any literal sense other than what the saints approve and confirm*"

[43] *Primitive Constitutions* XXXVI, http://www.op.org/sites/www.op.org/files/public/documents/fichier/primitive_consti_en.pdf

Augustine drew on Albert the Great for the idea of the couplet, proposing first the effect that Augustine's formula had. "But the learned Dominican, in those verses does none other than place in a brief and easy formula a doctrine already widespread in the schools."[44] Vaccari pondered Albert's influence upon Augustine of Dacia:

> Albert the Great, whenever he speaks of it, constantly goes with the verses of Augustine of Dacia; you can't find two authors from that time who are so much in agreement. The agreement is not accidental. Albert and Augustine were not only contemporaries, but they lived together for some time, probably in Cologne, where Albert taught for many years, and Augustine had entered into the Order of Preachers. Granting the dependence of the one on the other, there can be no doubt both who gives and who receives; Albert is the teacher, and Augustine the disciple. Whence it is noticed that the great Albert not only held the common doctrine of the four senses, but contributed in no small way to define it and to propagate it.[45]

---

[44] http://www.padrealbertovaccari.it/Vaccari served as Professor of Old Testament Exegesis at the Pontifical Biblical Institute from 1912-1959. A. Vaccari, "S. Alberto Magno e l'esegesi medievale," in *Biblica* 13 (1932) 257-272, 369-384, esp. pp. 261[= *Scritti di erudizione e di filologia. Bd. 2: Per la storia del testo e dell'esegesi biblica*, Roma: Edizioni di Storia e Letteratura Istituto Gráfico Tiberino, 1958, 317-346, esp. pp. 319-320]. "Ma il dotto domenicano in quei versi non fa che porre in breve e facile formula una dottrina già invalsa nelle scuole." This was noted by A. Walz, "das berühmte Distichon über Schriftsinne, das Aage bringt, spiegelt nach Vaccari die bereits in der Schule allgemein geltende Lehre wieder ("Des Aage," 1954, p. 248, quoting A. Vaccari, "S. Alberto Magno," *Biblica* 13 (1932) 261 [= *Scritti di Erudizione e di Filologia, Vol. 2, Per la Storia del Testo e dell'Esegesi Biblica*, Rome: Edizioni di Storia e Letteratura, 1958, p. 319-320]).

[45] Vaccari, "S. Alberto Magno," p. 265 [= *Scritti*, p. 323-324]: "Alberto Magno ogniquavolta ne parla, va constantements coi versi di Agostino di Dacia; non si trovino tanto d'accordo. Nè l'accordo può essere fortuito; Alberto ed Agostino erona non soltanto contemporanei, ma hanno covissuto per qualche tempo insieme, probabilmente a Colonia, dove Alberto insegnò molti anni, ed Agostino era entrato nell'Ordine de Predicatori. Posts la dipendenza dell'uno dall'altro, non può esser dubbio chi sia che dàe chi riceve; Alberto è il maestro ed Agostino

In contrast, Marie-Joseph Lagrange, O.P., founder of the École biblique in Jerusalem, argued that to determine the dependence of Augustine of Dacia upon Albert the Great, as Vaccari had done, was an insoluble matter because they had lived together in some Dominican community.[46] Having considered possibilities related to the origin of the couplet, let us examine how the distich has been assessed by exegetes and scholars of the 20th Century.

6. The Reception of Augustine's Distich by Exegetes in the 20th Century

a. *The Catechism of the Catholic Church*

The Catechism of the Catholic Church (1997) contained a distich and referred to Augustine of Dacia as the author. This is found in the section in Chapter Two "God Comes to Meet Man," Article 3 "Sacred Scripture," which offered a presentation summarizing the senses of Scripture. The prelude to this section begins: "According to ancient tradition, one can distinguish between two *senses* of Scripture: the literal and the spiritual, the latter being subdivided into the allegorical, moral, and anagogical senses. The profound concordance of the four senses guarantees all its richness to the living reading of Scripture in the Church."[47] However, as it is written, it contains the

---

   il discepolo. Donde rilevasi che il grande Alberto non solo tenne la commune dottrina dei Quattro sensi, ma contribuì non poco a definirla e propagarla."

[46] "Aussi bien ces questions de priorité sont peut-être isolubles, précisément à cause de l'amitié qui unissait ces deux puissants esprits dans la fraternité d'un cloître dominicain" (M.-J. Lagrange, "Bulletin," in *Revue biblique* 42 (1933) 284. This debate had not escaped the notice of A. Walz. "Lagrange meint in der Revue biblique 42 (1933) 284 die Abhängigkeit des Augustinus von Albert dem Grossen sei nicht so einfach zu bestimmen, wie Vaccari es tue. Vgl. P.A. Vaccari Auctor versuum de quattuor Scripturae sensibus: Verbum Domini 9 (1929) 212-214. Walz, "Des Aage," p. 248, n. 242.

[47] *Catechism of the Catholic Church*, Washington, D.C.: USCCB – Libreria Editrice Vaticana, 1997, p. 33, §118.

formulation attributed to Nicholas of Lyra, "*quo tendas anagogia*," rather than that of Augustine of Dacia, "*quid speres anagogia.*"

b. Joseph Ratzinger, Pope Benedict XVI

Pope Benedict XVI, who guided the writings of *The Catechism*, referred to Augustine of Dacia and his distich in two works: first, his address when he met with representatives of the World of Culture at the Collège des Bernardins, Paris in September, 2008; second, in the post-Synodal address, *Verbum Domini* in 2010.[48] In the 2008 address Pope Benedict wrote that Augustine of Dacia's couplet could be "rather disconcerting": "From this perspective one can understand the formulation of a medieval couplet that at first sight appears rather disconcerting: *littera gesta docet – quid credas allegoria* ... (cf. Augustine of Dacia, *Rotulus pugillaris*, I). The letter indicates the facts; what you have to believe is indicated by allegory, that is to say, by Christological and pneumatological exegesis."[49] Though the Pope does not elaborate, he seems to indicate that the first strophe would be the troubling part, but only at first sight. In *Verbum Domini* he writes more positively, proposing that the couplet highlights "the unity and interrelation between the literal sense and the spiritual sense, which for its part is subdivided into three senses which deal

---

[48] The occasion was the 150th anniversary of the apparitions of the Blessed Virgin Mary at Lourdes (September 12 - 15, 2008). It will also be remembered that Cardinal Joseph Ratzinger was Prefect of the Congregation for the Doctrine of the Faith when the document, *The Interpretation of the Bible in the Church*, was composed and promulgated. Other than a preface to the document, it is unknown whether he had contributed in any way to the final composition.

[49] Address of His Holiness Benedict XVI, Collège des Bernardins, Paris, Friday, 12 September 2008. https://w2.vatican.va/content/benedict-xvi/en/speeches/2008/september/documents/hf_ben-xvi_spe_20080912_parigi-cultura.html.

with the contents of the faith, with the moral life and with our eschatological aspiration."⁵⁰

c. Joseph Fitzmyer, S.J. and Peter Williamson

Jesuit Father Joseph Fitzmyer, international scholar and member of the Pontifical Biblical Commission at the time the document, *The Interpretation of the Bible in Church*, was written and promulgated, wrote a commentary on the document since the curial document quoted the distich and mentioned "Augustine of Denmark (13th Century)." In his note Fitzmyer indicated that it is "usually attributed to Augustine of Dacia, O.P., who was of Scandinavian origin (Denmark) and died in 1282."⁵¹ Fitzmyer pointed out that the fourfold sense of Scripture grew out of a three-part sense derived from Origen (*historia, moralis, allegoria*). The issue he raises here is that there are some Christian interpreters through the ages who have "reacted against such allegorizing or spiritualizing of Scripture."

Several years later Fitzmyer termed the distich "problematic." He also mentioned Augustine of Dacia's couplet in his book, *The Interpretation of Scripture: In Defense of the Historical-Critical Method*.⁵² He described the problem in the following way: "...but in

---

⁵⁰ Benedict XVI, Post Synodal Exhortation *Verbum Domini* (Sept. 30, 2010), §37, at The Holy See, http://w2.vatican.va/content/benedict-xvi/en/apost_exhortations/documents/hf_ben-xvi_exh_20100930_verbum-domini.html.

⁵¹ Fitzmyer, *The Biblical Commission's Document*, pp. 117-118. He refers to works of Walz and Vaccari both of which were published in 1929.

⁵² J.A. Fitzmyer, *The Interpretation of Scripture: In Defense of the Historical-Critical Method*, NY: Paulist, 2008, p. 94. This chapter "is a reduced combination of two articles, "Problems of the Literal and Spiritual Senses of Scripture" in *Louvain Studies* 20 (1995) 134-46, and "The Senses of Scripture Today," in *Irish Theological Quarterly* 62 (1996-97) 101-117" (p. ix). In n. 42 (p. 116) Fitzmyer noted: "The distich is usually ascribed to Augustine of Dacia, O.P., who really was of Scandinavian origin (+ 1282). It merely formulated in a distich what was already distinguished earlier, by Augustine of Hippo." In a previous book, *Scripture, the Soul of Theology*, New York, Paulist, 1994, p. 67, Fitzmyer mentioned Augustine of Dacia and quoted the couplet but did not offer a negative appraisal.

reality it is the connotations of the medieval senses that create the problem, when *littera* is set over against *allegoria* and *moralis*." Fitzmyer contends: "That medieval distich, which many quote with approval, is problematic, because it asserts that the *littera*, or 'literal sense,' would have nothing to do with faith or with what one is to believe. Astoundingly, it says rather that the Christian faith is to be governed by the allegorical meaning of Scripture: *quid credas allegoria!*"[53] In support of his position he cites Avery Cardinal Dulles and his comments on the Biblical Commission's document: "...this effort [of the Commission] to set forth the sense of Scripture will surely evoke further discussion. The distinctions are not as clear as one might hope."[54] Fitzmyer faulted not only *The Interpretation of the Bible in the Church*, but "with the way the question of the senses of Scripture has been discussed up until now."[55]

Peter Williamson addressed Fitzmyer's concerns in *Catholic Principles for Interpreting Scripture: A Study of the Pontifical Commission's The Interpretation of the Bible in the Church* (2001).[56] He did not believe that the couplet should provide such difficulties as Fitzmyer saw:

> Fitzmyer also maintains that this usage of the term 'spiritual sense' in II.B.2.d means something different than the Christological sense intended by the Commission's definition. He says that it would perhaps be better to refer to this meaning for Christians of the OT as 'the 'religious import' of what has

---

[53] Fitzmyer, *Interpretation*, p. 94.

[54] Ibid., p. 96, quoting A. Dulles, "The Interpretation of the Bible in the Church. A Theological Appraisal," in W. Geerlings and M. Seckler (eds.), *Kirche sein: nachkonziliare Theologie im Dienst der Kirchenreform: Für Hermann Josef Pottmeyer,* Freiburg im B.: Herder, 1994, 29-37, pp. 31-32 [= "The Senses of Scripture Today," *ITQ* 62 (1996-97) p. 111].

[55] Fitzmyer, *Interpretation*, p. 96.

[56] Rome: Gregorian and Biblical Press, 2001, p. 193, n. 11.

been literally expressed ("Literal and Spiritual Senses," 144-145). But Fitzmyer feels prevented from referring to it as the literal sense on account of the traditional understanding of the senses summarized in Augustine of Denmark's couplet ('Littera gesta docet, quid credas allegoria, / moralis quid aga, quid speres anagogia', quoted by the PBC in II.B.a) which grants only 'gesta', i.e. deeds or events, to the littera, and instruction for faith and morals to allegoria and moralis. Fitzmyer is right not to want to refer to the non-christological religious meaning of the OT as the spiritual sense. To do so is to deprive the inspired literal sense of the OT of its religious meaning and to undermine the univocity of the Commission's helpful new definition of the spiritual sense. However, Fitzmyer need not be stopped by Augustine of Denmark's couplet. That division of the senses really only applies to narrative texts – not psalms, wisdom literature, or other OT genres. Likewise, the spirit-letter dichotomy which characterizes some patristic and medieval interpretation and which reserves all the important signification for Christian faith and life to the spiritual sense does not harmonize with the Biblical Commission's definitions of the literal and spiritual senses.[57]

d. Carolyn Osiek, RSCJ

Carolyn Osiek, RSCJ, quoted the distich of Augustine of Denmark in her Presidential Address to the Society of Biblical Literature in 2005 followed by a translation and analysis.

> For those whose Latin is a little rusty, I give Roland Murphy's translation: 'The letter (or literal sense) teaches facts; the allegorical, what we are to believe; the moral, what we are to do; the anagogical, what we are to hope for'. As Murphy goes on to note, it does not always work this way, Sometimes the literal

---

[57] Ibid.

sense teaches what we are to believe or even hope for, and spiritual meaning cannot be limited to allegory.[58]

Thus Osiek's position is similar to that of Fitzmyer. Both scholars noted how Christian and Jewish interpreters might similarly or differently apply and might understand the fourfold sense of Scripture. Osiek observed further that the moral sense may be lacking in certain passages. "It is doubtful that an adequate moral or spiritual sense could be retrieved today, for example, from prescriptions that slaves obey their masters, as found in the household codes of the NT."[59]

e. Further References to Augustine of Dacia's Distich

Augustine of Dacia's distich is mentioned in various other publications, but the authors generally do not elaborate on it.[60]

---

[58] C. Osiek, "Catholic or catholic? Biblical Scholarship at the Center" in *Journal of Biblical Literature*, Vol. 125, No. 1 (Spring, 2006), pp. 19 [= *Presidential Voices: The Society of Biblical Literature in the Twentieth Century*, H.W. Attridge and J.C. VanderKam (eds.), Atlanta: Society of Biblical Literature, 2006, p. 339. R.E. Murphy, "What is Catholic about Catholic Biblical Scholarship – Revisited," in *Biblical Theology Bulletin* 28/5 (1998) 116.

[59] Ibid., p. 19 [= *Presidential Voices*, 339].

[60] R.E. McNally, "Medieval Exegesis", in *Theological Studies* 22.3 (1961), p. 447 and "Medieval Exegesis", in Editorial Staff at Catholic University of America (eds.), *New Catholic Encyclopedia*, Vol. 1, NY: McGraw-Hill, 1967, col. 708a; "Augustinus", in Svend Cedergreen Bech (ed.), *Dansk Biografisk Leksikon* [*Danish Biographical Lexicon*], 1979-84, third edition http://denstoredanske.dk/Dansk_Biografisk_Leksikon/Kirke_og_tro/Munk/Augustinus; K. Schatzgeyer, *Schriften zur Verteidigung der Messe* (Corpus Catholicorum), Münster: Aschendorff, 1984, p. 411, n.108, identifying Augustine of Dacia as the author, but noting the variation in phrasing from a citation of Nicholas of Lyra; R. Peppermüller, "Schriftsinne", in R-H. Bautier (ed.), *Lexikon des Mittalters*, Vol. 7, Munich/Zürich: Artemis, 1986, col. 1569; M. Dubois, "Mystical and Realistic Element in the Exegesis and Hermeneutics of Thomas Aquinas", in B. Uffenheimer and G. Henning Reventlow (eds.), *Creative Biblical Exegesis: Christian and Jewish Hermeneutics Through the Centuries*, Sheffield: Sheffield Academic Press and NY: Bloomsbury Publishing, 1988, pp. 40; A.J. Minnis, *Medieval Theory of Authorship. Scholastic Literary Attitudes in the Later Middle Ages*, Philadelphia: University of Pennsylvania Press,[2]1988, p. 232, n. 153, referred to the distich on p. 34. Though stating that the "distich has been attributed to Augustine of Dacia", citing the article by F. Chatillon, he recorded it employing the language of Nicholas of Lyra. He also

indicated 1282 as the date of Augustine's death. J.H. Martin, "The Four Senses of Scripture: Lessons from the Thirteenth Century", in *Pacifica* 2 (1989), p. 87, n. 1, using Nicholas of Lyra's phrase "quod tendas anagogia", though attributing the couplet to Augustine of Dacia; Augustine, Saint, Bishop of Hippo, *St. Augustine on Genesis. Two Books on Genesis. Against the Manichees and On the Literal Interpretation of Genesis: An Unfinished Book*, trans. R.J. Teske, Washington, D.C.: Catholic University of America Press, 1991, p. 33, n. 61; R.E. Brown "Hermeneutics", in R.E. Brown, et al. (eds.), *The New Jerome Biblical Commentary*, Englewood Cliffs, NJ, 1991, p. 1155, not attributed to any author, but using the phrasing of Nicholas of Lyra; H. Haag, "La Palabra de Dios se hace Libro en la Sagrada Scritura" in J. Feiner and M. Löhrer (eds.), *Mysterium Salutis. Manual de Teologia como Historia de la Salvacion*, trans. M. Villanueva Salas, Madrid: Ediciones Cristianidad, Vol. 5, ⁴1992, p. 463, n. 335. P. Walter, "Shriftsinne", in W. Lasprer (ed.), *Lexikon für Theologie und Kirche*, Freiburg: Herder, 1993, Vol. 9, col. 268; W.-D. Hauschild, *Lehrbuch der Kirchen- und Dogmen- geschichte*, Bd. 1, *Alte Kirche und Mittelalter,* Gütersloh: Gütersloher Verlaghaus, 1995, p. 627, §10.17.3.1; L.J. Smith, "Bible, Christian Interpretation of", in W.W. Kibler, et al. (eds.). *Medieval France: An Encyclopedia*, NY: Routledge, 1995, pp. 232-233; J.M. Rovira Belloso, *Introducción a la Teología*, Madrid: Biblioteca de Autores Creativos, 1996, p. 208, n. 27; M. Walter, "Den Glauben verstehen mit J.S. Bachs Kantaten – am Beispiel der Taufe", in Albert Clement (ed.), *Das Blut Jesu und die Lehre von der Versöhnung im Werk Johann Sebastian Bachs. Proceedings of the International Colloquium The Blood of Jesus and the Doctrine of Reconciliation in the Works of Johann Sebastian Bach. Amsterdam 14-17 September 1993* (Koninklijke Nederlandse Akademie von Wetenschappen Verhandelingen, Afd. Letterkunde, Nieuwe Reeks, deel 164), Amsterdam 1996, p. 161, n. 22. J. Grondin, *Introduction to Philosophical Hermeneutics*, trans. by J. Weinsheimer, New Haven, CT: Yale University Press, 1997, pp. 31-32; P. Beauchamp, "Sens de l'Eciture", in J.-Y. Lacoste (ed.), *Dictionnaire critique de théologie*, Paris: Presses Universitaires de France, 1998, p. 1087. He maintained that the distich is a summary of the teaching of St. Thomas Aquinas, as de Lubac had argued. Beauchamp noted further that Augustine's distich contained the variant *quid speres* for anagogical; R.E. Murphy, "What is Catholic", pp. 112-119, esp. p. 116; S.K. Wood, *Spiritual Exegesis and the Church in the Theology of Henri de Lubac*, Grand Rapids: Eerdmans and Edinburgh: T&T Clark, 1998, reprint Eugene, OR: Wipf&Stock, 2010, p. 27, n. 5, where she quoted Nicholas of Lyra's version in the text, but in the footnote observed that the "couplet actually concludes 'quid speres anagogia'" referring to McNally and Walz; J. Dyer, "The Psalms in Monastic Prayer", in N.E. Van Deusen (ed.), *The Place of the Psalms in the Intellectual Culture of the Middle Ages*, Albany, NY: State University Press, 1999, p. 69, citing Augustine of Dacia, but quoting the version of Nicholas of Lyra as found in de Lubac; E. Cousins, "The Fourfold Sense of Scripture in Christian Mysticism", in S.T. Katz, ed., *Mysticism and Sacred Scripture*, Oxford: Oxford University Press, 2000, p. 123; M. McNamara, *The Psalms in the Early Irish Church*, Sheffield: Sheffield Academic Press, 2000, p. 95, who stated: "according to some by Augustine of Dacia, O.P., died 1282, according to others by Nicholas of Lyra"; A. de D. Mercedes, *Retórica, Predicación y Vida Cotidiana en la Ciudad de México (1735), según Francisco de la Concepción*

Barbosa, O.F.M., STD Dissertation, Pamplona: Universidad de Navarra, 2002, p. 196, n. 196; B.S. Benfell, "Biblical Exegesis", in C. Kleinhenz, *Medieval Italy: An Encyclopedia* (Routledge Encyclopedias of the Middle Ages), London and New York: Routledge, 2003, p. 122; H. Crouzel, "Biblical Exegesis", in K. Rahner (ed.), *Encyclopedia of Theology: A Concise Sacramentum Mundi*, London: Burns & Oates, 2004, col.132; Craig Bartholomew, Mary Healy, Karl Möller, Robin Parry (eds.), *Out of Egypt: Biblical Theology and Biblical Interpretation*, Grand Rapids, MI: Zondervan, 2004, p. 78; S. Disalvo, "«Atal allur a catade» : Recuperación figural de la antigüedad pagana en las cantigas de Santa María de Alfonso X" in *Olivar* vol .5 no.5 La Plata jul./dic. 2004, p. 1, n. 1, who identified it as the work of Nicholas of Lyra, but in a footnote stated that the distich is also attributed to Augustine of Dacia. W. Yarchin, *History of Biblical Interpretation. A Reader*, Peabody, MA: Hendrickson, 2004, p. 101. J. Greisch, *Entendre d'une autre oreille. Les enjeux philosophiques de l'herméneutique biblique*, Paris, Bayard, coll. « Bible et philosophie », 2006, p. 145; A.E. McGrath, *The Intellectual Origins of the European Reformation*, Malden, MA and Oxford: Wiley, 1987, ²2004, p. 149; J.M. van der Meer and S. Mandelbrote, *Nature and Scripture in the Abrahamic Religions: Up to 1700*, Vol. 1, Leiden: Brill, 2008, p. 185; P. Viviano, "The Senses of Scripture", Washington, D.C.: USCCB, 2008, p. 3; M. Frascari, J. Hale, B. Starkey (eds.), *From Models to Drawings: Imagination and Representation in Architecture*, London and New York: Routledge, 2008, p. 27; M. Frascari, *Eleven Exercises in the Art of Architectural Drawing: Slow Food for the Architect's Imagination*, London and New York: Routledge, 2011, p. 59. T. Kirby, E. Campi, and F.A. James III (eds.), *A Companion to Peter Martyr Vermigli*, Leiden: Brill, 2009, p. 83, n. 67, stipulated that though "famously cited by Nicholas of Lyra", de Lubac attributed the "description of the four senses to Augustine of Dacia". C. Kourie, "A Mystical Reading of Paul", in *Scriptura* 101 (2009) pp. 239, n. 8; T.M. Seebohm, *Hermeneutics. Method and Methodology*, NY and Heidelberg: Springer, 2010, p. 29; R.N. Soulen, *Sacred Scripture: A Short History of Interpretation*, Westminster/John Knox, 2010, p. 99; M.T. Gerlach, *Lex Orandi, Lex Legendi: A Correlation of the Roman Canon and the Fourfold Sense of Scripture*, Ph.D. dissertation, Marquette University, 2011, p. 27, n. 93, pointing to Pope Benedict XVI's use of the distich in *Verbum Domini*; I. Levy, *The Letter to the Galatians* (Medieval Commentary series), Grand Rapids: Eerdmans, 2001, p. 252, n. 18; P. O'Callaghan, *Christ Our Hope. An Introduction to Eschatology*, Washington, D.C.: Catholic University of America Press, 2011, p. 331, referencing only the anagogical sense. See n. 12 where he references the IBC, II, B. and see his study: *La Biblia en la configuración de la teologia*, p. 873-874; C.S. Morrissey, "A Model for the Many Senses of Scripture. From the Literal to the Spiritual in Genesis 22 with Thomas Aquinas", in *Contagion* 19 (2012) p. 232, who argued, "But Scripture has many senses, a truth famously expressed in the medieval distich of Augustine of Dacia, best known in the version of Nicholas of Lyra". R. van Nieuwenhove, *An Introduction to Medieval Theology*, Cambridge: Cambridge University Press, 2012, p. 47, stated that Augustine phrased it and that Nicholas of Lyra had quoted it, though it reflected the phrasing of Nicholas; E. Falque, "¿Es Fundamental la Hermenéutica? Is Hermeneutics Fundamental?", in *Ideas y Valores*, 62.152 (2013):199-223, p. 201; T.R. Hatina, *New Testament Theology and its Quest for Relevance. Ancient Texts and Modern Readers*, New

York, Bloomsbury T&T Clark, 2013, p. 96; W. Otten, "On Sacred Attunement, Its Meaning and Consequences. A Meditation on Christian Theology", *The Journal of Religion*, 93.4, 2013, p. 486; K. Froehlich with Mark Burrows, *Sensing the Scriptures. Aminadab's Chariot and the Predicament of Biblical Interpretation*, Grand Rapids: Eerdmans, 2014, p. 9, n. 16; G. McLarney, *St. Augustine's Interpretation of the Psalms of Ascent*, Washington, D.C.: Catholic University of America Press, 2014, p. 57, n. 184, crediting Augustine of Dacia but employing the phrasing of Nicholas of Lyra; A. Puig I Tàrrech, "L'Hermenèutica de l'Escriptura. Estudi de Dei Verbum 12", in *RCatT* 39/1 (2014), p. 162; E. Bianchi, *Lectio Divina: From God's Word to Our Lives*, Brewster, MA: Paraclete Press, 2015, p. 83; D. Klepper, "Historicizing Allegory: The Jew as Hagar in Medieval Christian Text and Image", in *Church History* 84/2 (2015) 327, n. 48: "This poem seems to have originated with a Dominican friar, Augustine of Dacia (d. 1282), around 1260, Nicholas of Lyra employed it repeatedly in his fourteenth-century commentaries, with the last line reading instead 'quo tendas anagogia'...". T. Bushlack, "Lectio, Intentio, and the 'Twofold Tropological Sense': Lectio Divina as a Guide to the Cultivation of Practical Wisdom", *The American Benedictine Review* 67/1 (2016), p. 32, n. 7. Though he attributed the couplet to Augustine of Denmark he quoted the text which used the phrasing of Nicholas of Lyra. In the note he cited *The Interpretation of the Bible in the Church*, which correctly quoted Augustine's distich. T. Toom, *Patristic Theories of Biblical Interpretation: The Latin Fathers*, Cambridge: Cambridge University Press, 2016, p. 46, asserted that Nicholas of Lyra "invoked the four senses of Scripture from Augustine of Dacia's famous couplet". Others cite the work, but without attribution: R. Grant, *A Short History of Interpretation*, NY: Macmillan, 1960, p. 100; R.A. Muller, *Dictionary of Latin and Greek Theological Terms*, Grand Rapids: Baker, 1985, s.v., "Quadriga"; S. Schneiders, "Scripture and Spirituality", in B. McGinn and J. Meyendorff (eds.), *Christian Spirituality. Origins to the Twelfth Century*, NY: Crossroad, 1985, p. 15, "a famous medieval couplet of uncertain authorship". She quoted the Nicholas of Lyra version, "quo tendas anagogia". H. Caplan, "The Four Senses of Scriptural Interpretation and the Mediæval Theory of Preaching", in *Speculum*, Vol. 4/3 (1929), p. 286, credited Nicholas of Lyra and cited his phrasing, while noting "made famous by Nicholas of Lyra and perhaps used by others before him". He also observed that "*Speres* sometimes appears for *tendas*" (n. 12); W. Otten, "The Power of the Bible in the Middle Ages", in W. Farmer, ed., *The International Bible Commentary*, Collegeville: Liturgical Press, 1988, p. 50; F. Hahn, *Theologie des Neuen Testaments: Die Einheit des Neuen Testaments*, Vol. 2, Tübingen: Mohr Siebeck, ²2005, p. 138; J.C. Warner, *The Augustinian Epic, Petrarch to Milton*, Ann Arbor, MI: University of Michigan Press, 2005, p. 7, who noted that "This distich is often attributed to Nicolas of Lyra but is traced by Lubac to Augustine of Dacia"; D. Bergant, *Scripture. History and Interpretation*, Collegeville, MN: Liturgical Press, 2008, p. 115, without attribution though utilizing the language of Nicholas of Lyra; A.L. Harvey, *Spiritual Reading: A Study of the Christian Practice of Reading Scripture*, Durham: Durham University: eTheses, 2012 (http://etheses.dur.ac.uk/3916), p. 130; L. Trainor, "Palindromic Structure in the Pardoner's Tale", in *Michigan Academician* Vol. 41, No. 1 (2012) 56, observed that Augustine of Dacia "reduced the 'senses' of medieval exegesis to a

7. Conclusion

Augustine of Dacia's distich has perdured and is still often quoted. While a few scholars have taken issue with the formulation pertaining to the literal sense, and the allegorical as the only sense deserving of belief, none have offered a suitable alternative. There have been no counter-proposals generally received that have replaced the distich. Though the idea is not original to Augustine of Dacia, the articulation in the form of a mnemonic distich may well be. It remains significant that a Dominican provincial in the 13th Century was concerned with the theological education and pastoral formation of the friars, preparing them in particular for the ministries of preaching and hearing confessions. He is a witness to a systematic program of education in the province. The *Rotulus pugillaris* provides a window into practical pastoral and theological training in Dominican priories in the 13th Century.

8. Bibliography

Augustine, Saint, Bishop of Hippo, *St. Augustine on Genesis. Two Books on Genesis. Against the Manichees and On the Literal Interpretation of Genesis: An Unfinished Book*, trans. R.J. Teske, Washington, D.C.: Catholic University of America Press, 1991.

"Augustinus," in Svend Cedergreen Bech (ed.), *Dansk Biografisk Leksikon* [Danish Biographical Lexicon], 1979-84, third edition. http://denstoredanske.dk/Dansk_Biografisk_Leksikon/Kirke_og_tro/Munk/Augustinus

---

little couplet, which was popularized by Nicolas of Lira"; S.M. Holmes, *Sacred Signs in Reformation Scotland: Interpreting Worship, 1488-1590*, Oxford: University Press, 2015, p. 24. In n. 50 he identified Augustine of Dacia as the author, but used the phrasing of Nicholas of Lyra; D. Vessey, "Medieval Hermeneutics", in N. Keane and C. Lawn (eds.), *The Blackwell Companion to Hermeneutics*, Chichester, West Sussex, UK and Malden, MA: John Wiley & Sons, 2016, p. 41; K. Madigan, "Catholic Interpretation of the Bible", D. Senior et al. (eds.) *Catholic Study Bible* (NABRE), New York: Oxford University Press, ^{3}2016.

Beauchamp, P. "Sense de l'Ecriture," in J.-Y. Lacoste, *Dictionnaire critique de théologie*, Paris: Presses Universitaires de France, 1998, cols. 1083-1089.

Benedict XVI, Address of His Holiness Benedict XVI, Collège des Bernardins, Paris, Friday, 12 September 2008. https://w2.vatican.va/content/benedict-xvi/en/speeches/2008/september/documents/hf_ben-xvi_spe_20080912_parigi-cultura.html.

--------. Post Synodal Exhortation *Verbum Domini* (Sept. 30, 2010), §37, at The Holy See, http://w2.vatican.va/content/benedict-xvi/en/apost_exhortations/documents/hf_ben-xvi_exh_20100930_verbum-domini.html.

Bergant, D. *Scripture. History and Interpretation*, Collegeville, MN: Liturgical Press, 2008.

Benfell, B.S. "Biblical Exegesis," in C. Kleinhenz (ed.), *Medieval Italy: An Encyclopedia* (Routledge Encyclopedias of the Middle Ages), London and New York: Routledge, 2003, p. 122.

Bianchi, E. *Lectio Divina: From God's Word to Our Lives*, Brewster, MA: Paraclete Press, 2015.

Boyle, L. "Notes on the Education of the 'fratres communes' in the Dominican Order in the Thirteenth Century," in F. Creytens and P. Künzle (eds.), *Xenia medii Aevi Historiam illustrantia oblata T. Kaeppeli*, (Storia e letterature raccolta di Studi e Testi 141), Rome: Edizioni di Storia e Letteratura, 1978, 249-269.

Bretzke, J.T. *Consecrated Phrases: A Latin Theological Dictionary; Latin Expressions Commonly Found in Theological Writings*, Third Edition, Collegeville, MN: Liturgical Press, 2013, p. 131.

Brinkmann, H. *Mittelalterliche Hermeneutik*, Tübingen: Max Niemeyer Verlag, 1980.

Brown, R.E. "Hermeneutics," in R.E. Brown, et al. (eds.), *The New Jerome Biblical Commentary*, Englewood Cliffs, NJ, 1991, p. 1146-1165.

Brož, J. "From Allegory to the Four Senses of Scripture. Hermeneutics of the Church Fathers and of the Christian Middle Ages," in P. Pokorný and J. Roskovec (eds.), *Philosophical Hermeneutics and Biblical Exegesis*, Tübingen: Mohr Siebeck, 2001, pp. 301-09.

Bushlack, T. "*Lectio, Intentio*, and the 'Twofold Tropological Sense': Lectio Divina as a Guide to the Cultivation of Practical Wisdom," *The American Benedictine Review*, 67/1 (2016) 29-57.

Caplan, H. "The Four Senses of Scriptural Interpretation and the Mediæval Theory of Preaching," in *Speculum*, Vol. 4/3 (1929) 282-290.

Catechism of the Catholic Church, Washington, D.C.: USCCB - Libreria Editrice Vaticana, 1997.

Chatillon, F. "Vocabulaire et prosodie du distique attribué a Augustin de Dacie sur les quatre sens de l'Écriture," in *L'Homme devant Dieu. Mélanges offerts au Père Henri de Lubac* (Théologie 57), Paris: Aubier, 1964, pp.17–28.

Cizewski, W. "Biblical Interpretation" in J.R. Strayer (ed.), *Dictionary of the Middle Ages*, NY; Charles Scribner's Son, 1982-.

Cousins, E. "The Fourfold Sense of Scripture in Christian Mysticism," in S.T. Katz (ed.), Mysticism and Sacred Scripture, Oxford: Oxford University Press, 2000, p. 118-137.

Crouzel H. "Biblical Exegesis. II. New Testament Exegesis," in K. Rahner (ed.), *Encyclopedia of Theology: A Concise Sacramentum Mundi,* London: Burns & Oates, 2004, pp. 124-133.

De Lubac, H. *Medieval Exegesis. Vol. 1: The Four Senses of Scripture,* trans. M. Sebanc, Grand Rapids: Eerdmans and Edinburgh: T&T Clark, 1998 [= *Exégèse Médiéval. Le quatre sens de l'écritures. Premierè Partie*, Paris: Éditions Montaigne, 1959].

-------. *Théologies d'occasion*, Paris: Desclée de Brouwer, 1984.

-------. *Typologie, Allegorie, Geistiger Sinn. Studien zur Geschichte der christlichen Schriftauslegung,* Rudolf Voderholzer, Freiburg: Johannes Verlag Einsiedeln, 1999, ²2007.

De Wilde, V. "Augustin de Dacie," *Dictionnaire de'Histoire et de géographie ecclésiastiques*, A. Baudrillart, M.A. Vogt and M.U. Rouziès (eds.), Vol. 5, cols. 535-536, Paris: Letouzey and Ané, 1912-<2015 >.

Disalvo, S. "«Atal allur a catade »: Recuperación figural de la antigüedad pagana en las cantigas de Santa María de Alfonso X" in *Olivar* vol. 5 no. 5 La Plata jul./dic. 2004, pp. 1-17.

Donahue, J. "Things Old and New in Biblical Scholarship," in *The Way Supplement* 72 (1991) 20-31.

Dubois, M. "Mystical and Realistic Element in the Exegesis and Hermeneutics of Thomas Aquinas," in B. Uffenheimer and G. Henning Reventlow (eds.), *Creative Biblical Exegesis: Christian and Jewish Hermeneutics through the Centuries*, Sheffield: Sheffield Academic Press and NY: Bloomsbury Publishing, 1988, pp. 39-54.

Dulles, A. "The Interpretation of the Bible in the Church. A Theological Appraisal," in W. Geerlings and M. Seckler (eds.), *Kirche sein: nachkonziliare Theologie im Dienst der Kirchenreform: Für Hermann Josef Pottmeyer*, Freiburg im B.: Herder, 1994, 29-37.

Dyer, J. "The Psalms in Monastic Prayer," in N.E. Van Deusen (ed.), *The Place of the Psalms in the Intellectual Culture of the Middle Ages*, Albany, NY: State University Press, 1999, p. 59-89.

Falque, E. "¿Es Fundemental la Herméneutica? Is Hermeneutics Fundamental?," in *Ideas y Valores*, 62.152 (2013):199-223.

Fedalto, G. "Dominkaner, Dominkanerrin," in R-H. Bautier (ed.), *Lexikon des Mittalters*, Vol. 3, Munich/Zürich: Artemis, 1986, col. 1214.

Fitzmyer, J. *Scripture, the Soul of Theology*, New York: Paulist, 1994.

-------. The Biblical Commission's Document *"The Interpretation of the Bible in the Church." Text and Commentary*, Rome: Editrice Pontificio Istituto Biblico, 1995.

-------. "Problems of the Literal and Spiritual Senses of Scripture" in *Louvain Studies* 20 (1995) 134-46.

-------. "The Sense of Scripture Today," *ITQ* 62 (1996-97): 101-17.

-------. *The Interpretation of Scripture. In Defense of the Historical-Critical Method*, NY: Paulist, 2008.

Frascari, M., J. Hale, B. Starkey (eds.), *From Models to Drawings: Imagination and Representation in Architecture* London and New York: Routledge, 2008.

-------. *Eleven Exercises in the Art of Architectural Drawing: Slow Food for the Architect's Imagination*, London and New York: Routledge, 2011.

Froehlich, K. with M. Burrows. *Sensing the Scriptures. Aminadab's Chariot and the Predicament of Biblical Interpretation*, Grand Rapids: Eerdmans, 2014.

Gerlach, M.T. *Lex Orandi, Lex Legendi: A Correlation of the Roman Canon and the Fourfold Sense of Scripture*, Ph.D. dissertation,

Marquette University, 2011. http://epublications.marquette.edu/dissertations_mu/122

Grondin, J. *Introduction to Philosophical Hermeneutics*, trans. by J. Weinsheimer, New Haven, CT: Yale University Press, 1997.

Haag, H, "La Palabra de Dios se hace Libro en la Sagrada Scritura" in J. Feiner and M. Löhrer (eds.), *Mysterium Salutis. Manual de Teología como Historia de la Salvación*, trans. M. Villanueva Salas, Madrid: Ediciones Cristianidad, Vol. 5, ^{4}1992.

Hagen, K. "Biblical Interpretation in the Middle Ages and the Reformation" [Bethany Lutheran College, S. C. Ylvisaker Fine Arts Center, Mankato, Minnesota, October 26 and 27, 2000], pp. 1-15, available at http://essays.wls.wels.net/bitstream/handle/123456789/2084/HagenMiddle.pdf?sequence=1.

Hahn, F. *Theologie des Neuen Testaments: Die Einheit des Neuen Testaments*, Vol. 2, Tübingen: Mohr Siebeck, ^{2}2005.

Harvey, A.L. *Spiritual Reading: A Study of the Christian Practice of Reading Scripture*, Durham: Durham University, eTheses, 2012 (http://etheses.dur.ac.uk/3916).

Hatina, T.R. *New Testament Theology and its Quest for Relevance. Ancient Texts and Modern Readers*, New York: Bloomsbury T&T Clark, 2013.

Hauschild, W.-D., *Lehrbuch der Kirchen- und Dogmen- geschichte*, Bd. 1, *Alte Kirche und Mittelalter*, Gütersloh: Gütersloher Verlaghaus, 1995.

Holmes, S.M, *Sacred Signs in Reformation Scotland: Interpreting Worship*, 1488-1590, Oxford: Oxford University Press, 2015.

Jakobsen, J.G.G. email, website Centre for Dominican Studies of Dacia http://jggj.dk/CDSD.htm; Department of Nordic Research, University of Copenhagen.

-------. *Prædikebrødrenes samfundsrolle i middelalderens Danmark*, Ph.D. Dissertation, University of Southern Denmark on 31 January 2008 and defended on 12 June, 2008.

Jensen, K.V. "Augustinus de Dacia," Wikipedia article https://wiki.uib.no/medieval/index.php/Augustinus_de_Dacia.

Kirby, T., E. Campi, F.A. James III (eds.), *A Companion to Peter Martyr Vermigli*, Leiden: Brill, 2009.

Klepper, D. "Historicizing Allegory: The Jew as Hagar in Medieval Christian Text and Image," in *Church History* 84/2 (2015) 308-344.

Kourie, C. "A Mystical Reading of Paul," in *Scriptura* 101 (2009) pp. 235-245.

Levy, I. *The Letter to the Galatians* (Medieval Bible Commentary series), Grand Rapids: Eerdmans, 2011.

McGrath, A.E. *The Intellectual Origins of the European Reformation*, Malden, MA and Oxford: Wiley, 1987, ²2004.

McLarney, G. *St. Augustine's Interpretation of the Psalms of Ascent*, Washington, D.C.: Catholic University of America Press, 2014.

McNally, R.E. "Medieval Exegesis," *Theological Studies* 22.3 (1961), p. 445-454.

-------. "Medieval Exegesis," Editorial Staff at Catholic University of America (eds.), *New Catholic Encyclopedia*, Vol. 1, NY: McGraw-Hill, 1967, co. 708a.

McNamara, M. *The Psalms in the Early Irish Church*, Sheffield: Sheffield Academic Press, 2000.

Madigan, Kevin. "Catholic Interpretation of the Bible," in D. Senior et al. (eds.), *Catholic Study Bible* (NABRE), New York: Oxford University Press, ³2016, p. RG 73-87.

Martin, J.H. "The Four Senses of Scripture: Lessons from the Thirteenth Century," in *Pacifica* 2 (1989), p. 87-106.

Mercedes, A. de D. Retórica, *Predicación y Vida Cotidiana en la Ciudad de México (1735), según Francisco de la Concepción Barbosa, O.F.M.*, STD Dissertation, Pamplona: Universidad de Navarra, 2002.

Mills, M.S. *Concise Handbook of Literary and Rhetorical Terms*, Lexington, KY: Estep-Nichols Publishing, 2010.

Minnis, A.J. *Medieval Theory of Authorship. Scholastic Literary Attitudes in the Later Middle Ages*, Philadelphia: University of Pennsylvania Press, 1988.

Morin, G. "IX. Le *Rotulus Pugillaris* du Dominicain Augustin de Daice (XIIIᵉ s.)," in *Basler Zeitschrift für Geschichte und Altertumskunde* 26 (1927) 222-223.

Morrissey, C.S. "A Model for the Many Senses of Scripture. From the Literal to the Spiritual in Genesis 22 with Thomas Aquinas," in *Contagion* 19 (2012) 231-248.

Mulchahey, M.M. *"First the Bow is Bent in Study...:"* Dominican Education Before 1350. *Studies and Texts* 132, Turnhout, Belgium: Brepols, 1998.

Muller, R.A. *Dictionary of Latin and Greek Theological Terms*, Grand Rapids: Baker, 1985, s.v., "Quadriga."

Murphy. R.E. "What is Catholic about Catholic Biblical Scholarship – Revisited," in *Biblical Theology Bulletin* 28/3 (1998) 112-119.

O'Callaghan, P. *Christ Our Hope. An Introduction to Eschatology*, Washington, D.C.: Catholic University of America Press, 2011.

Olszewski, M. "St. Albert the Great's Theory of Inspiration of the Bible" in Walter Senner (ed.), *Albertus Magnus: Zum Gedenken nach 800 Jahren: Neue Zugänge, Aspekte und Perspectiven*, 2001, Berlin: Akademie Verlage, pp. 467-478.

Osiek, C. "Catholic or Catholic? Biblical Scholarship at the Center," in *Journal of Biblical Literature*, Vol. 125, No. 1 (Spring, 2006), pp. 5-22 [= *Presidential Voices: The Society of Biblical Literature in the Twentieth Century*, H.W. Attridge and J.C. VanderKam (eds.), Atlanta, GA: SBL, 2006, pp. 325-342].

Otten, W. "The Power of the Bible in the Middle Ages," in W. Farmer, ed., *The International Bible Commentary*, Collegeville: Liturgical Press, 1988, pp. 48-52.

———. "On Sacred Attunement, Its Meaning and Consequences. A Meditation on Christian Theology," in *The Journal of Religion*, 93.4 (2013), p. 478-494.

Peppermüller, R. "Schriftsinne," in R-H. Bautier (ed.), *Lexikon des Mittalters*, Vol. 7, Munich/Zürich: Artemis, 1986, col. 1568-1570.

Primitive Constitutions of the Order of Preachers, http://www.op.org/sites/www.op.org/files/public/documents/fichier/primitive_consti_en.pdf

Puig I Tàrrech, A. "L'Hermenèutica de l'Escriptura. Estudi de Dei Verbum 12," in *RCatT* 39/1 (2014) 153-197.

Ratzinger, J.A. (Pope Benedict XVI), *Principles of Catholic Theology: Building Stones for a Fundamental Theology*, trans. M.F. McCarthy, San Francisco: Ignatius Press, 1987.

Rovira Belloso, J.M. *Introducción a la Teología*, Madrid: Biblioteca de Autores Creativos, 1996.

Schatzgeyer, K. *Schriften zur Verteidigung der Messe* (Corpus Catholicorum), Münster: Aschendorff, 1984.

Schneiders, S. "Scripture and Spirituality," in B. McGinn and J. Meyendorff (eds.), *Christian Spirituality. Origins to the Twelfth Century*, NY: Crossroad, 1985, pp. 1-20.

Schütz, J. *Hüter der Wirklichkeit: Der Dominikanerorden in der mittelalterlichen Gesellschaft Skandinaviens*, Göttingen: V&R unipress, 2014.

Seebohm, T. *Hermeneutics. Method and Methodology*, NY and Heidelberg: Springer, 2010.

Senner, W. "Augustinus (Aage) v. Dänemark, O.P.," in W. Kasper (ed.), *Lexikon für Theologie und Kirche*, Freiburg: Herder, 1993, Vol. 1, col. 1247.

Smith, L.J., "Bible, Christian Interpretation of," in W.W. Kibler, et al. (eds.). *Medieval France: An Encyclopedia*, NY: Routledge, 1995, pp. 230-234.

Soulen, R.N. *Sacred Scripture: A Short History of Interpretation*, Westminster/John Knox, 2010.

Spicq, C. *Esquisse d'une Histoire de L'Exégèse Latin: Au Moyen Age*, Paris: Librairie Philosophique J. Vrin, 1944.

Trainor, L. "Palindromic Structure in the Pardoner's Tale," in *Michigan Academician* Vol. 41, No. 1 (2012) 53-67.

Toom, T. *Patristic Theories of Biblical Interpretation: The Latin Fathers*, Cambridge: Cambridge University Press, 2016.

Troelsgård, C. email, new critical edition of the Latin text of the *Rotullus*, Copenhagen.

Vaccari, A. "Auctor versuum de quattuor Scripturae sensibus," in *Verbum Domini* 9 (1929) 212-214.

-------. "S. Albert Magno e l'Esegesi Medievale," in Biblica 13 (1932) 257-272 [= *Scritti di Erudizione e di Filologia*, Vol. 2, *Per la Storia del Testo e dell'Esegesi Biblica*, Rome: Edizioni di Storia e Letteratura, 1958, p. 317-346].

van der Meer, J.M. and S. Mandelbrote, *Nature and Scripture in the Abrahamic Religions: Up to 1700*, Vol. 1, Leiden: Brill, 2008.

van Liere, F. *An Introduction to the Medieval Bible*, Cambridge: Cambridge University Press, 2014.

van Nieuwenhove, R. *An Introduction to Medieval Theology*, Cambridge: Cambridge University Press, 2012.

Vessey, D. "Medieval Hermeneutics," in N. Keane and C. Lawn (eds.), *The Blackwell Companion to Hermeneutics*, Chichester, West Sussex, UK and Malden, MA: John Wiley & Sons, 2016.

von Bormann, C. "Hermeneutik I," in G. Krause (ed.), *Theologische Realenzyklopädie*, Bd. 15, 113-114.

Viviano, P. "The Senses of Scripture," Washington, D.C.: USCCB, 2008.

Walter, M. "Den Glauben verstehen mit J.S. Bachs Kantaten – am Beispiel der Taufe," in Albert Clement (Hrsg.). *Das Blut Jesu und die Lehre von der Versöhnung im Werk Johann Sebastian Bachs. Proceedings of the International Colloquium The Blood of Jesus and the Doctrine of Reconciliation in the Works of Johann Sebastian Bach.* Amsterdam 14.-17. September 1993 (Koninklijke Nederlandse Akademie von Wetenschappen Verhandelingen, Afd. Letterkunde, Nieuwe Reeks, deel 164), Amsterdam 1996, p. 151-162.

Walter, P. "Shriftsinne" in W. Kasper (ed.), *Lexikon für Theologie und Kirche*, Freiburg: Herder, 1993, Vol. 9.

Walz, A.M. *Augustini de Dacia, O.P. "Rotulus Pugillaris." Examinatus atque Editus*, Rome, Angelicum, 1929.

-------."Des Aage von Dänemark 'Rotulus Pugillaris' im Lichte der alten dominikanischen Konventstheologie," in *Classica et Mediaevalia* 15 (1954) 198–252.

Warner, J.C. *The Augustinian Epic, Petrarch to Milton*, Ann Arbor, MI: University of Michigan Press, 2005.

Weisheipl, J.A. "The Place of Study in the Ideal of St. Dominic," River Forest, IL, 1960.

Williamson, P., *Catholic Principles for Interpreting Scripture: A Study of the Pontifical Commission's The Interpretation of the Bible in the Church* (Subsidia Biblica 22), Rome: Editrice Pontificio Istituto Biblico, 2001.

Wood, S.K. *Spiritual Exegesis and the Church in the Theology of Henri de Lubac*, Grand Rapids: Eerdmans and Edinburgh: T&T Clark, 1998, reprint Eugene, OR: Wipf&Stock, 2010.

Yarchin, W. *History of Biblical Interpretation*. A Reader, Peabody, MA: Hendrickson, 2004.

Chenu's Vision of the Gospel and Church Institutions[1]

Paul Philibert, O.P.

M.-D. Chenu was a great medieval historian and a theologian focused on contemporary pastoral concerns. His writings drew upon a dialectic between the absolute authority of the word of God and human needs arising from transformations in society (the "signs of the times"). His life demonstrated the conflict between the essentialist Neo-Thomism mandated by the Roman Curia and "ressourcement" theology (a liberating expansion of theological concerns drawn from Scripture and early Christian sources). Censored by the Church in 1942 for his daring exploration of new pathways in theology, Chenu much later had significant influence as a theologian at Vatican II. He proposed to construct a "new Christendom" out of the interplay of the primacy of the word of God and attentive concern for the signs of the times.

Whether treating medieval culture as a historian, the nature and methods of theology as a theologian, or contemporary social and pastoral issues as a prophet, M.-D. Chenu always focused upon both the inexhaustible abundance of the word of God *(forma evangelii)* and the historical evolution of ecclesiastical institutions *(forma ecclesiae)*. His writings address a number of questions. How does the absolute authority of God's word relativize the institutional power of hierarchical figures and ecclesiastical structures? How can the failures and the aging of institutions awaken consciousness of the vital power of God's word? How does the word of God allow new generations to

---

[1] From *Cristianesimo nella storia : ricerche storiche, esegetiche, teologiche = Studies in history, exegesis and theology* 36 (2/2015) 429-444. Reprinted with permission of Giuseppe Ruggieri, Director.

discern what is essential and permanent in institutional structures? How can social change and cultural transformations awaken fresh understandings of the fruitful abundance of God's word?[2]

Chenu's characteristic question was how to identify the "signs of the times," how to recognize new possibilities to embody essential values. For him two things were clear: God's word will always have more to tell us, and transformations in social structures are inevitable and are guided mysteriously by the Holy Spirit. Chenu used these two principles to understand ecclesial life and to resolve ecclesiastical difficulties.[3] However, these same principles were unacceptable to his Roman critics and censors who caused Chenu a lifetime of grief. Yet Vatican II vindicated Chenu by adopting these ideas as sources of insight for its discussions. Part of Chenu's legacy is that these ideas (the primacy of the word of God and the adaptation of institutions to social change) became expressed in many ways in the council's final documents.

1. Background and Influences

Marie-Dominique Chenu was born in 1895 in Soisy-sur-Seine, a village near Paris where forty years later the Dominican school of theology, *Le Saulchoir*, would be transferred from its Belgian exile. His parents were middle class Catholics who ran a metalworking business. His early education was placed in the care of his maternal grandmother, a teacher in the state schools. Her liberal attitudes shaped his own and provided him with a free spirit of inquiry.[4]

---

[2] See M.-D. Chenu, *La Parole de Dieu*, vol. I, *La Foi dans l'intelligence;* vol. II, *L'Evangile dans le temps*, Paris 1964.

[3] See G. Alberigo, M.-D. Chenu et al., *Une école de théologie: le Saulchoir*, Paris 1985.

[4] O. De La Brosse, *Le Père Chenu: La liberté dans la foi*, Paris 1969. Also J. Duquesne, *Un théologien en liberté. Jacques Duquesne interroge le Père Chenu*, Paris 1975. Baptized Marcel-Léon, Chenu was given the name Marie-Dominique on entering the Dominicans.

When a friend at his Lycee entered the Dominicans, Chenu went to the investiture and saw *Le Saulchoir* (the Dominican house of studies in exile in Belgium) for the first time. That visit captured his imagination with "a beautiful liturgy that matched a life of study and a harmonious and attractive community life."[5] Eighteen months later he too would enter as a novice, prepared by his temperament and his early education to make the most of this Dominican center of learning that was creative, free, and solidly grounded.

Chenu's life replicates the clash between the Catholic Church and modernity that marked the nineteenth and early twentieth centuries. The case of Lacordaire offers an example. The Order of Preachers (Dominicans) was re-established in France in 1843 by Henri-Dominique Lacordaire out of a conviction that profound doctrinal preaching could revive popular confidence in a church that had become discredited for most French people because of its ultramontane spirit and its inability to address the post-revolutionary age. Lacordaire espoused *Dieu et liberté* in the face of integralist denunciations. He founded a Dominican house of studies attuned to the challenges of a new age and deeply rooted in the wisdom of St. Thomas Aquinas.[6] Chenu's own daring initiatives were grounded on the spirit of Lacordaire which he encountered at *Le Saulchoir*.

When Chenu came to *Le Saulchoir*, Dominican leaders and mentors had already shaped its ethos. Fr. Ambroise Gardeil (†1931) was the school's guiding spirit. He insisted upon the primacy of biblical revelation *(le donné révélé)* with an emphasis that became Chenu's own. At that time dogmatic propositions, presented as *theses* (doctrinal positions) in seminary manuals, were generally considered to be the substance of Catholic theology. By contrast, Gardeil taught Chenu

---

[5] Duquesne, U*n théologien, cit.*, 27.

[6] *Une école de théologie,* cit., 110f.

the maxim "back to the sources" that would shape his understanding of theology.[7] Later an elder colleague, Fr. Pierre Mandonnet (†1936), who founded *Le Saulchoir*'s institute for medieval studies in 1921, taught Chenu how to pursue theological sources with accuracy and understanding by focusing on the Middle Ages in the West as the milieu in which Catholic theology developed as a coherent system. While the Roman schools saw Catholic theology as timeless metaphysical truths independent of historical or cultural influences, Chenu and Mandonnet saw that such a perspective rendered theology impotent for dialogue with living philosophy and culture.[8]

Chenu went to Rome in 1914 for studies at the Angelicum[9] while German troops invaded Belgium. He received a solid grounding in the theology of Aquinas in Rome, but he also learned a lot about the manners of Romanità. His major professor was Reginald Garrigou-Lagrange in whom he saw a gifted mind captivated by the ahistorical spirit of an ideological Neo-Thomism. Chenu said of him: "he was too much filled with Aristotle and not enough with the Gospel, and so his theology ran the risk of being only a sacred metaphysics."[10] But in Rome Chenu also met Fr. Leonard Lehu, a Dominican from Lyons who was a member of the Holy Office. Lehu took Chenu under his wing, and on long walks gave him an insider's view of Catholic Rome and the Vatican culture. This twofold initiation into the Roman world would provide perspective for Chenu's future dealings with the Vatican. Later Lehu, as the assistant to the Dominican Order's Master General, would aid Chenu in one of his early conflicts with the Holy

---

[7] Ibid. Also Chenu, *La Foi dan l'intelligence,* cit., 269-275.

[8] Duquesne, Un théologien, cit., 41f.

[9] The Pontifical University of St. Thomas Aquinas directed by the Order of Preachers.

[10] Duquesne, *Un théologien*, cit., 38.

Office.[11] Chenu took away from Rome a well-founded mistrust of its ecclesiastical luminaries.

Chenu's doctoral thesis (1920), directed by Garrigou-Lagrange, was a psychological and theological analysis of contemplation. It was innovative in addressing the psychology of faith, and it gave an impressive demonstration of Chenu's theological development.[12] Impressed, Garrigou-Lagrange invited Chenu to stay on at the Angelicum as his assistant with a view to beginning a new program in spiritual theology. Instead Chenu opted to return to *Le Saulchoir* where he was named professor of the History of Doctrines (preferring that to the usual phrase History of Dogmas).[13]

Chenu might have become the protégé of one of Rome's most esteemed theologians. But by turning down his offer of patronage, Chenu became suspect and worrisome for Garrigou-Lagrange and would pay a price for this disloyalty.[14] Yet from him Chenu appropriated an understanding of the supernatural quality of revealed faith as the source of theology (the *forma evangelii* of our theme). He complemented that with a firm conviction about the historicity of the human condition (the *forma ecclesiae*), influenced by another Angelicum professor, Reginald Schultes.[15]

These two poles of reference would shape Chenu's thought. In 1932 Chenu was chosen as director of *Le Saulchoir* after being named "Master of Sacred Theology" by the General Chapter of the

---

[11] Ibid., 35.

[12] C.F. Potworowski, Contemplation and Incarnation: The Theology of Marie-Dominique Chenu, Montréal 2001.

[13] Y. Congar, "Le Pere M.-D. Chenu," in *Bilan de la theologie du XX' siècle*, dir. par R. Van Der Gucht, H. Vorgrimler, 2 vol., Tournai-Paris 1970, 772.

[14] R. Peddicord, The Sacred Monster of Thomism: An Introduction to the Life and Legacy of Reginald Garrigou-Lagrange, South Bend, IN, 2005.

[15] Congar, Le Père M.-D. Chenu, cit., 772.

Dominicans held at *Le Saulchoir* in August of that year.[16] He oversaw the development of one of the most influential academic programs in the Catholic world, educating among others Yves Congar, Edward Schillebeeckx,[17] Pierre-André Liégé, Pierre-Marie Gy, Irenée Dalmais, the Dubarle brothers, and many more influential thinkers.

The historical approach of Marie-Joseph Lagrange and the *École Biblique* in Jerusalem became a model for *Le Saulchoir*. Just as Lagrange had shown that the biblical text cannot be fully understood except in the context of the history and languages of the ancient Middle East, so Chenu insisted that Aquinas had to be understood as a theologian of the 13th Century – as someone shaped by the factors of social change, confrontation with Aristotle and his Arab commentators, and the spiritual awakening among the laity.[18] Not only was history integral to doing theology, but it opened areas of dialogue between theology and the scientific world.

During the decade 1932-42, Chenu, through his articles, reviews, and notices in the *Le Saulchoir*'s journals of philosophy and theology which he edited, became recognized as an insightful historian of the Christian Middle Ages.[19] Friendship with Étienne Gilson, the preeminent medievalist at the Sorbonne, grew out of that work and led to Chenu's increasing involvement in medieval studies. At the urging of Gilson, Chenu founded an institute of medieval studies at

---

[16] De La Brosse, Le Père Chenu, cit., 42.

[17] Schillebeeckx followed Chenu's course at the École des Hautes Études in 1946.

[18] Ibid., 38.

[19] Chenu edited the *Bulletin thomiste* (founded in 1924), and from 1927 to 1934 the *Revue des sciences philosophiques et théologiques* [RSPT] (founded in 1907).

the Dominican studium in Ottawa (transferred in 1942 to the University of Montreal).[20]

Chenu's scholarly trajectory, based on the methods and intuitions he inherited from Mandonnet and Lagrange, led him to move backward from Aquinas' 13th Century into the 12th Century, its culture and its thinkers. From this research and its dissemination of ideas came the four remarkable historical works for which Chenu is justly famous: *La théologie comme science au XIIIe siècle* (1927), *Introduction à l'étude de S. Thomas d'Aquin* (1950), *La théologie au XIIe siècle* (1957), and *S. Thomas d'Aquin et la théologie* (1959). In these works, Chenu analyzed the shift at the end of the 12th and the beginning of the 13th centuries from rural feudalism to urban communes, from monastic and cathedral schools to universities, from agricultural economies to international markets, from the ideal Platonic world of 12th-century thought to the empirical Aristotelian world of the 13th. Theology shifted from commentaries to questions, from exposition to inquiry. Each of these changes, as Chenu saw it, required a renewal of institutions and of categories of thought.

2. The Roman Crisis and Its Aftermath

These insights may appear positive today, but they were not considered that way everywhere at the time. The Pope's theologian, Fr. Mariano Cordovani, wrote that Chenu's approach relativized Aquinas' theology by inserting it inside historical and cultural contexts,[21] whereas the Roman viewpoint was that Aquinas delivered timeless, eternally valid theological propositions. Those, thought the

---

[20] See the articles in tribute to Chenu in the special issue of *Revue des sciences philosophiques et théologiques*, 81, 3 (1997) written by J. Le Goff, J. Jolivet, J.-C. Schmitt, and A. Boureau.

[21] Fouilloux, *Le Saulchoir en procès (1937-1942)*, in Une école de théologie, cit., 50-59. It is worth noting that in the Roman universities not only the texts but also classroom lectures were in Latin.

Romans, had to be articulated, studied, and accepted as true. A confrontation was in the works.

After 1918, the French Dominicans received a large influx of new members, many of them veterans of the war. Chenu, after 1920, as a professor and later as director, inspired scholarship and fellowship, and the faculty of *Le Saulchoir* was enriched with important young theologians, Yves Congar among them. Biblical studies were nourished through contact with professors from Jerusalem. St. Thomas was taught within a framework of both history and pastoral life. Writing about this period, Congar said: "We thought that theology could have something to say to people today if it turned away from repeating tired formulas and faced up to the real problems of our time."[22] Further, the *Bulletin thomiste* and the *RSPT* brought the school an international reputation for genuine scholarship. *Le Saulchoir* was becoming a major school of theology.[23]

In 1936, to celebrate the feast of St. Thomas Aquinas, Chenu gave an address to a large gathering that aimed to describe the goals, the program, and the spirit of the house of studies. Chenu was urged to publish these remarks. Amplifying, clarifying, and deepening his text, Chenu produced a brochure entitled *A School of Theology: Le Saulchoir* (1937). Fewer than 1000 copies were printed, and distribution was made only through the school itself. Yet copies found their way to Rome, where Chenu's view was so antithetical to the approach of the professors at the Angelicum and of other highly-placed Dominicans in Rome that it caused a stir.

In 1937, *Le Saulchoir* became a Pontifical Faculty and Chenu was named the first Rector. Nonetheless the following year he was summoned to Rome to answer for his 'heterodox' views, and he was forced

---

[22] Congar, *Le Père M.-D. Chenu*, cit., 774.
[23] Duquesne, *Un théologian*, cit., 118; Fouilloux, *Le Saulchoir en procès*, cit., 40f.

to sign a set of ten propositions renouncing his 'mistakes' in the little book.[24] That same year, 1938, Hitler occupied Austria and the Second World War began to expand. By 1940, the Franco-German armistice established the Vichy government, and the Resistance dug in and began its vigorous exertions of destabilizing the occupying German forces and the Vichy regime. At just that moment, in 1942, Chenu's book was placed on the Index of Forbidden Books by the Holy Office; he was deposed as Regent and forbidden to teach or live at *Le Saulchoir*.[25]

In Paris, he began to teach at the École des Hautes Études and soon also at the Institut Catholique. His circle of colleagues and friends in Paris expanded as did his influence and his publications. After the war, Chenu offered pastoral leadership to the Priest-Worker movement, the Young Christian Workers (IOC), and other initiatives, such as the *Semaines Sociales* (annual conventions of Catholic intellectuals).

Chenu published a book on the spirituality of work and a great many occasional pieces and chapters in edited volumes. But his concern for a theology of work and his support of the worker priests raised Roman suspicions that he was advocating Marxism; clearly his Roman opponents were on the look-out for any pretext to blacken his reputation. In 1950, Pope Pius XII published his encyclical *Humani Generis* to put a stop to what he called 'the new theology' that departed from Neo-Thomism and that went beyond the church's official teaching. As Jürgen Mettepenningen's important study shows,

---

[24] F. Kerr, *Twentieth-Century Catholic Theologians,* Oxford 2007. Kerr carefully contextualizes this punitive action by the Vatican.

[25] De La Brosse, *Le Père Chenu*, cit., 98-103; Duquesne, *Un théologien*, cit., 120-131.

Chenu was clearly on the Vatican's list of offenders, even though no names or specific texts were cited in *Humani Generis*.[26]

Chenu's pastoral involvements incited the Vatican to yet another foray into condemnation and punishment. In 1954, the Master General of the Dominicans was forced to depose the three French Provincials and to exile Chenu and three other theologians.[27] Chenu was sent off to Rouen, exiled from his Paris commitments. He was not able to reside in Paris again until 1962, although he did return periodically to work with colleagues and to minister to his pastoral groups. He also continued publishing new editions of his works, many reviews, and completed *S. Thomas et la théologie*, a work that he especially liked.[28]

In 1958, Pope John XXIII was elected and he decided to convoke an ecumenical council. So Chenu's interests turned to the council and to various ways to prepare for it. In 1995 Alberto Melloni prepared a critical edition of Chenu's council notes for 1962-1963,[29] a work that brings to light Chenu's wide influence at Vatican II. Chenu went to the council as the personal theologian of a bishop from Madagascar, and this assistance to his bishop sponsor quickly became guidance for the bishops of Madagascar, and then spilled over into involvement with the bishops of Africa and (through a personal relation with Bishop Helder Camara) with the bishops of Latin America. He was never accepted formally as a *peritus* for the council, but he gave seminars for the bishops, drafted speeches for some of them, and assisted Yves Congar and other *periti* in their research and writing. He also assisted

---

[26] J. Mettepenningen, *Nouvelle Théologie, New Theology: Inheritor of Modernism, Precursor of Vatican II*, London 2010.

[27] F. Leprieur, *Quand Rome condamne: Dominicains et prêtres-ouvriers*, Paris 1989.

[28] Duquesne, *Un théologien*, cit., 157f.

[29] M.-D. Chenu, *Notes quotidiennes au Concile*, critical edition by A. Melloni, Paris 20122.

the commission that organized and developed Schema XIII (which was to become the pastoral constitution *Gaudium et Spes*). He was the instigator of the council's first public document, its Message to the World (an episode that his council notebook describes in detail).[30]

This is a bare outline of a long life filled with both scholarly and pastoral achievements. Through all of it, Chenu's focus on the primacy of the word of God and the provisional quality of theological propositions was consistent. He applied this insight to interpreting Aquinas from the perspective of his own culture, to urging *ressourcement* in theological method, and to taking the risks needed to create new pastoral solutions.[31] Both baroque Catholicism and the French revolution had focused on the destiny and interests of individuals; in the one case in pursuit of holiness, in the other in pursuit of freedom. By contrast, Chenu insisted that both the Gospel and healthy Catholic theology should be concerned with the collective health of the Body of Christ – a view that came to dominate the documents of Vatican II. His interest in what he called "sacred sociology"[32] reinforced his bias toward a collective explanation of social phenomena and a corporate feeling for the people of God.

The present number of "*Cristianesimo nella storia*" focuses on the question of how true reform in the church is a work of building human solidarity, translating the Gospel into new life in emerging situations, and extending the ferment of grace into the fabric of culture. Instead of seeing new ideas and new language as a threat for a closed system of Catholic rituals and ideas, Chenu saw them as a chance for the

---

[30] Ibid.

[31] J. Gray, *Marie-Dominique Chenu and Le Saulchoir: A Stream of Catholic Renewal*, in *Ressourcement: A Movement for Renewal in Twentieth-Century Catholic Life*, ed. by G. Flynn, P. Murray, Oxford 2011, 205-218.

[32] Chenu, *L'Evangile dans le temps*, cit., 39; De La Brosse, Le Père Chenu, cit., 216f. 32Potworowski, Contemplation and Incarnation, cit., 113-115.

Gospel to become relevant again. What were the conceptual tools that allowed him to ground his vision? Can they still be dynamic for us today?

3. Key Structures in Chenu's Thinking

Chenu knew that his understanding of theology was different from the static orthodoxy of the Angelicum and of the Roman theologians. He wanted not only to give theology broader expression, but to do so in language that would be contemporary and provocative. So we find neologisms in his writing, among them, the law of faith, the law of the gospel, and the law of the incarnation. By the term 'law' he meant to indicate not some kind of precept, but rather a sense of the order and relationships between gospel and society.[33]

He wanted to explain the dialectic between the divine and the human that posits divine grace as present in the midst of characteristically human situations. His reading of the Incarnation insists upon the transformed destiny of human beings and their situation because of God's entry into humanity. Chenu gave this mutual vulnerability of the divine and the human not just spiritual but embodied significance, not just individual but collective meaning, not just personal but social implications.

Using the following three themes, this synthetic vision of the mutual implication of the human and the divine became practical and pastoral.

a. The Dialectic between the Transcendent and the Provisional

The phrase 'the law of faith' is a metaphor that evokes the twofold aspect of the object of faith: the dogmatic proposition that engages the intelligence with language, and the divine reality that is known in

---

[33] Chenu, *L'Evangile dans le temps*, cit., 39; De La Brosse, *Le Père Chenu*, cit., 216f. Potworowski, *Contemplation and Incarnation,* cit., 113-115.

itself.[34] Faith always occurs in a historical context. For the word of God to be grasped by human beings, it must be spoken in human words that are historically, culturally, and socially conditioned. Because it is the word of God, however, it awakens the 'obedience of faith' spoken of by St. Paul – an obedience which is more a mode of becoming than a mode of doing, a transformation in the form of a communion.[35] Those who listen and believe find themselves in the presence of God. In several places Chenu cites a key text of Aquinas, ST 2^a2^{ae} 1, 2 ad 2: "The act of the believer does not terminate in the dogmatic proposition but in the divine reality itself."[36]

So in any experience of faith there are two poles: one a human utterance, the other divine revelation. Recalling the principle used by Aquinas, (*cognita sunt in cognoscente secundum modum cognoscentis* – ST 2^a2^{ae} 1, 2 c.), Chenu says that in knowing God, we know God humanly. Infused faith is neither given nor developed in human beings outside this anthropological reality. The transcendent object of faith "is manifested through the elevation of our faculties, and not through some derangement of our psychological being."[37] Ordinary people know God in ordinary ways.

So the psychology of faith involves a committed adherence to a truth articulated in a doctrine or formula, but it also involves a personal confidence in God's self-gift that is being continually enriched. Chenu describes these as "the *formalism* of adherence and the *realism* of communion."[38] Every aspect of the supernatural life is an 'incarnation' of the divine. People are not required to set aside normal,

---

[34] Chenu, *La Foi dan l'intelligence*, cit., 290-300; Chenu, L'*Évangde dans le temps*, cit., 366-368.

[35] Chenu, *La Foi dan l'intelligence,* cit., 293.

[36] See Congar, *Le Père M.-D. Chenu*, cit., 776-779.

[37] Chenu, *La Foi dan l'intelligence*, cit., 98. Also *Une école de théologie*, cit., 136-139.

[38] Chenu, La Foi dan l'intelligence, cit., 14.

human experience to enter into supernatural life. "Everything that is characteristically human has to be lifted up to the supernatural plane and find its fulfillment there."[39]

Inversely, Chenu observes something that sounds like recent utterances of Pope Francis, saying that there are two kinds of transmission of Christian truth: one rational and systematic that proceeds didactically, another existential that proclaims a 'kerygmatic' message that awakens people to the ways God is present in their lives.[40] Instead of focusing on the logical clarity of the message, we do well in many cases to draw people into communion by showing them the gracious humanity of faith-filled lives.[41]

This dialectic between transcendent experience and the provisional articulation of that experience in human words becomes a hermeneutical perspective. Theology is always impatient to embody its inspiration in signs and witness, recognizing the ephemeral character of the logical formulas that articulate divine truth. Chenu does not deny that human language can speak truly of the experience of God; he simply recognizes that the truth we speak needs to restate itself in new social and cultural conditions. This was his 'mortal sin' for which his *Une école de théologie* was put on the Index. But it is also the insight that allowed him to recognize how the theology of Thomas Aquinas owed its richness to a great plurality of sources and influences.

b. The Primacy of the Word of God

In 1937, Chenu grounded his explanation of theology upon the primacy of the revealed word of God. God's word is expressed in an

---

[39] Ibidem, 18.

[40] Chenu, *L'Évangile dans le temps*, cit., 326.

[41] Ibidem, 330. See the remarkable parallel with Pope Francis, *Evangelii Gaudium*, §164-168.

exterior mode in texts but also in an interior way by the light of faith, and it becomes a living and sanctifying word only when so illumined.[42] Chenu developed the insights of his predecessor, Ambroise Gardeil, whose book *Le donné révélé et la théologie* became a kind of handbook for *Le Saulchoir*. The phrase *donné révélé* can be translated loosely as 'revealed data,' suggesting that what is communicated has to be understood and interpreted. The revealed data is never just words but also an inner word – *lumen fidei* – a gift of the Holy Spirit. That light of faith 'illumines' not only rational assent to the biblical text, but extends to the entire enterprise of theological savoring and reasoning about the word of God.[43]

For Chenu the Roman obsession to control Catholic theology by, for example, the anti-modernist oath and the 24 Thomistic theses, was a perversion of theology that locks up theological production within a closed box of official pronouncements and fails to stress the dynamic influence of the light of faith.[44] Thomas Aquinas, a medieval doctor, then becomes a positivist and the patron saint of integrists. But the act of faith can never be denied its divine origin, even at work within theology, for from the light of faith comes theology's never-ending yearning for a fuller and more adequate expression of the divine mystery as well as the spiritual dynamic of loving contemplation.

When deprived of its mystical grace, faith will be reduced simply to obedience to a teaching authority. Theology then becomes language cut off from living religious experience and articulated in theses that become part of a propositional calculus. This leaves

---

[42] Chenu, *La Foi dan l'intelligence*, cit., 279.

[43] Ibid. Also *Une école de théologie*, cit., 130-134; Potworowski, *Contemplation and Incarnation*, cit., 44-46.

[44] Kerr, *Twentieth-Century Catholic Theologians*, cit., 21. Cf. Duquesne, *Un théologien*, cit., 30-32.

theology locked up in a closed system.[45] There is no *development* of theology seen that way – an absurdity for Chenu, but precisely what Roman theologians wanted to insist upon. Chenu saw theology as a "construction" that draws upon an inexhaustible source. The inexhaustible character of the word of God allows theology, faith, and the Christian life to *live.*

The primacy of the word of God highlights the importance of the theme of prophecy as well. This relates to the historical studies in this issue, since a prophetic charism is embodied in the evangelism of Francis, Dominic, and later Luther and Erasmus, even down to Lacordaire.[46] Chenu's most dramatic statement concerning the prophetic charism appeared in his article of February 1954 on the priesthood of priest workers. The context for the priest-worker experiment was, of course, the loss of the working class in France to a bourgeois church.

Chenu took as his theme the "church on mission,"[47] and explained that priesthood is not defined exclusively by sacramental functions, but is essentially missionary and has the potential to awaken a spiritual renewal. Further, this prophetic charism can be expressed by a primary act of "presence," a presence realized through a communion of life and fellowship with people who thus meet the word of God.[48] For Chenu, the word of God assured access to communion with God as really as the Christian sacraments do. The word also impels believers to embody the word "that sets people free" in

---

[45] Congar, *Le Père M.-D. Chenu,* cit., 777.

[46] M.-D. Chenu, "Rôle du prêtre dans la civilisation industrielle: Prophétiser avant d'évangeliser," in *Concilium* 43 (1969), 113: "Prophétiser avant d'évangeliser, évangeliser avant de catéchiser, catéchiser avant de sacramentaliser: telles sont les étapes [...]". Cf. Chenu, *L'Évangile dans le temps,* cit., 201-212.

[47] Chenu, *L'Évangde dans le temps,* cit., 277.

[48] Ibid., 279-280.

compassionate initiatives. Such a vision keeps believers alert for possibilities to bring the word to life. Chenu's never-ending fascination with evangelism is rooted here.

c. Attending to the Signs of the Times

The phrase "signs of the times," taken from Mt 16:3, became a theological category in the texts of Vatican II. God is active in the world and in the changing events of human history in such a way as to modify the human predicament and so require a new agenda for theological reflection. *Gaudium et Spes* n. 4 notes that "the church has always had the duty of scrutinizing the signs of the times and of interpreting them in the light of the gospel." (That would have been news for the Holy Office in 1942).

As early as *Une école de théologie,* Chenu wrote about the *loci* where grace, incarnation and redemption bear upon the meaning of human experience. Among these *loci* are pluralism in human cultures that call for Christianity to transcend itself, the world's opening to the East making its cultural riches accessible in the West, the ecumenical movement, and the new role of the laity in the church – all of this inviting the church to rediscover its evangelical power.[49] The Council gave the following examples of "deep-seated changes": transformations of the social order, new attitudes in morals and religion, economic imbalances in the world, the aspirations of women to claim parity with men, the phenomenon of atheism, etc. *(Gaudium et spes,* 4-10).

In reflecting on the "signs of the times," Chenu said that *time* itself must be taken seriously as a factor that modifies the life of the spirit. Here is the question of human historicity. Social changes are speeding up in human experience, from the economic structures in

---

[49] *Une école de théologie*, cit., 142. P. Michel Castro, "Un théologien des signes des temps," in *La Vie spirituelle* 808 (Sept. 2013), 409-420.

which we live to our habits of thinking. This creates a new moral situation. "Human beings are being-in-the-world: people are both historical and spiritual. Given human historicity, transformations in the world affect the church, and its evangelization must pay attention to the changing world it hopes to address."[50]

In the essay *Réformes de structure en chrétienté,* Chenu describes what are effectively historical "signs of the times," calling them critical opportunities for grace.[51] His examples are the clash of secular and ecclesiastical power in the 11th Century, the hunger of the laity for spiritual growth in the 12th Century, the transformation of urban centers and universities in the 13th Century, and the impatience for reform in the 16th Century. Here change challenges both "church" and "institution." The church as the custodian of God's word must look beyond its dogmas and its canons to reroot itself in the radical energy of its divine source; whereas institutions, both sacred and secular, must understand themselves as living models of social experience. "Human beings discover themselves in the plasticity of their nature as always inventive, always creative. Despite terrible excesses, the grandeur of revolutions or reforms comes from these moments of consciousness-raising in which little by little the potential of humanity is discovered along with resources to transform the human world."[52]

In his last years, Chenu took special delight in remembering his participation in inserting this prophetic (but also subversive) category into the *Constitution on the Church in the Modern World.*[53]

---

[50] M.-D. Chenu, *Peuple de Dieu dans le monde*, Paris 1966, 36.

[51] Chenu, *L'Évangile dans le temps*, cit., 38.

[52] Chenu, *Peuple de Dieu*, cit., 41.

[53] In his Preface to *Une école de théologie*, cit., historian and Academician René Remond wrote: "Exactly twenty years [after Chenu's work was put on the

4. New, Successive Christendoms

Chrétienté, the French word for Christendom, is present in the title "Structural Reform in Christendom."[54] The usual understanding of this term is the one given to the social-political organization that Chenu describes as 'Constantinian' in one of his essays, where spiritual powers dominate the temporal, power structures are authoritarian, and traditional Christian institutions exercise hegemony. In that essay, Chenu argues that Vatican II represents the end of the Constantinian era even though, he says, "the Constantinian era gave us a magnificently successful Christendom." He goes on to say, however, that "Christendom is not the church..."[55] In a world in which human experience transcends western culture, history leads us far beyond the organizational structures, graced though they were, that evolved in the Middle Ages. Yet Chenu goes on to speak of his "hope for a new Christendom" that will embody evangelical awakening, give primacy to the word of God, revive a missionary spirit, and show privileged concern for the poor.[56]

In another essay, Chenu writes that "the church, as a mystical community that is the sacrament of Christ, becomes realized in *successive Christendoms* which are linked to history and to historical change."[57] He then reiterates his hopes for what this new Christendom might look like, including a civilization of meaningful

---

Index], John XXIII opened the council that lifted up and affirmed the same positions that had earned Fr. Chenu disgrace and condemnations".

[54] "Réformes de structure en chrétienté," Chenu, *L'Évangile dans le temps*, cit., 37-53.

[55] Chenu, *L'Évangile dans le temps*, cit., 17-36. See G. Alberigo et al., *La chrétienté en débat: Histoire, formes, et problèmes actuels*, Paris 1984.

[56] Congar, *Le Père M.-D. Chenu*, cit., 803-804, reflects on the ambiguity of Chenu's usage of the term 'Christendom.' See Potworowski, *Contemplation and Incarnation*, cit., 146-148.

[57] Chenu, *L'Évangile dans le temps*, cit., 115.

work, a life that transcends rationalism, a return to the gospel and its missionary force, and the possibility for the poor to be evangelized and to live free in the spirit.[58]

Here we have a kind of synthesis of all the elements that we have recognized in Chenu: the interplay of the transcendent and the provisional, the primacy of the word of God, and an attentive concern for the signs of the times. Whether or not Chenu's use of the term "Christendom" is viable or productive in the 21st Century, the idea of a renewal that draws light and inspiration from the word of God to promote human development and solidarity is present here. Chenu's ideas are remarkably in tune with the "revival" being promoted by Pope Francis, and they can help us interpret the "newness" into which we are being invited.

Aquinas Institute of Theology
St. Dominic Priory
3407 Lafayette Avenue
Saint Louis, Missouri 63104, USA.

---

[58] Ibid., 122-129. On pp. 166-167, Chenu also reflects on the possibilities for "une chrétienté profane," best translated perhaps as "a secular Christendom".

Engaging Modernity Through Art: The Dominicans and *L'Art Sacré*

Mark E. Wedig, O.P.

After the 1926 papal condemnation of *Action Française*, a renewal of Catholicism was generated in the urban centers of France. A uniquely modern perspective on the Church was disseminated especially by burgeoning mass media campaigns. Publishing crusades gave voice to a minority vanguard Catholic outlook that opted for dialogue with the secularism, liberalism, and pluralism of modernity instead of a rigid apologetics against these forces. Several Paris-based publications strategically aligned themselves with this emerging Catholic avant-gardism which offered new interpretations of the Church for the modern world.

The place of the Dominican Order in this reformulation of French Catholic identity through the communications media was fundamental. Its publishing efforts at *Les Éditions du Cerf* represented the determinative nucleus of a growing crusade for the advancement of a modern urban-intellectualist interpretation of Church and society. The Dominicans of the Province of France (Paris) designed and developed a multi-layered communications network which aimed at deliberately activating an expressly modern Catholic viewpoint.[1]

It is from this ecclesial context that the friars' inspiration to interact with the modern art world emerged. In 1936, the Dominicans through *Cerf* purchased *L'Art Sacré*, a periodical that had been founded by Joseph Pichard eighteen months earlier. The founder had

---

[1] Mark Wedig, O.P., "The Fraternal Context of Congar's Achievement: The Platform for a Renewed Catholicism at Les Éditions du Cerf (1927-1954)," *US Catholic Historian* 17 no. 2 (Spring 1999) 106.

designed *L'Art Sacré* to circumvent the development of "eclectic academicism" that had embodied church architecture and decoration since the revival of Catholicism in the mid-Nineteenth Century. In his estimation that aesthetic academicism was holding back the church through derivative forms, Pichard aimed at informing French Catholic culture about a new and more authentic church art and architecture that were embodied in the projects of Maurice Denis and George Desvailliéres, and associates.[2] The renewed ecclesial mission of *Cerf* resonated with Pichard's inspiration of *L'Art Sacré*. In its new and invigorated incorporation into *Cerf*, *L'Art Sacré* would announce to French Catholic society the social consequences of aesthetics. The church would no longer retreat from the modern world through its derivative and anachronistic artistic and architectural styles, but instead would engage it.

1. Pie-Raymond Régamey (1900–1996) and Marie-Alain Couturier (1897-1954)

The Dominicans of the Province of France handpicked two of its young confreres to co-edit the journal. These friars' backgrounds in the arts prior to their entrance into the Dominican Order perfectly served the mission of *L'Art Sacré*. After World War I, Raymond Régamey (in religion: Pie) had trained as an art historian at the *Sorbonne* and art critic at the *École du Louvre* and was a disciple of the art historian Henri Focillon. His aesthetic training and historical studies, specializing in nineteenth-century developments in European art and architecture, positioned him to authentically critique contemporary developments in ecclesial art and architecture.

His confrere Pierre Couturier (in religion: Marie-Alain) also had trained after the First World War in Paris, but as a visual artist at the

---

[2] Joseph Pichard, *L'Art Moderne*, (Paris: B. Arthaud, 1953) 77-82.

Academie de la Grande Chaumière and later in the *Atelier de L'Art Sacré* of Maurice Denis.[3] Couturier's artistic vision followed the inspiration of his mentor Denis whose aesthetic dictum had become one of the central manifestoes of modern art itself.[4] Consequently, the concerns of non-figurative abstraction, painterly impressionism, and primitivism captured his artistic imagination as a religious painter. Moreover, Couturier had trained shoulder to shoulder with many of the emerging giants of the modern art world in post-war Paris. It would be his lasting interaction with that art community, better known as the "School of Paris," that would in turn generate a new movement in the life of the church all of which first materialized through the platform of *L'Art Sacré*.

2. The Aesthetic Enemy: Kitsch

Much of the artistic agenda of *L'Art Sacré*, first under Pichard and then under the Dominicans, involved a vehement aesthetic critique of "kitsch." For *L'Art Sacré*, the term kitsch stood for an overall aesthetic dysfunction in culture and was understood to be the by-product of artistic academicism that had plagued much of the work produced by nineteenth-century art schools. Régamey especially authored detailed diatribes against the low-brow, machine-generated church images and shoddy architectural decoration that increasingly seemed to clutter nineteenth and early twentieth-century church interiors. Kitsch as an ecclesial reality was portrayed

---

[3] Denis, who was a member of the Dominican Laity, and Jacques Maritain, who was closely aligned with the Order of Preachers together inspired aesthetic and ecclesial guidelines to eradicate the church of artistic decadence in the creation of the *Atelier de L'Art Sacré*.

[4] Traditionally histories of modern art have acknowledged the significance of Denis' manifestoes. His famous dictum: "We must never forget that any painting – before being a warhorse, a nude woman, an anecdote or whatnot – is essentially a flat surface to be covered with colors arranged in a certain order. Maurice Denis *Théories 1890-1910: du symbolism et de gaugin vers un novel ordre classique* (Paris: L. Rouart et J. Watelin: 1920), 38.

as the enemy of authentic church artistic and interior expression. Furthermore, kitsch supplanted the development of new forms that would renew the church from its tendency to settle for saccharine and mediocre interpretations of itself.[5]

It was during the period between the wars that the friars would seek out the collaborative scholarly contribution of art historians, theologians, and artists who offered alternative interpretations to the academicism that church and society had embodied in its comfortable, bourgeois, and romantic forms. Many of those contributions were facilitated by the Dominicans' interaction with new cultural and intellectual movements in Post-World War I French society. They saw that art and architecture had ecclesial significance and new aesthetic sensibilities would purge the church of its decadence. The friars turned enthusiastically to their friends at the crossroads of modern culture for answers to social, intellectual, and artistic problems.

3. World War II and Couturier's Expatriate Resistance

World War II drastically circumvented the momentum the French Dominicans had made in their cultural engagement with the modern world. The Third Reich saw modern art as "degenerate," and gathered up what it considered "Judeo-Marxist, decadent art" from Paris museums.[6] The "School of Paris" painters scattered or went underground. The onset of national socialisms, the Nazi invasion of Paris, and the destruction of dialogue with modernity destroyed the transnational agenda of the Paris avant-garde. The war compelled the friars to focus their efforts on French Resistance, involving themselves in systematic insurgency against right-wing forces in

---

[5] Régamey, "Le 'Kitsch' dans l'art et la vie chrétiennes," *L'Art Sacré* 3-4 (1950); 26.

[6] Sarah Wilson, "La vie artistique à Paris sous L'Occupation," in *Paris Paris, 1937-195,* Pontus Hulten, editor (Centre George Pompidou: 1981).

Europe. Yves Congar and other Dominicans participating in that Resistance were captured and incarcerated by German forces. Others' involvement centered on the French Worker-Priest movement and varieties of social activism.[7] The Dominicans strategized against the onslaught of the new nationalisms and their attempt to destroy modernity's quest for new universal languages and art forms that transcended national boundaries.

L'Art Sacré interrupted publication between 1939 and 1945. Couturier had traveled to the United States on December 29, 1939 to give lectures to French-speaking communities in New York. While there, France was invaded by Germany and its occupation ensued. Consequently, Couturier remained in the US and Canada until the early fall of 1945 offering conferences on modern art and decorating the novitiate chapel of the Dominican sisters in Elkins Park, Pennsylvania.[8] It is during that time that Couturier's friendship with expatriate avant-garde artists and intellectuals reached new plateaus and his strong belief in abstraction as a church expression was honed.[9]

Key to Couturier's development as an artistic entrepreneur was his renewed and developing relationship with John and Dominique de Menil. Like Couturier, the Menils were exiled from Paris in 1941, and had moved to Houston, Texas, the headquarters of their family business, Schlumberger, Ltd. Their movement among exiled French expatriate intellectuals in New York, notably with Catholic intellectuals like Raïssa and Jacques Maritain, during the war

---

[7] François Leprieur, *Quand Rome condamne: Dominicains et prêtres-ouviers* (Paris: Plon/Cerf, 1989).

[8] Marie-Alain Couturier, Dieu et l'art un vie (Paris: Les Éditions du Cerf, 1965) 235-237; 309.

[9] Monique Brunet-Weinmann, "Le Père Couturier au Québec" (1940-1941), RACAR 14 (1987): 243-261; Robert Schwartzwald, "The Civic Presence of Marie-Alain Courturier," Quèbec Studies 12 (1990): 234-261.

coincided with their interaction with Couturier.[10] Moreover, their social activism for civil rights and social change coalesced with their aesthetic platform to renew society through art. That belief in transformative qualities of art was spurred on by this newfound nexus of interest in new visual expression. The activist aesthetic vision opened to Couturier new ideas for collaborating with artists for a new church expression and would set both the de Menils and Couturier on a trajectory to bring about social change through a new sacred art after the war.

4. The Dominicans in Paris after World War II

After World War II, one witnessed extended collaboration between Catholic and non-Catholic neo-vanguard intelligentsia, literati, and activists. Once again avant-garde cultures overlapped and the Dominicans were a determinative force in such developments. A specific post-war generation of Dominican intellectuals extended and intensified its crusade against the French Right. A new leadership at *Les Èditions du Cerf* established a militant agenda for church and society.

At *Cerf* the emergence of what can be understood as an incipient program for a militant Catholic church came about at "le Carrefour" of worker priests,[11] growing youth movements,[12] liturgical research

---

[10] Pamela G. Smart, "Aesthetics as a Vocation," in *Art and Activism: Projects of John and Dominique de Menil*, edited by Josef Helfenstein and Laureen Schipsi (New Haven: Yale University Press, 2008) 21-39.

[11] The efforts of Louis Lebret, OP (1897-1966) and Jacques Loew, OP (1908-1999) who founded in 1941 the association *Èconomie et Humanisme*, together set in motion an extensive modern missionary effort among the working-class people of Marseilles.

[12] This was presented most extensively through the reflection and action of Maurice Montuclard, OP in his organization *Jeunesse de l'Èglise* and the review *Cahiers de Jeunesse de l'Èglise* both of which he founded.

endeavor and activism,[13] aesthetic crusade,[14] and ever-greater interdisciplinary theological reflection.[15] An urban Catholic activist vanguard bent on reconstructing church and society devised practices and norms from more "critical" philosophical, literary, aesthetic and religious foundations.

As this new cultural mediation emerged, it met strong opposition from Catholic forces. By the late 1940's the papal curia, by its influence over the major superior of the Dominican Order, attempted systematically to crush such French Dominican activism. The Roman curia aimed at destroying the foundations of what it perceived to be social and ecclesial extremism. In 1954 the Worker-Priests were suppressed; the projects pertaining to *L'Art Sacré* were censored; Yves Congar, M.D. Chenu, and H.M. Féret were silenced from teaching; the three French provincial superiors were dismissed; and the publishing efforts at *Cerf* were under close watch.

In retrospect, scholars have viewed the 1954 events as a battle between two radically different interpretations of the church in the modern world.[16] Even though the suppression of the French Dominicans can be understood as a systematic attempt to destroy a singular interpretation of church, each of the particular efforts tethered to *Les Éditions du Cerf* can be evaluated in relation to its own particular contribution to modern Catholicism. Each negotiated specific criteria

---

[13] I suggest that the ongoing developments of the Paris liturgy movement throughout the 1950's embodied its own church politics. See: Bernard Botte, *From Silence to Participation: An Insider's View of Liturgical Renewal*, Translated by John Sullivan (Washington, D.C.: The Pastoral Press, 1988).

[14] As mediated by *L'Art Sacré*.

[15] As embodied in the activities and extensive literary output of *Le Saulchoir* especially through the influences of MD Chenu, OP, Yves Congar, OP, and HM Féret, OP.

[16] Thomas O'Meara, O.P. "Raid on the Dominicans: The Repression of 1954," *America* 170 no.4 (February 1994): 8-16.

advancing a uniquely modern Catholicism in France after World War II.

5. "Parier pour le genie:"[17] Couturier's Inspiration for New Church Forms

It would not be until after World War II that the aesthetic ideas first addressed in the 1930's in the pages of *L'Art Sacré* would take new and fervent form through the inspiration and charismatic leadership of Marie-Alain Couturier. He returned to France with vigor to build a new church using new forms. By commandeering the aesthetic genius of his avant-garde friends for explicitly religious purposes, a modern church could be achieved. Couturier dreamed of a new aesthetic patronage in the church that would expropriate the artistic talent that had found refuge in Paris previous to the war. The tentative and mediocre aesthetics of nineteenth-century academicism would be overshadowed by the church's courageous new interaction with a host of avant-gardes willing to collaborate with the church.

For Couturier, the rhetoric of genius would play a major thematic function in his practices and writings of the post-war period. For Couturier, even though genius was not equivalent to faith, it was analogous to it. The aesthetic freedoms of truly creative artists were capable of leading spiritual or religious pilgrimages of their own. Couturier addressed the subject in *L'Art Sacré*:

> ...we do not know what goes on in the most secret recesses of the heart – nor what substitutes the intuitions of genius give faith. But there is between mystical inspiration and that of the heroes and great artists too profound an analogy for that favorable

---

[17] "To Bet on Genius."

presumption not to be in their favor. Always 'bet on genius,' as Delacroix used to say.[18]

The truly intuitive person, personified in the artist, innately would venture toward the sacred.

Access to genius required putting on the eyes of intuition and learning to see the unadulterated purity of forms. This could not happen without the wisdom of artistic masters. Modern art forms demanded the guidance of artists and art patrons who would provide roadmaps for more "difficult works" of the age. Couturier illustrated that point in referring to his new patronage of the avant-garde for the church:

> I would like to justify here what people have called our temerity. If we have chosen to go as far as we possibly could in a direction defined clearly enough by the names of Léger, Bazaine, and Miró, it was not for the vain desire to be or to appear to be progressive. It was simply that we were trying to reach a certain height, because below that height our effort seemed to us less worthy of the One for whom we undertook it – less worthy, too, of the men who had asked us to help them in a very wearing task. [19]

It was necessary for Couturier to demonstrate how to follow the mind of the aesthetic master.

In their post-war writings in *L'Art Sacré*, both Régamey and Couturier stressed that the aesthetic acumen of the master-genius would serve no purpose for the church unless the faithful would learn

---

[18] Marie-Alain Couturier, "Aux grands homes, le grandes choses," *L'Art Sacré* 9-10 (1950) 8. All French to English translations are the author's.

[19] Couturier, "Aunque es noche," *L'Art Sacré* 3-4 (1951): 10.

to trust these difficult, obscure visions and forms inspired by contemporary artists. Such trust necessitated a courageous leadership who would wager on the new forms themselves to redeem the church of its decadence. Couturier emphasized:

> A positive determination: 'Great men for great works,' Must a cathedral be built? We should say to ourselves, 'Somewhere in the world there must be an architect who is the greatest. He's the one we must find. We'll get him to do the cathedral, because he's the one man who is worthy to do it and capable of doing it...'[20]

A revival of church art in the Twentieth Century necessitated that a Catholic world become captivated by the miraculous idioms that only these masters could create.

6. The New Patronage: Plateau d'Assy; Vence, and Audincourt

Between 1948 and 1954, through an extensive collaborative effort among modern artists and architects and a new church patronage, Couturier set in motion the building of several important religious monuments designed according to specific modern religious-aesthetic standards. Couturier solicited for the sake of the church what he perceived to be the best modern artistic talent of the School of Paris, regardless of the individual artist's religious identity. By creating an explosion of landmark church decoration and architecture, inspired by modern aesthetic methods, Couturier intended to change the course of history. Even though he envisioned an even greater explosion of future projects, the Dominican involved the skill and insight of many of the towering personalities of the

---

[20] Couturier, "Aux grands homes, les grandes choses," 7.

French vanguard culture at mid-century to initiate a new aesthetic patronage for the church.

Couturier believed that these projects would not transform society or church without an extensive visual presentation of their uniqueness. From the winter of 1950 until his death in January 1954, Couturier alternated with Régamey, the editorial supervision and layout of *L'Art Sacré*. According to Couturier, the review would convert its readership to the aesthetic forms embodied in new projects by simply exposing their "truth." This would be achieved by clearing away the commentary and allowing new forms to simply speak for themselves.[21] Utilizing his aesthetic pedagogy, Couturier designed large bordered black and white photographs of the monuments accompanied by simple poetic descriptions about them. Even though Couturier avoided what he understood to be theoretical excursus, he nevertheless articulated an extensive aesthetic method for encountering his projects.

a. Assy

The first of Couturier's projects involved the decoration of a small church in the French alpine village of Assy. Couturier introduced the impact of the church to his readership in *L'Art Sacré*:

> Now this little church is finished. And even before it was finished, it had been talked about in every country in the world. That has not happened for any church for well over a century: the largest and most sumptuous basilicas have been built without attracting the slightest attention in artistic circles, or even, let's admit it, among genuinely cultured people.[22]

---

[21] Couturier, "Pour les yeux," *L'Art Sacré* 5-6 (1950) 3-5.

[22] Couturier, "La leçon d'Assy," *L'Art Sacré* 1-2 (1950) 16.

This church had been constructed through the efforts of a Canon Devémy before World War II using the architect Maurice Novarina. Couturier featured several separate issues dedicated to the project. Under Couturier's guidance the overall aesthetic schema of the church environment was shaped as a decorative collage of modern styles, representing various biblical and sacramental contexts or themes. Very different modern designs were incarnated through various media, leaving the onlooker with a variety of Catholic theological subjects.

Assy displayed an imposing marquee-façade depicting Mary surrounded by French ecclesial insignia, all presiding over the approaching pilgrim. In the façade, artist Fernand Léger characterized the church's patroness by designing an icon of her reminiscent of his "machine art." As one entered the church nave through a small narthex, the altar area demanded attention because of two major compositions. Germaine Richier's tree-like crucifix rose up from the altar area like a battered yet beautiful gargoyle. Above the crucifix a large colorful tapestry by Jean Lurçat illustrated the queen of heaven encountering a terrible beast. Many other compositions encircled the nave. Henri Matisse's simple line drawing of St. Dominic was positioned over Georges Braque's minimally designed tabernacle relief sculpture. Three windows by Georges Rouault each featured a colorful rendering of a heavily-laden figure imbued with the paradox of sorrow and serenity. In addition, the little church featured a sculpture by Jacques Lipchitz and a baptistery wall painting by Marc Chagall.

b. Vence

Couturier's second project encompassed a masterpiece which arose out of the unique aesthetic-theological collaboration between Dominican cloistered nuns, their chaplain, L.B. Rayssiguier,

Couturier and Henri Matisse.[23] Together they outlined the ground-plan for a monastery chapel at Vence, set in the hills of the Alps Maritimes between Nice and Antibes, France. The plan was for the entire undertaking to be designed and executed by a single master. As Couturier worked alongside Matisse he was convinced that his genius had found its rightful place. Couturier wrote:

> ...So true is it that the sincerity of one lone man, if it goes deep enough in him, reaches, for all other men, a universal substratum of truth which nothing else can ever penetrate. Anyone who knows how to look will find borne out here what was Matisse's constant law: he never did anything without first impregnating himself body and soul with what he wanted to paint, identifying with the object he wished to represent, then expressing it in one outpouring, rapid and in a way uncontrolled, so he might give himself to it whole and entire, without reticence or precaution, as he himself had become transformed by that other life within him.[24]

Matisse implemented his intense aesthetic doctrines of form, aiming at a harmony of design. The artist's aesthetic preoccupation with color that had been perfected in his cut-out designs was transmuted into organic shapes of the chapel's stained glass. Moreover, furnishings, vestments, and vessels were incorporated into the chapel's overall composition according to the same organic principles.

At Vence, the artist's fixation on the freedom of the sketched line drawing was embodied in the dance of black on white blueprint of Christ's passion in fourteen Stations of the Cross. Couturier

---

[23] See the entire issued dedicated to the project: "Vence," *L'Art Sacré* 11-12 (1951).
[24] Couturier, "Vence," *L'Art Sacré* 11-12 (1951) 15-16.

commented on what he believed to be its rare and exceptional language.

> I want to try to say, as simply as I can, what I think of this work of art: I think it is the most important and most beautiful thing in the chapel. I also think that it is what will most deeply disturb the public of our time. I say "of our time" because I already see the youngest among us, the twenty-year-olds, accepting and living it readily. It belongs to the world. It speaks a language they understand. But I also see people as different as Picasso and Bazaine appreciating it just as the young do.[25]

Couturier believed that Matisse had created a modern religious idiom through what he referred to as "this violence, this total absence of the slightest concern for beauty..."[26]

c. Audincourt

In January 1951 the Diocesan Commission for Sacred Art of Besançon, France approved the construction of two uniquely modern church structures that involved the collaboration of Couturier and a Canon Ledeur. Both of these structures, like Assy and Vence before them, generated a new paradigm of church patronage of modern art and architecture. The first of these two modernist structures was created for a small rural church at Audincourt in the Franche-Comté region of Burgundy. *L'Art Sacré* particularly viewed the unique contribution of Audincourt as a new frontier in abstract art for the church all in a single creation.[27] Couturier explained how the people were introduced to these new forms:

---

[25] Couturier, "La chemin de croix," *L'Art Sacré* 11-12 (1951) 24.

[26] "La chemin de croix," 25.

[27] See the issue: "Audincourt," *L'Art Sacré* 3-4 (1951).

> ...you have to go and live with the people you are working for. Let them see with their own eyes that into these strange works of art that they do not yet appreciate you have put all your love and the best you have and are... It generates strong friendships and mutual confidence which ambient malice, envy, and stupidity cannot corrode.[28]

The strange forms produced by the free interior visions of the artist would themselves germinate and sprout in the imagination of the people.

At Audincourt a starkly designed semicircle nave housed a modest altar and ambo encircled by a colorful clerestory band near the ceiling edge. The artist Fernand Léger solicited the assistance of parishoners of Audincourt to help create stained-glass abstractions of liturgical and biblical themes. The other decorative trait of this church was its façade-mosaic. Above the portals artist Jean Bazaine created a highly lyrical interpretation of the Tree of Jesse.

7. Posthumous Projects: Ronchamp and L'Arbresle

Two of the projects both involving the architect Le Corbusier,[29] that were initiated by Couturier before his death, have endured comprehensively in the annals of art history. Unfortunately, he would not see these two projects to completion because of his tragic death. Couturier sought out the famous architect for the creation of explicitly religious design for a pilgrimage church at Ronchamp and a large convent for the formation of Dominican friars outside of Lyon,

---

[28] Couturier, "Aunque es de noche," *L'Art Sacré* 3-4 (1951) 16-17.

[29] Charles-Édouard Jeanneret-Gris, better known as Le Corbusier was born October 6, 1887 and died August 27, 1965. Jeanneret-Gris was Swiss-French architect, designer, painter, and urban-planner and is considered one of the pioneers of modern architecture.

France in Èveux. Couturier convinced Le Corbusier to translate his aesthetic into explicit religious formulation.

a. Ronchamp

The Besançon diocese had set in motion the construction of the pilgrimage church of Notre-Dame-du-Haut at Ronchamp. Couturier became increasingly enthusiastic about the new paradigm of church architecture that was being brought about at Ronhamp. In one of the last issues of *L'Art Sacré* edited by Couturier, he announced the plans for project:

> At first sight one will be surprised by the extreme originality of these forms. But it will quickly be seen that plans and forms are developed here with the suppleness and freedom of living organisms, and at the same time with the exactness that their purpose and function demand. The sacred character can be felt throughout, and first of all in the originality itself, the unusualness.[30]

Here the purist machine-age abstractions of the architect gave way to a new sculptural architectural lyricism. The church design mixed the metaphors of monument and landscape. Le Corbusier molded a sagging slab-like roof upon white-washed curving walls that met at right-angles.

Couturier declared that the pilgrim's passage into a sacred world involved movement into a mysterious and primitive cave of concrete. He heralded a pilgrimage to the sacred recesses of genius:

> Naturally this passage from the secular to the sacred in the forms themselves is brought about by minute and variations

---

[30] Couturier, "Le Corbusier: Ronchamp," *L'Art Sacré* 11-12 (1953) 29-39.

with formulas, but these are nonetheless perfectly perceptible to the soul. All the masterpieces bear witness to this fact. These marvelous purifications, these priceless advances, are not effected by engineers' calculations or exact logic: they come from the soul itself.[31]

According to Couturier the Spirit breathed on such creations.

b. La Tourette

The Dominican priory of Sainte Marie de La Tourette, designed to house the seminary/house of studies for the Dominican Friars of the Province of Lyon, was the brain-child of Couturier and Le Corbusier's collaborative inspiration. Nevertheless, the house of studies' construction between 1956 and 1960 would come into being considerably after Couturier's death. Today La Tourette is considered one of the most important buildings of the late Modernist style.

On a hillside in the rural topography of Èveux, France, the rough reinforced concrete structure that dominates the landscape houses a hundred bedrooms for teachers and students, study halls, recreations rooms, a library, refectory, and a large chapel for common prayer. The structure, built on a steep slope of a hill, encompasses two levels acoustically separating private cloistered areas from more public ones. The building's design captures and circulates the cool air of the countryside. All together the building opens a new logic for engineered space.

8. Conclusion

Couturier's premature death from the lifelong disease of *Myasthenia gravis* on February 9, 1954 at age 56, unfortunately circumvented a ground-breaking movement kept alive uniquely by

---

[31] Couturier, "Le Corbusier: Ronchamp," *L'Art Sacré* 11-12 (1953) 31.

his charismatic and entrepreneurial spirit. That same year his confrere and friend, Pie Régamey, would resign his editorship of the review. Even though the Dominicans at *Cerf* would maintain *L'Art Sacré* until 1969, attempting to carry out the original inspiration set in motion by its two founders, the sacred art movement uniquely facilitated by Couturier and embodied in the pages of their review, abruptly ceased.

The Dominicans through *L'Art Sacré*, between 1936 and 1954, had managed to change the course of aesthetic and ecclesial history. Even though not the only movement of its kind in Europe in the first half of the Twentieth Century, their uniquely French avant-garde approach managed to rid the church of academicism and replace it with new aesthetic forms of the "School of Paris." That relatively short-lived movement, modest in its volume of projects, nevertheless managed to impact the aesthetics of the sacred in modern world like no other.

Dominican Initiatives in Bolivia: 1956 to 1973

Charles W. Dahm, O.P.

Indigenous peoples have long constituted nearly three-fourths of Bolivia's population. They have, however, been systematically excluded from the social and economic life of the country, before independence from Spain in 1825 and after. They have been constantly subjected to racial discrimination and political oppression. Poverty and near total marginalization prevented them from demanding or even making known their rights and needs while ruling elites and foreign interests monopolized power and exploited the country's wealth. One consequence of this system was extreme political instability; by 1980, 155 years after its successful war of independence, Bolivia had experienced more than 165 palace coups, and the political system was fractured by dozens of political parties and widespread corruption. In the 1960s Bolivia was considered the poorest country in South America.

1. The Reality of Bolivia in the Mid-Twentieth Century

In 1952, the *Movimiento Nacional Revolucionario* seized power from wealthy elites and foreign interests. It was a true revolution, achieving structural change that has lasted until today. For example, it implemented agrarian reform, returning land to the indigenous peasants, who constituted the vast majority of the population. It nationalized the tin mines, a valuable national resource at the time, even though on the verge of total exhaustion. It supported the labor movements of miners and farmers, reformed the tax code and extended the vote to indigenous people. The MNR ruled through elections until 1964 when, weakened by internal divisions, corruption and accommodations with traditional wealth, it fell to a military coup.

The Spanish *conquistadores* brought Christianity and the Catholic Church to Bolivia. The fact that the Christian religion came from outside and was imposed, to a great extent by force, meant that the Church would depend upon foreign clergy for most of its history; it meant that the faith would become profoundly syncretic; that religion would become a cultural reality rather than a personal choice; and that the institutional Church would become linked traditionally to the ruling classes, enjoying a position of social privilege and economic and political power. Priests lived from stipends for administering the sacraments, multiplying Masses and demanding donations for every kind of blessing, prayer or sacrament. In the 1950s, the Catholic Church in Bolivia was an old Church, badly in need of reform.

In the mid-Twentieth Century, the basic task for the Bolivian Church was to reform itself in the spirit of Jesus Christ and to respond prophetically to the injustices of the day. The most obvious sociological fact, theological problem, and pastoral concern involved institutional injustice and structural sin which supported exploitation and oppression of the masses. In the nineteenth and twentieth centuries, the Church fought against the Masons, Protestants and Communists, but those struggles were institutional battles led by the clergy rather than struggles of the people to be free. The Church often ignored the real problems of the people and their efforts to free themselves from subhuman conditions and unjust exploitation.

2. Italian, German, and North American Dominicans in Bolivia in the 1950s

Until 1826, Bolivia was part of the Peruvian Dominican Province of John the Baptist. There were Dominican communities in La Paz, Oruro, Cochabamba, Sucre, Potosi and Tarija. Fr. Vicente Bernedo, a friar living in Potosi during the Seventeenth Century, was so highly esteemed for his sanctity that his cause for beatification was introduced in Rome. However, the Dominican friars were expelled from Bolivia in 1826, the year after independence, and their convents and churches were closed or expropriated by the government, or given to diocesan clergy. Between 1826 and 1950, no Dominican apostolate was carried out in Bolivia.

In 1952, a group of twelve Italian Dominicans from the Province of Turin arrived in Bolivia. Six went to Sucre to take charge of the diocesan seminary, and six went to La Paz to establish a parish in the suburb of Calacoto that included a rural mission in Rio Abajo and the valley of Palco. It was under the direction of the Italian Dominican, Fr. Van Noenen, until 1959 when Dominicans left the parish.[1]

Dominicans from the German Teutonic Province also arrived in the 1950s and founded a vicariate. The Province of St. Albert the Great, U.S.A. arrived in Bolivia in 1956, four years after the 1952 revolution and soon thereafter established its own vicariate. The relationship with the German Dominicans in Bolivia was always cordial and fraternal even though the two groups had different theological and pastoral approaches and distinct fields of apostolic work. The German Dominicans took parishes in the area of Samaipata and Comorapa (halfway between Cochabamba and Santa Cruz) to carry out pastoral work in small towns and outlying rural areas. The two vicariates did not collaborate in specific apostolic works or in structuring a common formation program for future Bolivian Dominicans. In January 2013, however, the two vicariates joined to form a vice province.

In the early 1950s, Fr. Edward Hughes, O.P., Provincial of St. Albert the Great Province, USA, and his companion, Fr. Patrick

---

[1] In 1957, the Italian Dominicans who worked in the seminary in Sucre, the country's capital, terminated their work in Bolivia. Only two of their priests remained in Bolivia: Francisco Merlino, who joined the North American Dominicans in La Paz, and Antonino Lubatti who joined the mission of the German Dominicans.

Clancy, O.P., visited Bolivia and consulted the Apostolic Nuncio about the possibility of their province initiating a mission in Bolivia. They were responding to the Vatican's request that religious orders send ten percent of their members to work in the "missions." After a positive response, the Dominicans decided to establish a mission with Fr. Peter Houlihan, O.P. and the German Dominican, Fr. Athanasius Van Noenen, O.P. They developed a university apostolate by establishing a Dominican Newman Center near the state University of San Andres in La Paz. Fr. Houlihan was responsible for the Center while Fr. Van Noenen developed *"Cursillos de Cristiandad,"* (introduced from Spain around that time), and a communication apostolate through radio and the printed press.

3. Conceptual and Pastoral Change in Latin America

The disconnection of the Church in Latin America from its people began to change in the decades between 1930 and 1960. It started with the importation of the pastoral model, Catholic Action, developed in Belgium by Fr. Joseph Cardijn. This model emphasized the need for the Church to enter different sectors of society, such as labor, business, secondary or higher education, agriculture, medicine, etc., as the leaven for evangelization. Catholics gathered in small groups called cells to reflect on their lives and the scriptures through a process called *Revisión de Vida,* which employed the methodology of See, Judge and Act. First, the small group reflected on a problem or current situation in its area – whether community, church, or nation – and analyzed it. Then to "judge" or evaluate it through the eyes of faith, the members called on the scriptures to enlighten their analysis. Finally, they decided either jointly or individually to take some action regarding the situation in order to advance the Reign of God.

These groups began throughout Latin America, initially in Brazil, where they awakened the faith and mobilized the peasantry and working class. The members gradually grew into small Christian communities, called "*Comunidades Eclesiales de Base*," (CEBS). An ecclesiology developed around these communities, which included the claim that they were the fullness of Church written in miniature. The more they reflected on their "reality," the world of poverty and oppression, the more these communities became politically aware and active. Traditionalist clergy and laity accused the rapid growth of active Catholics in these communities of meddling in politics and often denounced them as influenced by or promoters of communism. Many of the developments in thought and experience in Europe that gave birth to the Second Vatican Council were operative behind the changes occurring in the Church in Latin America. Latin American economists working through the *Economic Council for Latin America* (ECLA) developed new economic analyses called "dependency theories" which explained the structural or systemic conditions that spawned and maintained poverty throughout the continent. They postulated that Third World countries that depended principally on primary resources (oil, metals, agricultural products, etc.) were losing economic ground in their trade or exchange with First World countries that excelled in manufacturing; consequently, poor countries were doomed to remain poor or underdeveloped, and hugely indebted to First World countries. The teaching of the Second Vatican Council gave additional impetus to these efforts which were reconnecting the Church with the People of God and allied it with their struggles. These developments led to the creation of "Liberation Theology," first articulated in Brazil and then in the late 1950s in Peru which spread across Latin America like wildfire.

The first theological reflections that led to liberation theology had their origins in a dialogue between a church and a society in ferment, between Christian faith and the longings for transformation and liberation arising from the people. The Second Vatican Council produced a theological atmosphere characterized by great freedom and creativity. This gave Latin American theologians the courage to think for themselves about pastoral problems affecting their countries. This process could be seen at work among both Catholic and Protestant thinkers with the organization *Church and Society in Latin America* (ISAL) taking a prominent part. There were frequent meetings between Catholic theologians (Gustavo Gutiérrez, Segundo Galilea, Juan Luis Segundo, Lucio Gera, and others) and Protestants (Emilio Castro, Julio de Santa Ana, Rubem Alves, José Míguez Bonino), leading to intensified reflection on the relationship between faith and poverty, the gospel and social justice. Their work was influenced by European thought, notably, the integral humanism of Jacques Maritain, the social personalism of Mounier, the evolutionism of Teilhard de Chardin, Henri de Lubac's reflections on the social dimension of dogma, Yves Congar's theology of the laity, and the work of Marie-Dominque Chenu. The Second Vatican Council then gave the most authoritative support to this movement.

By the time of the Second Latin American Bishops Conference in Medellin, Colombia in 1968, this theology of liberation had won supporters among bishops and theologians from Mexico to Chile and Argentina. Even today, the documents from that conference remain a watershed in the historical development of the Latin American Church, and, of course, greatly influenced the direction of the mission of Dominicans in Bolivia.

4. A Dominican Pastoral Vision

During the period from 1960 to 1970, the Dominicans, originally invited to Bolivia to support, strengthen, and extend institutional or traditional ministries, became conscious of the structural and pastoral deficiencies of the pre-Conciliar Church, and of the need to develop a new pastoral approach they called a *"Nueva Cristiandad"* – a New Christendom – a specifically "Christian culture" not tied necessarily to ecclesiastical institutions nor a political ideology. At the same time, they lacked clarity about what exactly needed to be done, and they suffered, like other missionary groups at that time, from the myopic limitations of the pre-Conciliar Church. However, they were beginning to perceive many of the challenging dimensions of the new Church that would be brought to life by the Second Vatican Council and their missionary and evangelical perspective helped them avoid involvement in strictly sacramental ministries. The Bolivian bishops wanted the Dominicans to take responsibility for parishes and offered them a number and even prelatures. The bishops found it hard to understand how a group of priests could work in Bolivia without parish commitments. Indeed, a few Dominicans did want to do parish work in order to learn more about the people and the culture.[2] The Bishop of La Paz also asked the Dominicans to participate in "flying missions" in the rural areas outside the city of La Paz. This invitation had greater appeal. The Dominicans formed teams composed of a priest, two or three religious sisters and lay catechists, who traveled each Sunday to three or four communities in the rural Altiplano and surrounding mountainous areas to celebrate the Eucharist, administer the sacraments, and give religious instruction. Frs. Jim Burke, Pat Rearden, Ed Cleary, and Kieran Redmond began this ministry, but it was Fr. Rearden who continued the work until 1966.[3]

---

[2] A few friars had a special interest in the parish of Buena Vista, to the north of Santa Cruz, both as a Dominican mission and as a place of pastoral training for seminarians. They were invited by the bishop of Santa Cruz to take responsibility for Buena Vista, and during the summers of 1959 and 1960, four priests (Burke, Cleary, Holachek, and Houlihan) worked there. Within a few years the parish was given to the priests of the St. James Society, a missionary society recently founded by Cardinal Richard Cushing in Boston.

[3] In 1959-61 Frs. James Burke, Jordan Bishop, Athanasius Van Noenen, Terrence Holachek, Edward Cleary, Patrick Rearden, Ralph Rogowski, Kieran Redmond, and Br. Kevin Carroll arrived in Bolivia in March of 1961.

To develop and implement a new vision for their ministry, the whole vicariate met at least twice a year to evaluate and plan. They were a band of Dominican brothers who prayed in community, read books and articles about changes proposed by the Second Vatican Council, challenged one another and planned together. After the closing of the seminary and a visit from a French Dominican, Fr. Paul Ramfot, O.P., director of the social institute in Montevideo, Uruguay in 1959, they decided to focus on the formation of laity for social apostolates organized according to the Catholic Action model. The experiences they had gained working outside the seminary led them to a growing awareness of the urgency to do something about the social conditions in Bolivia. They were becoming convinced that their apostolate should be "in the world." They sought new guidelines and avenues for responding to the problems in Bolivian society which were not being addressed in parishes. They were connecting with the movement of Church reform sweeping Latin America.

In 1959, the Italian Dominican, Francisco Merlino, was thinking in such terms when he founded the Bolivian branch of UNIAPAC for the Christian formation of business leaders. It functioned in La Paz, Oruro, and Cochabamba, and always had Dominicans as advisors. Fr. Tom Davy, experienced in forming cooperatives while assigned to the Irish Dominican mission in Trinidad, came to work with the cooperative movement in La Paz and other parts of Bolivia. The Dominicans also formed CETRA, a Labor School, which taught workers' rights based on the social teachings of the Church. It extended from La Paz to Oruro, Cochabamba, and Santa Cruz, and always had a Dominican *asesor* or advisor.[4] The Dominicans also worked with other Catholic groups, such as the *Cursillos de Cristiandad,* the Christian Family Movement, and diocesan and

---

[4] After Fr. Davy left Bolivia in 1974, this labor movement ceased to exist.

religious priests and sisters. For example, Fr. Jim Burke, who was named the first Dominican vicar provincial in 1962, later served as President of the National Conference of Religious from 1965 to 1966.

5. Growth and crisis

The vicariate grew rapidly in the first ten years: two friars in 1956, ten in 1958, twelve in 1960, thirteen in 1961-1963, fifteen in 1964, twenty in 1965-1968. All were from the United States with the exception of Frs. Merlino and Davy. In 1966, a period of vocational crisis began for the Dominicans. Between 1966 and 1972, twelve members of the vicariate left the Order.[5] These departures demanded serious community adjustments and took a toll on the ministry and on the men who remained. It was an exciting but stressful time. The loss of personnel and the lack of new missionaries from the Province gradually diminished the number of Dominicans in Bolivia: eighteen in 1972, fifteen in 1974, thirteen in 1975, twelve in 1977. Furthermore, some friars returned to the United States to carry on their ministries in the late 1960s and early 1970s, namely, Frs. Burke, Holacheck and Houlihan in 1968, Chuck Dahm in 1970, and Edward Cleary in 1971.

In the mid-1970s, the vicariate began to focus on developing native vocations. Although a number of young men in Cochabamba and in Santa Cruz expressed serious interest, Bolivians responded slowly to the Order. In the 1960s, the first three vocations were attracted to the Order by Dominicans' work in the universities: Oscar Uzin, Alfonso ViaReque, and Eduardo Zelaya. The two former ones were trained in the U.S., and the latter died tragically in a car accident while studying in Bolivia. A lively debate ensued about where

---

[5] Hyacinth Maguy, Maurice Johnson, Simon McCormick, Luke Sablica, Timothy Sullivan, Kieran Redman, Jordan Bishop, Tom Shanley, Bob McAuliffe, Bill Lange, Nicolas Thielen, and Art Sist.

candidates for the Order should study. After experimenting with sending students to Colombia and Peru, the vicariate decided that Bolivia was the appropriate venue and opened its own novitiate in 1976 in Cochabamba with only one novice after having prepared five postulants the previous year. Although the novice left during the same year, subsequent years saw more Bolivians join the vicariate, and by January 2013, when the vicariate became a vice province, it was solidly under the direction of Bolivian Dominicans.

6. Schools and Ministries

a. Seminaries

In 1957, on the occasion of the visit of the Provincial, Fr. John Marr, O.P., the Apostolic Nuncio invited the Dominicans to assume responsibility for the major seminary in La Paz, then conducted by Salesian priests from Italy. Fr. Marr accepted this invitation and sent four more Dominicans to accompany the two already there. Frs. Jim Burke, appointed the first superior of the house in La Paz, Matthias Mueller, Jordan Bishop, and Hyacinth Maguy. Shortly thereafter, he sent more friars: Frs. Ralph Rogowski, Terence Holacheck, Timothy Sullivan, Edward Cleary, Kieran Redmond, Patrick Rearden and Br. Kevin Carroll.

The Dominicans signed a four-year contract with the Archdiocese of La Paz to run the seminary (1958-1962). The archbishop also wanted the Dominicans to take charge of a high school, Colegio San Andres, in Calacoto, but the Dominicans declined because they wanted to avoid being tied to traditional apostolates like schools and parishes in order to be free to respond to the needs of the seminary and other unattended needs of the Bolivian Church.

Because the number of seminarians was small (twenty-one in 1958, ten in 1959) and because there was another major seminary in Sucre, the country's capital, which had thirty seminarians, the bishops decided to combine the two seminaries in a new National

Seminary of San Jose in Cochabamba. The Dominicans were not unhappy because they had become aware of other apostolic needs, particularly the work with university students. They did offer to supply professors to the new seminary, and in fact, Fr. Jordan Bishop, O.P., after completing a sabbatical year of study (1963-1964) in new pastoral theology at Université Catholique in Lille, France with the prominent Dominican, Père Liégé, O.P., taught church history for a brief time in the new seminary, which was otherwise staffed by Spanish priests from OCSHA, a Spanish missionary organization of diocesan priests.

The OCSHA priests favored a model of formation that required seminarians to gain pastoral experience in parishes. The bishops, however, wanted a more traditional Tridentine approach to seminary formation which set the seminarians apart from societal involvement, and, consequently, dismissed the OCSHA priests and closed the seminary for a brief period in 1969. Fr. Bishop resigned in protest. In the early 1970s, the seminary was reopened as Seminario de San Luis and was connected to the new Catholic University's *Institute for Theological Studies* (ISET). Dominicans John Risley and Oscar Uzin, the first Bolivian to join the U.S. province, began teaching there in the early 1970s but left in October, 1977, when Frs. Risley and Uzin joined a group of professors and administrators who resigned in protest at the dismissal of two professors. Their dismissal stemmed from long-standing conflicts with the Episcopal Conference, which came to a head when the bishops accused a professor, a Spanish Jesuit, of teaching unorthodox theology, and there was no process by which he could defend himself. Frs. Risley and Uzin continued with an apostolate of teaching and theological reflection but outside the institute.[6]

---

[6] Fr. Uzin also developed a literary apostolate to convey his Christian and very humanitarian vision and theological themes, publishing novels, *El Ocaso de*

b. University Apostolates

As mentioned above, the friars had begun a ministry at the state University of San Andres, just up the street from the seminary. They had opened the University Center of St. Thomas Aquinas where students were welcomed to share breakfast and other meals. Some friars worked with university students to form small groups and implement the Catholic Action model. Some attended classes at the university to facilitate their contact with the students. In November 1958, however, the center was closed for lack of funds and because the drop-in center was considered an ineffective approach.

In January, 1961, Terence Holachek, Timothy Sullivan, Matthias Mueller, and later Jordan Bishop were sent to Cochabamba to establish a new community and focus on the university apostolate *Juventud Universitara Católica (JUC)* and to teach in the Catholic Normal School, a teachers' college, operated by the Dutch Augustinians. Brother Timothy Wrinn joined the group in March 1963 as the community's economic administrator and Fr. Mueller became its first superior. The Dominicans arrived when the JUC, under the direction of Fr. Lorenzo Perez, OFM, was abandoning the typical Catholic Action model. He developed a new approach which focused on organizing students to change unjust university structures and Christianize them. Fr. Bishop called this "the moral approach to

---

Orion, which won the Guttentag Prize in Bolivia in 1972, and the second novel, *La Oscuridad Radiante*, which was equally successful. He later published commentaries on the New Testament.

Fr. Risley conducted retreats for religious and clergy and also worked with the Bolivian Conference of Religious, attending various international meetings for Latin American religious men. He moved to La Paz to work with an ecumenical organization called ASEC (Ecumenical Association for Coordination and Cooperation in Social Development Work). He helped the team of ASEC reflect theologically on the orientation of their projects in rural areas and to work in a grassroots ecumenical project aimed at urging the different churches to unite forces in the field of social action.

political commitment" in which a student "front" campaigned for positions in student government in order to fight the double evil of corruption and communism, the "anti-Christian" forces and fronts. Frs. Sullivan and Holachek were designated by the Bishop of Cochabamba as responsible for university ministry, which functioned in the Dominican center, St. Martin De Porres, adjacent to the Dominican residence on Calle Colombia. There students had access to inexpensive daily meals, a noon Mass and weekly lectures on theological or catechetical subjects and social analysis. Small reflection groups were formed using the *Revisión de Vida* model. The friars combined the Catholic Action model of ministry (JUC) with the more political Catholic front called *Frente Universitario Revolunario Católico (FRUC)*. The latter inspired by Christian democracy and even connected to the Christian Democratic Party, won elections and snatched the student contingent on the university's board of directors away from the "reds." (In Latin America, students comprise half the membership of the universities' boards of directors.) And they, like the faculty, the other half of the boards, were elected through the work of the national political party, the Christian Democratic Party, which was searching for a "third way" between communism and capitalism.

Fr. Sullivan energized a vibrant university movement and provided Christian formation for the students. He was a charismatic priest who made the thought of St. Thomas Aquinas come alive for students. He organized quarterly retreats for about 50 students in a retreat house, *La Pascana*, outside Cochabamba where he enthralled students with his explanations of St. Thomas' tracts on the moral virtues. The students ate simply but abundantly and danced into the night, ultimately sleeping on the floor. When Fr. Chuck Dahm, O.P., replaced Fr. Sullivan in 1966, JUC and FRUC continued their efforts to change the university and added a service dimension of constructing clinics and schools in the poor rural areas of Bolivia. Catholic Relief Services lent the students shovels and pickaxes, wheel barrels and frames to make adobes and Dahm drove their truck along treacherous mountain roads as the students and bricklayer held on for dear life.

The university students were immersed in social action. The Cuban revolution in 1959 had inspired them and countless others throughout Latin America to work for a more just and egalitarian society, a socialist political system that avoided the pitfalls of a communist dictatorship. Che Guevara arrived in Bolivia in 1967 in attempt to organize a peasant-based uprising and revolution, but he sorely miscalculated the political consciousness of the population. The peasants rejected his invitation to revolt. His presence and the manhunt to capture him raised the level of national debate to hysterical levels. Bishop Gutierrez of Cochabamba displayed balance and common sense in his pleas for calm and peaceful resolution of conflict as well as steps toward promoting justice. Eventually, betrayed by a *campesino*, Guevara was captured and executed in October 1967.[7] Bishop Gutierrez held a Mass in the Cochabamba cathedral for the repose of his soul.

All the brethren working in the university movement had an extended meeting in 1964 to exchange ideas and formulate a unified

---

[7] An illustration of the students' rather radical approach was when the body of Simon Patiño, Bolivia's notorious tin baron, often referred to as "The Andean Rockefeller, who, after World War II, was considered possibly the richest man in the world, was brought back from Switzerland, where he had lived in exile after the 1952 revolution had nationalized the country's mines. The university students organized a demonstration at the Cochabamba airport to protest the return of his body, claiming that he had so greedily and brutally exploited and stolen from the Bolivian people that even his body should not be welcomed back into the country. The protest turned dramatic when the students, upon the arrival of his body at the airport, spilled cow's blood on the floor of the airport to symbolize the death of so many Bolivians at the hands of the Patiño family. Needless to say, the bishop called the Dominicans that evening quite upset with this form of Catholic Action.

concept of the meaning, objectives, and value of their apostolate. Their objective was to form a bona fide intellectual community in the university adequate to meet the demands and needs of Bolivian society. While all agreed on this vision, friars differed on how to put it into practice. Fr. Rearden moved to Cochabamba in 1968 to replace Fr. Dahm in the university work, which thereafter experienced a slow decline and ended when he began teaching theology at the Normal School.

The JUC movement in Cochabamba produced amazing results and assumed a leadership role in the country's universities. Students in these apostolates went in various directions, but many into areas of great social involvement. Some students got scholarships for advanced study in Chile where a few later died in 1973 when General Pinochet, overthrew President Salvador Allende in the bloody, CIA-orchestrated, coup. A few others died fighting in the guerrillas in Bolivia while others became active in Bolivian politics. Still others got scholarships to study in the United States and Europe, especially medical students, with the understanding they would return to serve their country. Unfortunately, only a few returned to Bolivia. This failure disheartened Dominicans who had planned for them to return and reform the medical system.

The Dominicans created the university apostolate in the mining city of Oruro when Frs. Bishop and Rogawski arrived in 1964. In the following three years, there was considerable turnover of Dominican personnel and eventually the Dominicans terminated their ministry there.[8] In Santa Cruz university work was opened to Dominicans

---

[8] A year later Fr. Rogawski moved to Santa Cruz and was replaced by Br. Mark Paraday, and Fr. Bishop moved to Cochabamba and was replaced by Fr. Holachek. A year later (1966), Fr. Sullivan joined them for a brief time in Oruro. Others ministered with workers as well – first Fr. Rogawski, then Fr. Mueller; and some dedicated themselves to working with high school students – Fr. Luke Sablica, who arrived in 1965, and then Br. Kevin Carroll.

when Fr. Rogawski arrived from Oruro in April 1965. At the invitation of the bishop, Fr. Rogawski created a Christian university center at *La Mansión* (a large estate donated to the Santa Cruz diocese) and began to work informally with small groups of students, but not organizing a movement as such. Dominicans wanted to develop Christian leaders throughout the national university system. In fact, in the 1960s, they formed strong leaders who impacted the leadership of the universities in La Paz, Oruro, Cochabamba, and Santa Cruz. The students they formed also took control of the national university student organization, *La Confederación Universitaria Boliviana*.[9]

c. Ministry in the Catholic Normal School

The Catholic Normal School, which trained elementary and high school teachers, welcomed Dominican professors from the time the Dominican community was established in Cochabamba. The Dominicans, Frs. Mueller, Holachek, Bishop and Redmond were influential in the activities of the Normal School and until 1966, taught all the philosophy and theology courses besides being involved in extracurricular activities. Fr. Redmond organized a drama club and conducted a variety of *jornadas* and retreats. When Frs. Holacheck and Redmond left Bolivia in 1968 and Fr. Mueller moved to Santa Cruz, Fr. Bishop was left alone to finish the school year. From 1969 until

---

[9] Since his return to Bolivia in 1972, Fr. Alfonso ViaReque, the second native Bolivian Dominican vocation, focused his apostolic endeavors on the university in Cochabamba from which he had graduated and where he had been formed in the university apostolate. He now worked informally with small groups of university students both from the University of San Simon in Cochabama and from the Faculty of Philosophy of the Catholic University where he taught philosophy. After becoming professor of philosophy in San Simon, he expanded his contact with both teachers and students and helped develop programs for them. His plan was to work for university reform from within, concentrating more on the faculty than on the students. He eventually left the Dominicans but continued working in the university.

1974, Fr. Rearden's activities in the Normal School included teaching religion and providing students with *jornadas* and retreats, social and pastoral activities, and facilities for study in St. Martin De Porres Center. After he left the Normal School in 1974 because of health problems, no Dominican worked there at the Normal School.

d. High School Apostolate

From the early l960's, the Dominicans believed that working in high schools was an important way to influence the future direction of the country. They helped develop ministries first in La Paz and Cochabamba, and then in Oruro and Santa Cruz. In La Paz and Cochabamba, they worked collaboratively with Dominican sisters teaching religion in the public schools, where most children were poor. They used the two centers, the seminary and later IBEAS (described below) in La Paz and St. Martin De Porres Center in Cochabamba. In both places they offered Christian youth formation through *jornadas,* or day- or week-long retreats, educational courses, liturgical, social, and recreational activities, and the availability of library and study facilities. Formation courses were also given for people who worked with youth. In 1962, Fr. Rearden began a high school student apostolate in La Paz, and in 1964, was appointed archdiocesan director of religious education for public schools and, then, in 1966, archdiocesan director of Catholic youth ministry, *Juventud Estudiantil Catolica (JEC)*.

The Dominican high school apostolate ceased to exist in La Paz when Fr. Rearden was transferred to Cochabamba in 1968 to work with university students.[10] He was joined by Br. Mark Paraday and then Br. Kevin Carroll who came from Oruro at the end of 1968. When Fr. John Risley arrived in Bolivia in June 1970, and Br. Carlos

---

[10] Fr. Houlihan had arrived in 1963 to establish JEC in Cochabamba. He continued this ministry until poor health forced him to return to the States in 1967.

Griego in October 1970, the Dominican team for high school apostolate in the Cochabamba center grew to include one priest, three brothers, and three Dominican sisters from Sinsinawa, Wisconsin. Between the years 1969 and 1973, the high school movement in the center remained strong, with nearly 150 boys and girls in organized groups and many more in informal groups. It ended in 1973 when the center began focusing on the charismatic renewal.

In Oruro the high school apostolate was directed originally by Br. Carroll and Fr. Sablica from 1966 to 1968. From religion classes in the public schools, small groups were formed to develop Christian leaders. It ended in 1968 with the closing of the Dominican community in Oruro. Br. Reginald Neu arrived in Santa Cruz in 1968 and began to work in a similar way with high school students.

7. Instituto Boliviano de Estudio y Acción Social (IBEAS)

The experience of forming groups of laity in different social and economic sectors to meet the social challenges in La Paz inspired the Dominicans to coordinate the activities of these groups. To accomplish this goal, in August 1963 the Dominican community in La Paz founded a center of social-economic research and theological reflection and formation called IBEAS (*Instituto Boliviano de Estudio y Acción Social*). They were influenced by the work of Père Lebret, O.P., who was the principal author of Pope Paul VI's 1968 encyclical, *Populorum Progressio*. IBEAS was approved by a commission of bishops who viewed it as a realization of the Bolivian Episcopacy's desire to put the social doctrine of the Church into practice. Some bishops, however, never favored IBEAS because it did not fit traditional church categories of pastoral work. In the early 1960s, Fr. Jim Burke worked with the U.S. Embassy and the Bolivian government to obtain USAID funds to build a new building for IBEAS, one of the only new buildings constructed in recent history in the center of La Paz, just down the block from San Andrés University.

The Dominicans, however, never reached complete agreement about exactly what IBEAS should be. Although the idea of a strictly technical institute was never an acceptable model, opinions were divided on three points: a) the degree of professionalism the institute should have, b) the degree of pastorally oriented programs it should provide and c) its authority in guiding other Dominican apostolates. The Dominicans recruited and then worked alongside Bolivian professionals who headed up IBEAS, raising funds and providing a theological perspective. They held workshops and conferences on social, economic and cultural matters, and conducted research of developments in different sectors, such as the failure of the agrarian reform to achieve its goal because of the excessive parceling of land among the indigenous and the lack of investment in supportive inputs for farmers, such as irrigation systems, tractors, and appropriate fertilizers. It provided training to small farmers in the principles of organizing cooperatives and challenged the unjust practices of U.S. companies, such as W.R. Grace for its exploitive gold mining.[11]

a. The Rise of IBEAS

IBEAS began with the assistance of experts from the University of Louvain and Frs. Geraets and Roach who arrived in Bolivia in January 1964 to work as Dominican advisors (*asesores*) in IBEAS. The Dominicans in LaPaz considered IBEAS a Dominican apostolate of national import that would coordinate and unify all the apostolic works of the vicariate seeking to influence key areas of society, especially where decisions capable of changing Bolivian society would be made. This national vision led to the establishing of Dominican communities in Oruro and Santa Cruz. Frs. Geraets and Roach

---

[11] In 1968, Frs. Burke and Dahm visited W. R. Grace in their New York City offices in a futile attempt to enlist support for a more supportive role of the company in Bolivia's economic development.

considered the social mission of Dominicans to be one of orientation and instruction, not one of execution. The idea of a nationally unified Dominican apostolate, however, never was completely accepted by all friars who worked outside La Paz, especially those in Cochabamba who thought such unification might lead to excessive centralization and would limit their own creative efforts. Thus, the idea of IBEAS as a national apostolate for all Dominicans was never realized.

The first year of IBEAS was difficult because of internal differences between the Dominican advisors and the first director of the center of research, a Belgian sociologist. In March 1965, he resigned and was replaced by a Bolivian professional, Dr. Eduardo Bracamonte, who helped IBEAS develop its programs and attracted other Bolivian lay professionals. Between 1967 and 1970, under his direction and a succession of Dominican advisors (Geraets, Roach, and Rogowski, then Holochek and Dahm, who arrived in Cochabamba in 1965 and moved to IBEAS in 1968), IBEAS had its most active and prestigious years. It was organized into three centers – research, formation, and communications – and four departments – education, economic administration, industrial relations, and socio-religious concerns. Other Dominicans who worked in IBEAS were Frs. Thomas Shanley of the Eastern Province, in industrial relations, Thomas Davy of the Irish Province, who taught the principles of cooperatives, Edward Cleary who directed research in education, Oscar Uzin, who attended to socio-religious concerns, and Brothers Simon McCormick who was the economic administrator for the La Paz community, Timothy Wrinn who served as the economic administrator of IBEAS, and Martin Hartung who worked on rural projects. Fr. Dahm worked as vice president of IBEAS from 1968 to 1970, accompanying the Bolivian president of IBEAS.

IBEAS successfully launched socio-pastoral projects in La Paz and the surrounding rural areas of Bolivia and even in the highlands of Peru. It conducted courses for laity both in IBEAS and wherever participants worked. These efforts helped the Bolivian Church implement the directives of the Second Vatican Council. For example, IBEAS conducted a study of the Maryknoll Fathers' missions in Peru and Bolivia in order to help them reorient their ministry based on the directives of the Second Vatican Council. This research was one of the first studies in Latin America about a major Catholic religious organi-zation that was trying to implement the teaching of the Council.

It should be noted that before 1965 the Catholic Church saw little need to adjust its pastoral approach or evangelization to the reality of the people it served. It was commonly believed that a missionary could give the same sermon in China, Chicago or Bolivia. Creating a parish community and administering the sacraments among indigenous people in Bolivia's Altiplano was no different than working a parish in a Chicago suburb. At IBEAS, the Dominicans developed an analysis of Bolivia's economic, social, political, and cultural reality and taught numerous U.S. and European religious missionaries about the importance of making their ministry more culturally sensitive to local conditions. The Dominicans also assisted the Bolivian bishops in writing their pastoral letters on development and other social problems. In the 1970s, Fr. Risley taught a few courses on pastoral orientation for newly arrived missionaries studying Spanish at the Maryknoll Language School in Cochabamba. When the Conference of Bolivian Bishops wanted to start a Catholic University (Bolivia was the only Latin American country without a Catholic University), the Dominicans opposed the effort because they believed, and predicted correctly, that the university would end up, like all Catholic universities in Latin America, serving the wealthier students. It would siphon funding from other church work among the poor into serving the elites. That stance cost the Dominicans much support among the bishops. Henceforth, the Dominicans ceased to serve as the bishops' theological consultants.

IBEAS also carried out a valuable research effort, developing, under the direction of Dahm, one of the best social science libraries in Bolivia. Its socio-economic and pastoral studies were published and widely distributed. It also inaugurated a professional journal of social studies on the Andean Region, *Estudios Andinos*, edited for many years by Frs. Cleary and Dahm in collaboration with the Center for Latin American Studies at the University of Pittsburgh. During that time the Dominicans also carried out other social apostolates which were integrated into the work of IBEAS. UNIAPAC, which was dedicated to the formation of business people in Christian ethics, functioned in La Paz, Oruro, and Cochabamba, and always had Dominicans as advisors. Fr. Davy, experienced in forming cooperatives while assigned to the Irish Dominican mission in Trinidad, worked with the cooperative movement in La Paz and other parts of Bolivia. He also worked in the labor school, CETRA, created in 1962 by Fr. Rogowski. The Dominicans also worked with other Catholic groups, such as the *Cursillos de Cristiandad* and the Christian Family Movement and always collaborated fully with diocesan and religious priests and sisters.

b. The Decline and Fall of IBEAS

In April, 1970, during the presidential regime of General Alfredo Ovando, a group of armed students from the University of San Andres took possession of IBEAS in the early morning hours. These leftist students, some known to the Dominicans through their university apostolate, wanted the government to seize the IBEAS building and donate it to the university which severely lacked space. But the pretext for the dramatic takeover (Dahm was led around the building at gun point to open all its doors) was the false accusation that IBEAS and the Dominicans were receiving money from Gulf Oil, the only major oil company in the country. Gulf Oil had become a pariah, a symbol of U.S. imperialism, and many groups were calling for its nationalization. In addition, the Dominicans were accused of working with the CIA. Fr. Dahm's photo was printed on the front page of the morning paper with the story accusing him of communicating with the CIA through his ham radio, a ludicrous accusation given that ham radio communication is open to all. After several hours, government soldiers removed the students and returned the building to the Dominicans.

In October 1970 during a military coup led by the leftist leaning General J.J. Torres, IBEAS was seized again by university students. The new military government allowed the university to keep the IBEAS building for its Department of Sociology. (Fr. Burke was assigned the task to return from the U.S. to help remove IBEAS and the Dominican community from the premises).[12] That action effectively brought about the end of the Institute despite the fact that a small group of laypeople from IBEAS continued to work at a greatly reduced level. Their effort eventually became the Center of Social Promotion of the Archdiocese of La Paz. Fr. Davy was its first advisor and continued in that role until he left Bolivia in 1974. Committed to the social apostolate of the Church, this group of laity was led by IBEAS employee, Jaime Virreira, who later was appointed Director of the Bishops' National Pastoral Office and ordained a priest. The Dominican community in La Paz was soon reduced to five priests – Frs. Burke, Cleary, Merlino, Uzin, and Davy – who had moved to new quarters in La Paz. A few years later, IBEAS was dissolved legally as a juridical entity by the decision of the Dominicans and the lay team.

---

[12] A right-wing military coup removed General Torres in August 1971, and General Hugo Banzer took power and remained there until 1978. The new government expelled the university and expropriated the IBEAS building for its own use as the Ministry of Planning.

The government decreed a payment for indemnification to the Dominicans, but no remuneration was ever received.

The community did not pursue indemnification because of the costs involved and the public criticism such an action might provoke. The Dominicans in the vicariate were divided on the question: some believed the remuneration should be pursued and the funds used for ministry to the poor, especially since the original funding of IBEAS came principally from people of modest income in the U.S. at the Shrine of St. Jude in Chicago. Furthermore, the Bolivian bishops worried that not demanding indemnification would establish a dangerous precedent for possible future state confiscations of property. Others saw the difficulty involved in a long, drawn-out process that would demand the full attention of at least one Dominican and hurt the already damaged public image of the Dominicans in Bolivia by seeming to use the influence of the Church to benefit the Order at the cost of the Bolivian people. Moreover, not pursuing the indemnification would present an evangelical testimony of granting forgiveness and not exacting money from a poverty-stricken government.

What were the real reasons for the takeover? Among groups opposing IBEAS there had been a convergence of interests: the students wanted the building for the university, but the U.S. Embassy was also unhappy with the Dominicans. In first place, the Dominicans had refused to accept the U.S. Ambassador's support for the military coup in 1964. In a meeting at the Ambassador's house, Fr. Jim Burke, in the name of the Dominicans, rejected his request that all U.S. expatriates support the military coup against the democratically elected government. The Dominicans' opposition caused a serious fall out between the U.S. Embassy and the Dominicans. The U.S. Embassy was also upset with the Dominicans because through CETRA they worked with independent labor groups that refused to align themselves with AIFLD, the Latin American arm of the AFL-CIO which enjoyed U.S. government financial support and through the influence of the CIA served to mollify more radical labor efforts throughout Latin America. Both the Archdiocese of La Paz and the government's Ministry of Interior set up commissions to investigate charges against IBEAS (of being an agency of the CIA; of being financed by U.S. corporations such as Gulf Oil; of being an organ of espionage for the U.S. government). Dahm worked with military officers investigating IBEAS in June and July 1970 as they futility searched IBEAS files looking for evidence. Neither commission found evidence to support these charges, but the results of the investigations were never publicized, much to the chagrin of the Dominicans. It is interesting to note that IBEAS was attacked from both sides: from the right, for making known and trying to effectively confront the social problems of Bolivia and for not accepting the reformist solutions advocated by national and foreign powers; and from the left, for not taking a more revolutionary, Marxist stance on social change.

8. Change of Direction:
Dominicans Initiate the Charismatic Movement

The fall of IBEAS spelled a change in the pastoral focus for Dominicans. It coincided with a new direction, the Charismatic Renewal. In 1969, Fr. Geraets, then vicar of Dominicans in Bolivia, visited his Benedictine brother in St. Benedict Abbey, Wisconsin while on vacation and was converted to being a charismatic Catholic. He subsequently wanted to bring the charismatic movement – it was rapidly gaining popularity in the U.S. – to the church in Bolivia. In July 1969, several Dominicans in Cochabamba formed a charismatic prayer group with other North American missionaries then studying at the Maryknoll Language School. In 1970 Fr. Gereats invited Francis McNutt, a former Dominican and a leader in the rising Catholic Charismatic Renewal Movement in the U.S., to come to

Bolivia to preach. With MacNutt's help, the priests in Cochabamba organized three retreats based on the charismatic model in 1970, 1971 and 1972. These retreats inspired other missionaries to form prayer groups in Cochabamba, La Paz, and Santa Cruz often directed by the Dominicans. These groups were at first composed of English-speaking priests, sisters, and brothers, but gradually the charismatic renewal or *renovación* took root among the Bolivian people.

In 1970, Frs. Geraets and Roach decided to leave La Paz and found a charismatic center in Santa Cruz diocese at the university center, *La Mansión*, basically abandoning IBEAS. Fr. Geraets' term as vicar had expired and Fr. Cleary succeeded him. The Dominicans' focus on Catholic Action which had targeted different social sectors now gave way to the charismatic approach to ministry. *La Mansión* had always been a university student center, providing a library and study rooms for individuals and groups and also, for a time, a small residence for students from the provinces. Most of this gradually disappeared because of the need to provide more space for the charismatic movement. In Cochabamba, the charismatic movement developed under the direction of Frs. Rearden, Risley and Paraday but at a more modest level than in Santa Cruz. In 1973 Paraday moved from Cochabamba to Santa Cruz and was replaced in the Cochabamba movement by the first Bolivian to study and be ordained a Dominican priest, Alfonso ViaReque.

The Sunday charismatic liturgies in Santa Cruz grew by leaps and bounds. In the beginning, people from the more privileged classes attended but within a few years more and more from the disadvantaged classes participated. On Palm Sunday, 1973, approximately 5,000 people attended the service. Increasing numbers meant the location for Mass changed from the large center patio inside the building to the huge yard outside where a *pahuichi* (an open-walled, grass-roofed pavilion) was constructed to accommodate the celebrations. The *pahuichi* soon became too small and more space was added each year by extending the roof and adding more benches. Extra Masses on Saturday and Sunday evenings were also required. Thousands listened to the Mass on the radio. In Cochabamba the charismatic Masses were attended by about 150 to 200 people each Sunday in the St. Martin De Porres Center.

The Dominicans involved in the charismatic renewal believed the movement was the key to renewing and transforming the Catholic Church in Bolivia, and through a renewed Church, to transforming the social order of Bolivia. They believed that the social transformation Dominicans had tried to effect in the past did not stress enough an important and even indispensable element: the power of the Holy Spirit that can profoundly change people and, through their strong sense of mission and charisms granted by the Holy Spirit, the structures of society. Ministry to the laity meant helping people develop a personal relationship with Jesus and facilitate their receiving the power and gifts of the Holy Spirit in order to transform the world.[13] The Dominicans in Santa Cruz preached about the coming of the "New Pentecost" for the Church in

---

[13] There have been two different charismatic approaches among the Dominicans in Santa Cruz. One was headed up by Fr. Rogowski and Sr. Helen Raycraft, O.P. of the Sinsinawa Dominicans and later with Sr. Guadalupe Sarfa, O.P. of the same community, and Br. Wrinn. They developed their model in Bolivia but in 1974 moved to Harlingen, Texas to carry out their ministry. As an itinerant missionary team they annually traveled to and preached in a few Latin American countries and other Spanish-speaking areas of the United States. Their model used iornadas or evangelical missions in poor sections or barrios of a city which then led to the formation of Christian base communities (comunidades de base) with a charismatic dimension: prayer groups, healing ministries, and social-communitarian assistance as an expression of Christian love. The second model of the movement, involved the Dominicans at the Mansion which emphasized creating, not specifically Christian communities, but an "assembly" of Christian prayer and celebration from which the participants return to their communities and gradually transform them both humanly and "Christianly," that is, as their human needs are perceived in the light of the Gospel and the presence of the Risen Lord.

Bolivia. They published articles in newspapers and distributed mimeographed flyers and pamphlets to advance the charismatic approach. On occasion, these articles contained questionable material, for example, "prophesies," such as the prediction that Jesus Christ would walk with people in procession to the central plaza, which of course never happened.

About half the members of the Dominican vicariate became actively involved in some aspect of charismatic renewal. Other Dominicans questioned the value of the movement, and others, though sympathetic, did not get involved. This division in the vicariate led to a period of tension that gradually diminished and was replaced by a spirit of mutual respect and understanding. The model of Catholic Action that had thrived was gradually abandoned. Direct involvement with groups in different sectors was judged too political or excessive involvement of the Church in the affairs of the world.

9. Further Ministries in the 1970s

In the 1970s some Dominicans branched out to other ministries that had little in common. Brother Carlos Griego, who had arrived in 1971, maintained an office for psychological counseling for the youth at the St. Martin De Porres Center. In 1971, upon the invitation of the Sisters of Charity he began to teach psychology in the Nursing School connected with Seton Hospital in Cochabamba and to help the student nurses in their training for work in the mental hospital, *Los Remedios.* Br. Carlos also collaborated in youth retreats with the diocesan *Pastoral Commission on Youth and Vocations* under the direction of Fr. Rearden. This commission maintained an office in the St. Martin De Porres Center.

In Santa Cruz Brothers Paraday and Neu worked among young soldiers who were completing their compulsory military service. They promoted evangelization in the military barracks where the young conscripts were trained, in the local prison and General Hospital, and in the city's *barrios,* using a charismatic and catechetical approach as opposed to the previous Catholic Action orientation. They used movies and film strips on religious themes as a means of evangelization. Fr. Vincent Blake, who arrived in 1969, worked with poor, working class youth and assisted them with various social needs.

In 1969, Fr. Mueller, after leaving at the Normal School, spent two years doing carpentry as a worker-priest in Santa Cruz, and in 1971 accepted the invitation of some Maryknoll Sisters to work in the northern part of Santa Cruz in a project of colonization sponsored by an ecumenical organization, United Churches. He helped in the settlement of colonists, indigenous people moving from the Bolivian highlands to the plains and jungles of Santa Cruz, specifically to a colony called Pirai. The colonists were being settled in the fertile eastern lowlands in order to alleviate the pressure on farmers whose small parcels had become increasingly incapable of sustaining their growing families. Fr. Mueller celebrated Mass, provided sacramental preparation and ran a small pharmacy until 1976 when he moved with a team of Fr. Risley and several religious sisters to Charomoco and Capinota in the Cochabamba valley, where they conducted evangelization until 1978 when a tragic car accident killed one of the sisters and decimated the team.

Work on justice and peace barely continued in the early 1970s. Fr. Arthur Sist arrived in 1971. After spending time with Fr. Mueller in the colony of Pirai and then in the major seminary in Cochabamba teaching philosophy, he was invited by Dr. Luis Adolfo Siles Salinas, the ex-President of Bolivia, to organize and then work for the Justice and Peace Commission in Bolivia. In this capacity he dealt with serious human rights abuses, such as torture of political prisoners, by the military regimes that succeeded one another in the 1970s.

Another Dominican interested in social action arrived in Bolivia in 1970 – the Belgian, Fr. Eric deWasseige. Because of his interest in indigenous people. he worked in La Paz with *CIPCA: Centro de Investigación y Promoción de Campesinad* and joined Fr. Sist on the Justice and Peace Commission. Because of his politically sensitive work on the Commission, Fr. Sist feared for his life and eventually resigned. Fr. deWasseisge replaced him. After the Commission published the pamphlet, "The Massacre of the Valley," a report of the killing of over 100 *campesinos* by military forces near Cochabamba during a peaceable protest over rising prices of basic commodities, government forces picked up Fr. de Wasseige in March 1975 along with an Oblate priest, and deported them. After spending almost two years helping other Bolivian exiles in Lima, Peru, he moved to Washington, D.C. where he worked in the Washington Office on Latin America which advocated for the poor and oppressed of Latin America before the U.S. Congress and administration. Years later he returned to Bolivia to work in a variety of development projects.

Fr. Sist eventually created a new group independent of the hierarchy: the *Office of Social Assistance of the Church* (*Oficina de Asistencia Social de la Iglesia*). It trained and organized migrant farm workers who traveled to harvests in Santa Cruz. Although he continued to help them, Fr. Sist left OASI to direct UNITAS, an organization in La Paz which coordinated the efforts to support *campesinos.* Soon after, Fr. Sist left Bolivia and the Dominicans, returning to the U.S. to work with the State University of New York in a social development program for Bolivia.

10. Conclusion

At times, differences in ministries and pastoral approaches caused tension and misunderstanding among Dominicans in Bolivia, but they worked to overcome them and achieve unity in the vicariate. The Dominicans became more aware that unity did not depend upon uniformity but upon dialogue and mutual support. There was always an effort to have regular community prayer, while respecting the different styles of prayer members needed. The friars recognized the need to improve communication within and among their communities, and, consequently, they were faithful in holding biannual vicariate meetings, which were marked by an atmosphere of brotherhood and mutual understanding. After the early years in Bolivia, there always was a diversity of spiritualities and lifestyles within the vicariate and even at times within the same community. But the different spiritualities, intimately related to a variety of personalities and apostolates, had common Dominican elements: commitment to study and theological reflection, community prayer, community life, and dedication to the Word of God and its proclamation as the fruit of a contemplative life incarnated in the temporal world. Communities in the vicariate were characterized by a spirit of study and prayer and of freedom and independence within the regulations that govern Dominican life. The members actively involved in the charismatic movement witnessed their spirituality gaining strength among others and especially attracting Bolivians to join the Order. With the entry of more Bolivians in the 1980s and 1990s, the Bolivians began assuming the leadership of the vicariate, which continued with a predominant focus of the charismatic renewal.

This paper is based largely on the document written first by Fr. Jordan Bishop, O.P., then revised in the 1970s by Fr. Jack Risley, O.P., and finally restructured and expanded by Chuck Dahm, O.P. in August, 2016.

Channeling the Divine
A Comparative Exploration of How Infinite Power Can Work Through Finite Human Persons within the Thought of Meister Eckhart, Tsongkhapa and Dolpopa
Scott Steinkerchner, O.P.

1. Introduction

From the beginning, Dominicans have entered religious life and undertaken its rigors "with the desire to attain [their] own salvation and the salvation of others."[1] While it might be obvious how specific religious practices help with our own salvation, it is less obvious how they might make us better able to assist others with their salvation. The Medieval Dominican mystical theologian Meister Eckhart (c. 1260-1328) had an intriguing answer to this question. He taught that as a capstone to all our religious practices, a prayer of absolute silence, beyond all images, methods and words, could unleash the power of God within us in a new and more direct way so that we would be better conduits of God's grace in the world.

Eckhart's views generated controversy in his day and some were condemned after his death. His ideas also have interesting parallels in other religions, a fact that has not gone unnoticed by scholars. There have been numerous studies of Eckhart and various Buddhist philosophies. I propose to go further down this path by looking at parallels between Eckhart's views and those of a particular Tibetan Buddhist scholar who was his contemporary – Dolpopa Sherab Gyaltsen (c. 1292-1361). Though they lived worlds apart and their religious world-pictures were essentially incompatible, their views interestingly overlapped in the importance of encountering a

---

[1] Order of Preachers 1984, §1.II.

divine/unlimited light through meditation only after leaving behind all images and ideas. For both Eckhart and Dolpopa, such a meditation would unleash in us a divine/unlimited power that would allow us to function more effectively for the sake of saving others, which is the highest religious goal.

2. Method

This chapter is a comparative reading of Eckhart and Dolpopa on the topic of how meditation beyond words can allow us to tap into a divine/infinite power to assist us in helping others. Specifically, we will look at Dolpopa's view of how the power of the buddha-nature within all sentient beings can be released to effect, in Dominican parlance, "their own enlightenment and the enlightenment of others." Dolpopa's view on this subject is called "*gzhan stong*" (pronounced "shen-tong"), signifying that our core is empty of anything other than itself. Dolpopa represents a minority opinion on this issue within Tibetan Buddhism, and his views have been vehemently and even violently opposed by the majority view called "*rang stong*" (pronounced "rang-tong"), which holds that our core is absolutely empty. Thus, to understand Dolpopa, we will first have a look at the majority opinion that he stood against through the work of its greatest expositor, Tsongkhapa. To minimize confusion, words that are used to designate important Buddhist concepts that have no English equivalent, such as "gzhan-stong" and "rang-stong," will be used as English loan-words and will be explained here.

In some ways, the questions investigated by Dolpopa are very similar to those of Eckhart, and, in some ways, they are quite different. Where their questions are similar, we can align their answers and see how they agree and do not agree. The similarities in their answers can help to extend the understanding of the arguments on both sides of the comparative reading. The differences in their answers to similar questions can help us to see how these two religious systems cannot be collapsed into each other, highlighting the uniqueness of their different views of ultimate reality. Thus both the similarities and the differences between the various answers to questions read comparatively add to our understanding.

But having different questions to ask is also of great benefit. If a particular question is deemed important enough to be thoroughly investigated on one side of the comparison and yet is not posed on the other side, we can now pose it. Some questions are simply too idiosyncratic to a particular system to even make sense elsewhere, but other questions reveal important new contours of a way of picturing the world when they are finally investigated. The questions brought up by one religion often lead to new and deeper understanding when they are given an answer in another religion.

In pursuing this comparative project, no theory of the overall connection between Christianity and Buddhism will be invoked or required. We will look at particular arguments of Eckhart and Dolpopa and align and contrast them according to principles that they themselves enunciate. Salvation and enlightenment are respectively ultimate goals in these two religions. We will productively parallel Eckhart's view of how imageless meditation transforms us towards being better mediators of God's grace and Dolpopa's view of how imageless meditation frees the buddha-nature within us without ever needing to discover what Eckhart might think about the buddha-nature or what Dolpopa might think of grace.

We will begin by looking at Buddhism, first Tsongkhapa's rang-stong view and then Dolpopa's gzhan-stong view. Although Tsongkhapa lived a generation after Dolpopa, his rang-stong position elaborates what was the predominant orthodoxy of Dolpopa's day, and against which Dolpopa defined his own position.

3. Tathagatagarbha: The Buddha Within

A fundamental aspiration of Mahayana Buddhism is to achieve enlightenment – in which one becomes a fully functioning buddha – so that one can help to free all sentient beings from suffering. This aspiration is embodied in the bodhicitta vow in which one pledges to become enlightened for the sake of all sentient beings.[2]

The buddha-mind has no limitations and thus has an infinite ability to respond to the needs of sentient beings in leading them out of the state of confusion in which we find ourselves. Buddhism offers no explanation as to why we are in a perpetual state of confusion; it is simply noted as what is in fact the case and has been as far back as we can know. This is denoted by the phrase "beginningless nescience." The Buddha's infinite knowledge is asserted to be non-discursive, meaning that in order to help someone, a buddha does not have to plan and decide how best to respond to an individual trapped in delusion. A buddha instantly, intuitively knows how best to respond and acts out of this non-discursive intuition in the best way possible to help suffering sentient beings. This is why the Buddhas' actions are so effective.

Something infinite cannot be created by expanding something finite. Though it might grow to be quite large, it would still be finite. Thus, our present minds, with their discursive reasoning and limited understanding cannot be expanded to become infinite buddha-minds. Nor can we create an infinite buddha-mind out of nothing. If what is

---

[2] The word "buddha" with a small "b" in this context signifies a type of person of which there are many rather than a singular, historical person. In the view of Theravadan Buddhism there is only one buddha, the Buddha, Siddhartha Gautama, the founder of Buddhism. In the view of Mahayana Buddhism there are a myriad number of buddhas. Siddhartha Gautama was the particular buddha that enlightened this world, but were buddhas before him and there are buddhas yet to come. When one becomes enlightened, one achieves the same abilities as Siddhartha Gautama, joining him in the panoply of buddhas. One does not become Siddhartha Gautama.

commonly designated as our "self" is to be properly spoken of as a buddha, having infinite omniscience, the designated "self" must already somehow have that ability hidden within itself. This line of thinking is called "*tathagatagarbha*," the idea that all sentient beings must already have the buddha-nature within themselves or else they could not become enlightened. This buddha-nature does not need to be created, it simply needs to be freed from whatever is keeping it from functioning.

4. Tsongkhapa's Rang-Stong View

What is the buddha-nature within each sentient being? This is highly contested. The majority position among Tibetan Buddhists is called "*rang stong*." This position was given a definitive treatment by Tsongkhapa (c. 1357-1419), the founder of the Dalai Lama's Gelukpa order. To understand Tsongkhapa's position on rang-stong, we must first understand his view of emptiness.

The Buddha taught *anatman*, that there is no fixed thing or "soul" at the core of a sentient being. Rather, what appears as a stable "you" or "me" are five aggregates (*skandhas*) that are constantly in motion: this body, with these sensations, causing these thoughts, forming these habits (*samskaras*), creating this fleeting consciousness. These five aggregates are superimposed on each other, appearing at the same place, giving the appearance of something fixed in which they adhere. That sixth thing, the fixed soul, does not actually exist, though it does appear to exist.

Here we must distinguish between two levels of truth, 1) what appears to be true about something and how it functions on the conventional level and 2) what is ultimately true about it, particularly its status regarding existence. The first is called "conventional truth," the second, "ultimate truth." Conventionally, there is a functioning self, a designated "me" that performs actions and thinks thoughts and is the object of karma. Ultimately, however, "I" do not exist as something distinct from my five aggregates. I exist in dependence upon my five aggregates, and my five aggregates give rise to the illusory unitary thing conventionally called "me."[3] My "soul" does not exist at all. It is simply illusory. It does not function even on the conventional level. When one closely examines conventional experience one can come to understand that there is no "soul." "You" and "I" exist conventionally, we function in the world, but our putative "souls" are simply illusory.[4]

The Buddha's teachings about dependent existence are considered to be the second turning of the wheel of dharma, which distinguishes Mahayana and Theravadan Buddhism. The first turning of the wheel of dharma was the Buddha's public teaching during his lifetime, centering on the Four Noble Truths: 1) that all life entails suffering, 2) suffering is caused by clinging desire, 3) ending clinging desire can end suffering, and 4) the Noble Eightfold Path to end suffering. Teachings of the first turning of the wheel of dharma are held in common by both Mahayana and Theravadan Buddhists. Only Mahayana Buddhists, however, acknowledge the authenticity of the second turning of the wheel and the teachings about dependent existence.

One of the important sources of teachings of the second turning of the wheel of dharma is the Lotus Sutra, written about 500 to 700 years after the life of Siddhartha Gautama, the Buddha.[5] The Lotus Sutra portrays itself as a secret teaching that was given by the historical Buddha just before his (apparent) death. The important notion of "skillful-means" is introduced in the Lotus Sutra to explain how new teachings could be given that contradict the original

---

[3] Tsongkhapa 2002, 122.

[4] Ibid., 215.

[5] Williams 2009, 150.

teachings. The Buddha uses skillful-means in teaching, telling people what they need to hear in order to help them do the things they need to do.

The Lotus Sutra offers several parables to explain skillful-means. The first is of unruly children living in a large mansion that is on fire.[6] Their father tells them of the danger and orders them to leave the house, but they do not listen and continue playing inside. In desperation, the father tells them that he has special toy chariots outside for them and that the first one out gets his pick. There are no toy chariots outside, but the children save themselves by running outside to find them anyway. In this parable, the father told the children what they needed to hear to motivate them to do what they needed to save themselves, thus using skillful-means to save them.

The objective truth-value of the father's words, whether they correspond to facts in the world, is irrelevant to their usefulness. The father employs words for their usefulness, and this determines their value. If one accepts the view of the Lotus Sutra, one can see that there could be many authentic teachings that are ultimately false but are yet essential in their original context to move followers in the right direction.

Another essential teaching of the second turning of the wheel is that all phenomena are empty of intrinsic existence. The objects we experience with our senses have conventional existence, but not ultimate existence. Phenomena exist on the conventional level; they function and can be identified, but they are transient and have no fixed nature. Everything exists in dependence upon other things. Things come to be because of causes and conditions, not because of some intrinsic nature or ability of their own. There is nothing that exists ultimately, nothing which has a stable identity apart from other

---

[6] Kumārajīva 2007, 54-58.

things. Not only do we not have ultimate existence, but even our skandhas and the elements of the world around us do not ultimately exist.

This is not how the world appears to us. When we look at the world, it appears to have a stable existence, an essence, a particular, fixed way of being. The world fools us in this way. As we take in impressions of things through our senses, we are fooled into thinking that these things ultimately exist in the same way that they appear to us.[7] Along with our true sense data something untrue slips in, a notion of intrinsic existence – that the thing we are sensing has a fixed, stable nature. This is called "*māyā*," the same Sanskrit word that denotes a magician's illusion. What appears to be real is actually an illusion, and our perceptions and misperceptions are all part of the magic trick. We are trapped in our fundamental confusion until we can see through this trickery of the world through embracing and implementing Buddhist teachings.

For Tsongkhapa, the teachings of emptiness contained in the second turning of the wheel of dharma are the highest, definitive teachings of Buddhism. They strike a middle ground between nihilism and essentialism. It would be nihilistic to simply proclaim the ultimate non-existence of things without also proclaiming their dependent existence.[8] Dependent existence allows us to explain our experiences as corresponding to something that exists, but something that exists on the conventional and not the ultimate level. Our experiences are always changing because there is nothing ultimate or fixed about reality. It would also be wrong to believe that things exist essentially the same way they appear to us. They do not. Things function and exist dependently upon other things. They do not ultimately exist

---

[7] Tsongkhapa, 2002, 175.
[8] Ibid., 143-146.

apart from other things. Nothing exists intrinsically, not even the Buddha. The Buddha exists conventionally and can affect things conventionally, being a cause of the liberation of other sentient beings who are still trapped in delusion by *māyā*. This is how the Buddha functions and how we are encouraged to function as well.

In the oldest Buddhist scriptures, the Buddha sometimes referred to himself as "*tathāgata*," meaning either "the one thus gone" (*tathā gata*), or "the one thus come" (*tathā āgata*). "*Garbha*" signifies a womb or an embryo. Thus Mahayana Buddhists use the word "*tathāgatagarbha*" (pronounced "ta-TA-ga-ta-garb-ha") to signify the idea that all sentient beings contain within themselves the buddha-nature. This is what makes it possible for sentient beings to become enlightened. For Tsongkhapa, "tathagatagarbha" signifies emptiness as applied to the self. There is nothing ultimately fixed about us, and thus we are able to become enlightened, transcending all conventional phenomena. Since we are not ultimately determined in any way, we can transcend all limitations.

A buddha's realization of the emptiness of the self is a pure negation "with no remainder," meaning that it does not assert anything. It does not imply that a buddha realizes the "existence" of emptiness. A buddha's embodiment of truth is "the elimination—through utter non-apprehension—of all signs which are elaborations of external and internal phenomena."[9] The non-existence of the self could never be experienced, it would be like seeing the son of a barren woman.[10] Only buddhas have such consciousnesses that see reality exactly as it is without any mistaken appearances arising.[11]

---

[9] Ibid., 121.
[10] Ibid., 343.
[11] Ibid., 200 and 257.

Enlightenment consists of achieving the perfect realization of selflessness.[12] This realization is necessarily beyond any idea or concept of what "selflessness" means. Words and concepts, like all phenomena, have dependent existence. Words have no fixed meaning and concepts have no eternal, fixed truth. Both words and concepts arise in dependence upon causes and conditions, arising from the things of experience that are themselves only dependently existent. Words, concepts and images have no absolute truth. Enlightenment comes when we finally see through words and concepts, recognizing them as ultimately empty of any fixed meaning. Enlightenment can be attained through a process of moving between sustained philosophical analysis of reality guided by Buddhist scriptures and one-pointed meditation on the self under the guidance of a master who has already traveled this path. In meditation we can learn to see our minds as they really are. We can subsequently use Buddhist philosophy to analyze and understand what we have experienced, and then return to improved meditation with this better understanding.[13] For instance, at the beginning we might think that we experience a "self" when meditating on our own experience. Through Buddhist philosophy, we can come to understand that there is no "self," just the appearance of a self. We can then return to meditation with this discriminating wisdom and see more clearly that it is indeed true, that there is only the appearance of a self. As we move back and forth between these processes of meditation and reflection under the guidance of a master our insight gradually becomes more stable and profound, and we see that all of our concepts and words are ultimately empty of any essence or fixed meaning.[14]

---

[12] Ibid., 108.
[13] Ibid., 327.
[14] Ibid., 341.

Summing up, for Tsongkhapa, we are trapped in this realm of suffering by our delusions, most notably our deluded notion that we "exist." There is nothing that is ultimately established, no word that has a fixed meaning, no thing that exists in its own right, no concept that can stand the scrutiny of rigorous analysis. Through a particular process of philosophical investigation coupled with focused meditation we can break through the delusion and free ourselves from attachment to all words, concepts, and things and thus end our suffering, finding that power beyond words, the buddha-nature within, which is the non-existence of the self with no remainder. We can the help free others from their delusions insofar as we free ourselves.

5. Dolpopa's Gzhan-Stong View

In Tsongkhapa's rang-stong view, the self is proclaimed to be empty of intrinsic existence. This was the majority position within Tibetan Buddhism in Tsongkhapa's day, but it had recently come under question through the teachings of Dolpopa Sherab Gyaltsen (c. 1292-1361), a charismatic mystic who taught a contrary position called "*gzhan stong*."

Dolpopa's views would have been shocking and almost unintelligible to many Buddhists of his day, yet he had a great authority because of his position as abbot of the Jonang monastery and his incredible mystical abilities. His teachings were attended by great crowds and wondrous signs.[15] Dolpopa taught that after the second turning of the wheel of dharma, there had been a third turning, well known in a previous golden age, in the mythical kingdom of Shambhala, but almost unknown in his own day.[16] Dolpopa was simply reviving this tradition in this age of manifestly inferior doctrine. As the second turning of the wheel of dharma

---

[15] Stearns 1999, 35-36.
[16] Ibid., 5, 27.

relativized the first turning as skillful-means – a provisional truth given at a particular time and place for a particular reason but having no definitive value – so the third turning of the wheel proclaims the second turning to be provisional and not absolute.

In affirming the provisional truth of the second turning, Dolpopa also affirms that all words and concepts point only to relative truth. They belong to the dependent, phenomenal world. Any concept or idea that can be put into words, therefore, can at most be relatively true. As Tsongkhapa argued, absolute truth has to be beyond words. To this, the third turning adds a higher teaching: that the buddha-nature exists with its qualities in a different mode of existence and is self-arising. Dolpopa rejects as nihilistic the idea that the buddha-nature does not ultimately exist.[17]

In his explanation, Dolpopa makes use of a central text of the third turning, the *Tathagatagarbha Sutra*. The *Tathagatagarbha Sutra* proclaims that the tathagatagarbha is like the sun shining in the sky. The clouds might block the sun from shining on the earth, but the sun itself is not affected. Further, the clouds could be cleared away so that the sunlight would reach the ground. In the same way, the buddha-nature with its luminosity and spaciousness is active at the core of every sentient being, though clouds of karmic dirt usually block its light. These clouds can be cleared away through tantric practices, exposing the previously obscured buddha-nature.[18]

In opposition to the rang-stong view, Dolpopa teaches that dependent origination is not the only mode of reality.[19] There is another, ultimate mode of existence, the absolute existence of the buddha-nature. The stains are relative; they are of the mode of

---

[17] Ibid., 152.
[18] Ibid., 144.
[19] Ibid., 151.

delusion and exist dependently as rang-stong. Nevertheless, the buddha-nature is not rang-stong, it is gzhan-stong, without causes, without change, without parts and omnipresent, containing nothing that is not itself, but existing in itself with its qualities.[20] The ground of purification, the buddha-nature complete with its qualities, is permanent and untainted and exists in the mode of gzhan-stong.[21] The objects of purification are the impermanent stains that are not united to the buddha-nature. The stains arise through relative dependent origination and exist in the mode of rang-stong, which is why they are impermanent and can be removed.

This entails a different two-truth theory compared to that of Tsongkhapa. For Tsongkhapa, the two truths are distinguished by what is conventionally true about the world and what is ultimately true about the world. Dolpopa adds that what is ultimately true about the world exists in a different mode than what is conventionally true about the world.

Buddha-nature is the ground, the basis of the stains, that which allows the stains to exist, but it is not the stains themselves. Buddha-nature exists before them and in a different mode. Here then is Dolpopa's philosophical critique of the rang-stong position that holds that the only existence is dependent existence: phenomena, all of which have merely dependent existence and are thus relative and rang-stong could not exist unless there was something that existed by itself, an absolute, self-existent.[22] This is the buddha-nature complete with its qualities. Drawing from the analogy, clouds cannot exist without the sky, but they are not the sky. Clouds exist in dependence upon the sky, but the sky does not depend on them. The absolute

---

[20] Ibid., 156.
[21] Ibid., 145.
[22] Ibid., 167.

pervades the relative, supports it, and allows it to exist. If there were no absolute, there could be no relative phenomena.

The sky metaphor points to an answer to two other philosophical dilemmas as well. First, it explains why something as ultimately powerful as the buddha-nature at the core of each sentient being could remain unnoticed. The buddha-nature is obscured behind a cloud of karmic dirt. Second, the buddha-nature cannot be created at the core of a sentient being by any effort of a finite sentient being. The buddha-nature is infinite, and an infinite reality cannot be created by a finite action. We do not, however, have to create the buddha-nature, we simply need to create a karmic wind to clear the metaphorical clouds from the sky and the buddha-nature will shine. Thus, with finite effort, we can unleash the power of the buddha-nature.

It is the need for these infinite effects that drives Dolpopa's concern. One cannot learn to become a buddha. One can only release that infinite gnosis that was always within yet was prevented from functioning. The buddha-nature within is that infinite power beyond words. It is the basis of the world of experience, but it is not the world of experience. It can manifest in the world of experience with infinite, non-discursive wisdom and power, suffering none of the limitations of dependent existence. The wisdom of the Buddha cannot be composite, a collection of discrete facts which a buddha sorts through to determine which action would be the most effective. Such knowledge necessarily exists on the level of relative phenomena in the mode of rang-stong. Whatever is ultimate exists in the mode of gzhan-stong, beyond all divisions and beyond creation, cause and effect. This manifestation of wisdom as a quality of the buddha-nature is non-discursive and non-conceptual. It is called "gnosis."

In agreement with the rang-stong position, Dolpopa taught that ultimate truth could only be found beyond words, concepts and images. Words, concepts and images all belong to the realm of phenomena and have only relative truth. But for Dolpopa, clearing away misconceptions, even of the existence of the self, was not the final step. It was a necessary step to clear away some of the clouds of karmic dirt, but the final clearing away of clouds could only be done through tantric practice, forms of deep meditation coupled with physical practices. Once undertaken these could unleash the ultimate power beyond words, the tathagatagarbha, the buddha-nature at the core of every sentient being, complete with its properties. This is where his gzhan-stong view parted ways with Tsongkhapa's rang-stong position. In rebuttal, Tsongkhapa would say that the second turning of the wheel was definitive and that the putative "third turning" was simply skillful-means employed by the Buddha to try to win over Hindus who were used to talking about souls or *atmans*. Against Dolpopa's assertion of the non-discursive gnosis of the Buddha, Tsongkhapa asserted the Buddha's realization of emptiness with no remainder.

6. Meister Eckhart in Comparison

Meister Eckhart was a medieval Dominican friar who lived at the same time as Dolpopa. Though operating in a very different religious and sociological context, Eckhart was also a famous preacher and noted scholar who often addressed the topic of how we might become transformed by religious experience. His sermons were so valued that many were written down and preserved so that we have them still today.

A classic locus of Eckhart's thought on the subject of religious transformation comes from his sermon on Jesus cleansing the temple in Matthew 21.[23] In this sermon, Eckhart begins with some comments

---

[23] Eckhart 2009, 66-71.

on prayer that are for a general audience, likening those who try to bargain with God in prayer to the dishonest buyers and sellers that Jesus threw out of the Temple. We have nothing to offer God that was not already a gift to us from God. Eckhart then makes a further move for those who have learned this lesson well and make their prayers with no intention of gain at all, simply for the love of God. While there is no sin in these prayers, they still hinder people from seeing the pure or highest truth. Eckhart asserts that a person who wants the highest truth should move to a wordless, imageless contemplative prayer: "without before and after, untrammeled by all his acts or by any images he ever perceived, empty and free, receiving the divine gift in the eternal Now, and bearing it back unhindered in the light of the same with praise and thanksgiving in our Lord Jesus Christ." Those who want to know the highest truth must abandon all images and ideas of God in order to find God in the emptiness beyond all such limitations. One must cast out of one's mind all images and ideas of God just as Jesus cast everyone out of the temple so that he could be alone in silence. "When the temple is thus free of obstructions (that is attachment and ignorance), then it glistens with beauty, shining out bright and fair above the whole of God's creation, and through all God's creation, so that none can equal its brilliance but the uncreated God alone." Eckhart then notes that such a prayer would entail risk, writing: "And when [the soul] emerges into the unmixed light, she falls into her Nothingness and in that Nothingness so far from the created Something, that of her own power she cannot return to her created Something." This experience can feel like losing one's self, all that one conceives of oneself as being, and everything one thinks of as "God" as the light that we have become merges with the unmixed light of God. But, Eckhart assures us, there is benefit beyond the sheer experience.

In that silence, and only there, Jesus would speak. What would he speak? He would speak himself, the Word of the Father, the divine nature and all that God is. "In speaking the Word, He utters the Word and all things in another Person to whom He gives the same nature that He has himself," giving us "the power to attain to likeness by the grace of the same Word." In this place beyond words, Jesus would speak the Word that eternally gives birth to the Son, eternally reconstituting both God and the person as parent-child in the eternal now, so that God might become incarnate here and now in and through that person.

This experience would change us. We would not gain any information or learn anything about God, but we would be changed in ways that would make us better able to live and act as Christians. Eckhart notes three specific ways in which we would be changed. The first and third effects are similar. The first effect is that it would strengthen and fill one with such power that, "neither joy nor sorrow, nor anything God has created in time, can destroy that man, but he stands mightily there as if with divine power, in face of which all things are puny and futile." The third effect is that Jesus would fill us with such "sweetness and richness" that we would have the strength to act with complete integrity, allowing our actions to follow our own inner directions "at all times" and "until death." Through this meditative encounter with God in that place beyond all words and signs, the divine power would become our power, enabling us to withstand adversity and restoring within us a blessing that was lost due to original sin, the ability to act with complete integrity.

The second effect is more controversial. This birth of God in the soul would give us "wisdom" such that "all doubt, all error, and all darkness are entirely removed; [the soul] is set in a bright pure light which is God Himself." This leads to Eckhart's boldest assertion: "Then God is known by God in the soul; with this Wisdom she knows herself and all things, and this same Wisdom knows her with itself; and with the same Wisdom she knows the power of the Father in fruitful travail, and essential self-identity in simple unity void of all distinctions." Note the language Eckhart is using here. It is not that the soul would come to know God better or receive some information. Rather, God would come into the soul in a new way such that it would be God knowing God "in the soul," in us, in the perfect, infinite way in which God knows God's own self and all things.

This birth of Christ in the soul and its effect on us sounds very much like Dolpopa's infinite non-discursive, non-conceptual gnosis of the buddha-nature once freed to act. Both are also pictured as unmixed light. They are not identical, but Eckhart's wisdom born in the soul functions strikingly similarly to Dolpopa's gnosis of the buddha-nature. A difference is that Dolpopa taught that this infinite wisdom that was always present but covered could be uncovered in the soul, while for Eckhart this infinite wisdom, not naturally present in the soul, could come to be present there. But both would affirm that infinite wisdom has to be uncreated.

Eckhart elaborates further on how specifically God would strengthen us through this encounter in the place beyond words in another sermon where he is commenting on Luke 2:49, "I must be about my Father's business." Noting that we normally think and reason and decide what to do with a power called our "active intellect," Eckhart states that: "what the active intellect does for the natural man, that and far more God does for one with detachment: He takes away the active intellect from him and, installing Himself in its stead, He Himself undertakes all that the active intellect ought to be doing."[24] In this, God operates quite differently than we normally would. We can only think of one thing at a time and slowly come to

---

[24] Ibid., 49.

understand what is best by considering many things one after another. When God takes over, such limitations are gone and we are instantly presented with a solution that "presents itself to you together in a flash, concentrated in a single point." For Eckhart, this proves that it is directly from God: "Surely, this demonstrates and proves that it is not the intellect's work, for it has not the perfection or the resources for this: rather it is the work and the offspring of Him who has all images at once in Himself." In fact, since such wisdom is so directly from God, we could not even take credit for our actions in these circumstances.

As explained above, Dolpopa also noted that to be infinitely effective a buddha's gnosis had to be non-discursive, an immediate intuition rather than the result of a reasoning process. Only someone guided by such an immediate, perfect wisdom could act in an ultimately perfect, effective way. Eckhart seems to be making a similar point, and one that goes right to the second part of our original question. How might religious practice assist in helping others to attain salvation? By creating in us God's divine wisdom that would more perfectly direct our activities than we ever could. For Eckhart, such a wisdom comes to be implanted in us through a profound prayer of silence in which we let go of all images, thoughts and activities. For Dolpopa, this wisdom can be uncovered by tantric practice, but only once we have, as Tsongkhapa notes, let go of all knowledge that comes from words and stilled all of our ideas.

Eckhart does not portray God's wisdom coming as an explanatory voice, God appearing through our senses and explaining what to do, or as implanting a fully formed idea in our minds. We get the sense that God indicates the best course of action from among a range of actions of our own choosing. Eckhart explains: "God bears the Word in the soul, and the soul conceives it and passes it on to her powers in varied guise: now as desire, now as good intent, now as charity, now as gratitude, or however it may affect you."[25] There is still need for the unique memory and creativity of the individual to come up with options from which God indicates the best route to take. God still relies on our learning that we have built up ourselves through experience and is stored in what he refers to as our "passive intellect." God's wisdom, once it is born in us, points to a particular path to take as the best one, or leads us to desire something that is conceived of by ourselves. But God highlights for us ideas and solutions that we have previously learned. This is a specific and limited view of what we might call "personal revelation." In this way, Eckhart could maintain the role of study for those who would want to best help others. If one understood more things, God would have more options and could wordlessly direct one more effectively.

God's wisdom is infinite, and human wisdom cannot be expanded so as to become infinite. Instead, as with Dolpopa's freeing of the buddha-nature, a finite action has made God's infinite wisdom available to us in an intimately effective way. The finite action in Eckhart's case is the quieting of all thoughts and images, allowing us to enter into the hidden, divine light that can only be entered to in profound silence. The unlimited power – God's very wisdom – is released in an interestingly limited though powerful way. We do not become God, though Eckhart's detractors accused him of holding this, we gain access to God's wisdom to direct our actions in the way that is most effective. This is an ability sought by any disciple trying to do the will of a master, and the best way to effectively work for one's own salvation and the salvation of others.

Dolpopa insists that the Buddha's gnosis is non-conceptual as well. Conceptual knowledge cannot be ultimate knowledge. Conceptual knowledge exists in the mode of rang-stong and is

---

[25] Ibid., 51.

ultimately empty. Eckhart's assertion that God leads us through emotions and desires rather than explanations affirms that this divine wisdom is in some sense non-conceptual, but not in the fullest sense that Dolpopa would affirm.

Like Dolpopa, Eckhart affirms that there is a necessity to study and learn before one could make use of this infinite gnosis. Eckhart offers this path to those who are already adept at the spiritual life and are now seeking the highest truth. Tsongkhapa explains that there is no shortcutting the long process of studying Buddhist scripture and taking on Buddhist practices. Also, when an accomplished bodhisattva becomes reborn through choice rather than karmic necessity, the new human person (called a "tulku") does not begin with access to the complete knowledge of the former life. The young tulku has to study Buddhism, and through this process, gradually, old experiences might be remembered and previously gained wisdom can once again come to the fore. For both Eckhart and the tulku, wisdom directs and enhances knowledge gained through conventional means.

Also, in both systems the absolute has the ability to act directly in the world. For Christians, it is not that God cannot become manifest through some miraculous vision or act directly in the world. Such occurrences are not unheard of, but they are extremely rare, and they are not what Eckhart is referring to. As in our opening question, we are seeking to understand how we might better help others to ultimate ends.

The answer is to become more transparent to God's infinite power working through us. We are invited to join in God's (or the Buddha's) saving work, becoming a part of it, like an axe in the hands of a forester cutting down a tree. Who cut down the tree? Watching, we would say the forester. If we were the tree, it would feel like it was the axe. In truth, both the forester and the axe were involved, but both in different ways. In the same way, Eckhart invites us to become better axes, sharper, easier for God the forester to use to chop down trees.

God does not have to use us. The forester can cut down trees in other ways and with other axes. But Eckhart's "highest truth," offered to those who are already committed and knowledgeable enough to forsake bargaining with God and simply live in praise of God, is to become more effective tools for God to use to accomplish God's divine purpose. This is ultimately that to which Eckhart exhorts his listeners – not simply an experience or even an inside track to salvation. We are invited to help extend salvific grace to others, and those who understand Christianity at the deepest level see this as the highest truth.

This is the core of Eckhart's vocation as a Dominican friar, and it is also what sets Mahayana Buddhism apart from Theravada Buddhism. It is not that the Buddha needs help in order to reach all sentient beings, as if he were limited in space and time. Such is true in the vision of Theravada Buddhism, which teaches that the only access we have to the Buddha is through his teachings. The vision of the Lotus Sutra is very different. In the Lotus Sutra the Buddha is revealed as transcending time, space, and alternative realms of existence, being manifest everywhere and all times. Further, the Lotus Sutra teaches that the goal of saving ourselves by entering a nirvana of quiescence is a provisional, even illusory goal. The only real final end is to unleash the buddha-mind hidden within each of us.

In one sense, joining in the salvific activity of the absolute is more optional for Christians than it is for Mahayana Buddhists. The Lotus Sutra is clear in stating that all other goals are simply illusory and provisional. If one seeks one of these lesser goals, once it is achieved, the further goal will then be revealed. Obtaining the omniscience of a buddha is the only stable, final religious end. For Christians, Jesus has already performed the work of salvation, and God has many means to extend that salvation to others. If a particular person does not wish to join in this effort we might wonder if God's salvific activity would be greatly hampered, but it would be difficult to believe that the individual's eternal salvation would be completely in jeopardy.

In another sense, joining in divine activity is just as optional in both systems. Eckhart is clear that this contemplative work is difficult and recommends it only for those who want the highest truth, implying that this is optional and would not be appropriate for many people. The Lotus Sutra is also clear that its teachings are not for everyone. Most people are not ready to hear them. The historical Buddha waited until the end of his last earthly life to reveal them. When he did, many of his closest followers left as he began because they could not bear to hear something so new. The Buddha then assured his listeners that he would have these stray followers reborn in another realm of his own making where he would then teach them this highest truth. So in both systems, adopting this viewpoint is optional for any particular person one might encounter in the here and now.

In Catholic Christianity, people collaborate with God in the salvation of the world through conventional means such as learning and teaching the faith as well as through divinely infused actions such as performing sacraments. These actions do not require any preternatural effort or knowledge on the part of Christians. God does the heavy lifting, channeling grace through these otherwise merely human actions. Eckhart offers a way to be more efficiently used by God as a tool through which to dispense grace – a way that in some sense makes you the unique child of God. But this level of collaboration with God is not required of everyone, since God exists before and independently of us. What Eckhart is offering, however, is something very much like Dolpopa's view of freeing the tathagatagarbha, infusing our actions with a supernatural wisdom that is perfectly suited to the situation. While this might not be everyone's cup of tea, it may be apparent why it would be appealing to heavily invested Christians, especially to those who vow to spend their lives working for their own salvation and for the salvation of others.

7. Conclusions

In his sermon on Jesus cleansing the Temple in Matthew 21, Meister Eckhart pointed the way for those who were looking for the highest truth, recommending that they forsake all words and actions and encounter God in the brilliant silence beyond all images, words and signs. In that brilliant light beyond words Jesus would speak the Word that he is, transforming them into the only Son of God and allowing God's very wisdom – the wisdom by which God knows God's own self – to more directly guide their actions. For Eckhart, the highest truth is not an insight into God, but a better ability to work for the salvation of others, a fundamental component of one's vocation as a Dominican.

This is strikingly parallel to Dolpopa's view of the ultimate truth of Buddhism being not knowledge, but the freeing of the buddha-nature inside us to work for the enlightenment of all sentient beings. For both of these thinkers, this infinite assistive wisdom is infinite, uncreated, and non-discursive, and is pictured as light rather than darkness. It can only be encountered after we have used our knowledge to gain a certain proficiency and then purposefully leave behind all images and thoughts and enter into a meditative state beyond words.

Dolpopa and Eckhart's views also contain differences that keep them from being able to merge. Dolpopa believed that the buddha-nature complete with its properties was ultimately inherently the core of every sentient being, a philosophy called "gzhan-stong." Thus this power was inherently present though only potentially active. Eckhart believed that this uncreated wisdom is not inherently part of the human person, but could come into a person through the divine power of God; potentially present and active. This difference leads to Eckhart's assertion that the divine wisdom functions in the human person in a limited way, giving them strength, feelings and good intentions, while Dolpopa saw almost no limitation on how the buddha-nature, once freed, could act.

8. Postscript: Questions for Buddhism

This comparative project used insights from Dolpopa to find new questions to ask to glean a better understanding of Meister Eckhart's theology of how we can be transformed through an encounter with the divine power beyond words. It also raised for me some new questions about Tsongkhapa's rang-stong view which beg for further study: 1) what is the point of tathagatagarbha teaching, and 2) what, in this view, is the essential difference between Theravada and Mahayana Buddhism? In contradistinction to Eckhart's view, the Lotus Sutra makes the claim that the ultimate goal of each of us is to become a fully functioning, fully enlightened Buddha, nullifying the previous Theravadan goal of "achieving nirvana." The gzhan-stong view embraces this and adds that the absolute buddha-nature is one, that it exists with its qualities at the core of every sentient being, and that to achieve the ends of the Lotus Sutra, sentient beings trapped in samsara simply need to free the buddha-nature inherently at their core. Tsongkhapa's rang-stong doctrine seems to undercut the functioning of the buddha-nature within. In this view, what does asserting tathagatagarbha add to the established principle that all existence is dependently arising? If tathagatagarbha is simply the doctrine of emptiness as applied to the self, then it is not "beyond" nor "higher" than emptiness. This has indeed been argued by Gelukpas, who believe that tathagatagarbha doctrine has no ultimate value, being simply a skillful means the Buddha used to win over Hindus who were used to talking about an atman. But if there are ultimately no distinct qualities to the buddha-nature, then what does the Lotus Sutra mean by proclaiming a new ultimate goal of becoming a Buddha? In what sense is this not simply a rhetorical flourish? If the buddha-nature is ultimately empty, isn't becoming a buddha the same as entering a nirvana of quiescence?

9. Works Cited

Eckhart, Meister. *The Complete Mystical Works of Meister Eckhart.* Translated by Maurice O'C Walshe. New York: Crossroad Pub. Co., 2009.

Kumārajīva. *The Lotus Sutra.* Translated by Tsugunari Kubo and Akira Yuyama. Berkeley, CA: Numata Center for Buddhist Translation and Research, 2007.

Order of Preachers. *Book of Constitutions and Ordinations of the Friars of the Order of Preachers.* Rome, 1984.

Stearns, Cyrus. *The Buddha from Dolpo.* Albany, NY: State University of New York Press, 1999.

Tsongkhapa. *The Great Treatise on the Stages of the Path to Enlightenment.* Translated by The Lamrim Chenmo Translation Committee. Vol. 3. 3 vols. Ithaca, New York: Snow Lion Publications, 2002.

Williams, Paul. *Mahayana Buddhism: The Doctrinal Foundations.* 2nd Edition. London: Routledge, 2009.

September 2016

Democracy in the Bible and in the Dominican Order

Benedict Thomas Viviano, O.P.

There is no fully developed theology of democracy yet in any church and such a theology is needed to help Christians find their political roots in our Christian tradition and their place in society. The Bible offers a number of starting points for such a theology. This essay presents some resources from the Old Testament and from ancient Greece as they had an impact on the New Testament. It invites others to join the effort for the construction of such a theology and its construction. We will begin with some definitions and prerequisites, and then go on to survey the Hebrew Bible, Athenian democracy, Paul, Matthew, Luke-Acts. Then we will pick up the story as it develops in the Dominican Constitutions and their influence, and in the theology of Thomas Aquinas.

1. Some definitions and prerequisites of democracy

Webster defines democracy as government by the people; government in which the supreme power is retained by the people and exercised either directly (absolute or pure democracy), or indirectly (representative democracy) through a system of representation. This definition implies what is called popular sovereignty. As history has developed, more and more prerequisites or conditions seem to be added.

Some of these conditions are: a minimal civic consensus; a rule of law, a constitution; a literate population; a free and private press and media (that is, not controlled by the government). Other elements are: separation of powers (Montesquieu; legislative, executive, judicial); academic freedom of research; an independent central bank. Auxiliary helps to a democratic polity are a common language and culture; common shared religious values, e.g., Christianity or Jewish-

Christian biblical values, e.g., the Decalogue; a two-party system (Schillebeeckx); toleration of eccentricity (J.S. Mill). The example of Switzerland indicates that a common language and religious confession are not absolutely necessary if there is enough of a civic consensus based on a common past history.

Broader considerations are the idea of an open society, capable of changing over time. This is the theme of Karl Popper's *The Open Society and its Enemies*, promoted since the fall of the Iron Curtain (1989) by the financier and disciple of Popper, George Soros. Another frequent element is equality before the law. This means that although aristocracy is not excluded, it does not exempt you from the common laws of the land. In earlier times, it was common to have weighted votes; one man, one vote, or egalitarian democracy has been a later achievement. This policy does not amount to an anthill leveling or erasure of all differences, whether of wealth or education or physical strength or talent or personality as some have feared, but it does mean that extreme disparity is reduced in favor of fairness. The extension of the franchise to women is the result of the First and Second World Wars. Let us now look at the biblical roots of democratic polity.

2. The Hebrew Bible

If one lives for some time in the Holy Land, it becomes evident that the Pentateuch serves the modern state of Israel as a sort of constitution or basic law. The biblical feast days are announced by sirens and traffic stops. Kosher restaurants are the norm in public services. The idea of the Pentateuch as a constitution is especially evident in the book of Exodus which describes the birth of a nation. The people assembled on the plain below mount Sinai twice accept the revealed law, once before sacrifice is offered, once after (Exod 24:3 and 7): "All the people answered with one voice, saying, All the things that the Lord has commanded we will do." "All that the Lord has commanded we will faithfully do, lit. do and obey." The idea of the consent of the governed, and popular sovereignty are rooted in these basic experiences and assents.

The history of community in Israel provides the basis for democracy among the people of God. Paul Hanson has studied this question at length.[1] Hanson found three persistent elements that are present in all thirteen periods of biblical history, from the Exodus to Jesus and the church. The three crucial elements that perdure are: 1) striving for justice leading to social harmony; 2) compassion for the weaker elements of society; 3) Yahweh God as sole Lord, redeemer and creator. This story begins around 1200 B.C., perhaps at Gilgal, and its goal is a life of *shalom*, peace and prosperity and social harmony. Throughout Israelite history there were popular assemblies alongside the leaders like Moses and Aaron and Joshua, assemblies at first divided by tribes, and consisting of all men of military age. Later on, in the books of Chronicles, and Ezra and Nehemiah, the assembly included women and older children. This is clear in the great liturgical scene in Nehemiah 8. This scene is the birth of the liturgy of the Word in the synagogue and the church. "And Ezra the priest brought the law before the assembly, both men and women and all who could hear with understanding." (Neh 8:2). Ancient Israel had a highly hierarchical priestly structure, but it also developed a simple structure for the synagogue, the local place of worship or house of prayer. This simple, nearly democratic, structure is reflected in the early church and in Paul in 1 Thess 5:12.[2] "We beseech you, brethren, to respect those who labor among you and are over you

---

[1] P.D. Hanson, *The People Called: The Growth of Community in the Bible* (San Francisco: Harper & Row, 1986; 2nd ed. 2001).

[2] J.T. Burtchaell, *From Synagogue to Church: Public Services and Offices in the Earliest Christian Communities* (Cambridge: Cambridge University Press, 1992), pp. 293, 349.

(*proistamenous hymon*, have charge of, rule over) in the Lord and admonish you." The letter of James also refers to a Christian synagogue: "If a person with gold rings...comes into your assembly" (*synagogen hymon*; Jas 2:2)... Authority in the synagogues accrued through money, social standing, literacy (for public reading), learning, ability to preach or expound Scripture. But there were no special sacramental powers. The synagogue was run by laymen (and possibly by laywomen).[3]

Let us say that the Hebrew Bible was completed around 424 BC (with the exception of Daniel). That implies that there was a long interval before the birth of Jesus and the writing of the New Testament. During this long interval, ancient Israel or as it could now be called, early Judaism, was surrounded by oriental despotism,[4] Egyptian Pharaohs, kings in Assyro-Babylonia and Persia, then Alexander the Great and his successors, his generals and their dynasties, Antigonids, Seleucids and the Lagides (Ptolemies), and then the might of Rome. All these different regimes contributed to the political experience of the people of God. They were largely despotic arrangements from which the Jews were trying to escape. The Greeks brought their culture that was in many respects superior into the intertestamental biblical world. This Hellenistic culture included Aristotle's analysis of societies as either monarchic, aristocratic or democracy. All three of these polities are to be found in the Bible. Aristotle favored a mixed polity, but not democracy.[5]

---

[3] Martin Hengel, *Judaism and Hellenism* (Minneapolis: Fortress, 1991); E.J. Bickerman, *From Ezra to the Last of the Maccabees* (New York: Schocken, 1962); Bernadette Brooten, *Women Leaders in the Ancient Synagogue: Inscriptional Evidence* (Missoula: Scholars Press, 1982).

[4] Karl August Wittfogel, *Oriental Despotism* (New Haven: Yale University Press, 1992).

[5] Ernest Barker, *The Politics of Aristotle* (Oxford: Oxford University Press, 1946).

The encounter of the Jews with Greek culture began in Egypt even before Alexander went on his campaigns. So they came to know the story of Athenian democracy, even after it had disappeared.

3. Athenian Democracy

In the early Jewish encounter with Greek civilization and polity, the best known and most admired polity was classical direct democracy as developed in Athens in the late sixth through the fourth centuries before Christ (508-322 B.C.). Greece was outgrowing the heroic age of the Homeric epics, where military values were paramount. Philosophers were discovering the significance of the individual person.[6] Greece in this period was a network of city-states that were small enough so that there was no need for representative or parliamentary democracy. Direct democracy was exercised in the popular assembly (called the *ekklesia*, the term later used by the early church for their assemblies).[7]

This Athenian system or polity included the rule of law, liberty and equality. Membership was restricted to free men, so no slaves or women or foreigners had a vote. Etymologically democracy comes from the word *demos*, which means the ordinary or common people and then the lower classes, the poor. *Demokratia* was even deified as a goddess. When the assembly had voted, the phrase to express their decision was *edoxe to demo*, it has seemed right to the people. We may compare this with what is said in Acts 15:28 at the conclusion of the council in Jerusalem: "it has seemed right to the holy Spirit and to us

---

[6] Bruno Snell, *The Discovery of the Mind* (German orig. 1946; Eng. transl. Cambridge MA: Harvard U.P., 1943); William Chase Greene, *Moira: Fate, Good & Evil in Greek Thought* (Cambridge MA: Harvard U.P., 1944); Erwin Rohde, *Psyche: the Cult of Souls and Belief in Immortality among the Ancient Greeks* (German orig. 1897; Eng. transl. Chicago: Ares, 1987).

[7] M.H. Hansen, *The Athenian Democracy in the Age of Demosthenes*, in H. Hayes Scullard, N. Geoffrey, and L. Hammond (eds.), *Oxford Classical Dictionary*, Oxford: Clarendon Press, ²1991, pp. 451-454.

(*edoxen...kai hemin*)". We see that the terminology used in the New Testament for the life of the church has been influenced by the vocabulary of Athenian democracy.

The most important freedom or democratic value in Athens was called *parrhesia,* freedom of speech, the freedom to say anything in the assembly. This virtue of *parrhesia* turns out to be an important value in the New Testament too. It occurs 31 times in the New Testament, mainly in Paul, John, Hebrews and Acts.[8] The debates in the assembly in Athens were about going to war or not, approving treaties and the like. There were also smaller bodies like a council (*boule,* 11x in the NT) or a senate of elders (*gerousia,* Acts 5:21, perhaps as a translation of Sanhedrin, mentioned in the same verse). The council met at times on the Hill of Ares, the Areopagus (Acts 17:19, 22, 34). Another important term is *synedrion,* already mentioned, a loan word in rabbinic Hebrew, which occurs 22 times in the New Testament. At times there was an election by lot, called sortition, as in the choice of Matthias to replace Judas, Acts 1:15-26.

The terms of Athenian democracy were thus familiar to the authors of the New Testament. The memories of that golden age and the golden age of Israelite charismatic leadership under the judges and under the direct government of God lingered in the minds of the authors. But Athenian democracy had long been demolished by Macedonian military dictatorship and then by the Roman principate.

Among the philosophers, democracy early acquired a bad reputation as little other than demagogy or mob rule. Plato had a negative view of democracy, and Aristotle had a classical analysis of

---

[8] *TDNT* 5, pp. 871-886 (Heinrich Schlier); S.B. Marrow, "*Parrhesia* and the New Testament," *CBQ* 44 (1982) 431-446. The Vulgate had a difficult time translating this word with a uniform equivalent. It offers: *fiducia, confidentia, constantia, audenter, manifeste, palam.* These terms do not quite catch the nuance of boldness combined with freedom of speech. The passage in Acts 4:23-31 shows the disciples praying for boldness.

the three main forms of government: monarchy, aristocracy and democracy. Aristotle favored a mixed constitution, but not democracy, as already mentioned.

Rome overran biblical Palestine by 63 B.C. Within the period of the early Church Roman government was predominantly of a military imperial type. The Romans were good at governing and legislating but they were less good in articulating their governing practice in works of theory. They tended to defer to their cultural superiors the Greek philosophers. But some think that their governing theory is eventually articulated by St. Augustine. The Roman contribution is called the *amicitia* system.[9] The Roman senatorial class regarded themselves as friends with one another and together they governed the subjects below. This loose system influenced institutions like the British House of Commons and the House of Lords and the College of Cardinals.

4. Paul

St. Paul in many ways created the vocabulary of the early church, as he travelled establishing churches. He thus contributed to the reception of the Athenian experience within the New Testament. St. Paul has made two main contributions to democratic political culture. One is the accent on equality as in egalitarian democracy, equality before the law. The other is the concept of charism, much developed by the sociologist Max Weber. Equality is made a theme in 2 Cor 8:14-15. This dense passage is part of Paul's efforts to make a collection of money to help the poor of Jerusalem (2 Cor 8:1-9:15). "I do not mean that there should be relief for others and pressure on you, but it is a question of a fair balance (*isotes,* equality) between your present abundance and their need, so that their abundance may be for

---

[9] Hannah Arendt, *Between Past and Future* (New York: Viking, 1968).

your need, in order that there may be a fair balance (*isotes*). As it is written, 'The one who had much did not have too much, and the one who had little did not have too little.'" (2 Cor 8:13-15, quoting Exod 16:18). The verse from Exodus is from a section on the fair distribution of the manna, and it inspired Karl Marx's ideals for distribution of goods and property.

Paul's second great contribution to political science is his teaching of charisms or spiritual gifts. His teaching in many parts of his letters but especially in 1 Cor 12-15 and in Rom 12:3-8 (cf. 1 Pet 4:10) speaks about an organic model of community (the body of Christ) composed of differing members, and this metaphor is then further explained as various *charismata* or talents for community service. The organic model is dangerous, because it does not respect that each individual person is a center of consciousness and not simply a finger or a hand or a cell. But the further explanation of the charisms protects the image from totalitarian abuse by underlining our personal diversity.[10] Paul's ecclesiology is received into the telling of the story of Jesus by St. Matthew, after Paul's death.

5. Matthew

Matthew is unique among the four gospels in mentioning the word "church" (*ekklesia)* as the term for the community that emerges from Jesus' ministry. The others do not mention it at all (Mark) or only in their second volume (Luke's Acts and John's letters). The structure of the church in Matthew does not translate directly to a political structure for civil society but it offers some analogies for application to civil society. Jesus first convenes a circle of 12 disciples called apostles (Matt 10:1-42) to whom he gives authority to heal (10:1); he also gives them further instructions on how to lead and to be financed,

---

[10] Max Weber, *Politics as Vocation* (Philadelphia: Fortress, 1972).

in this chapter. In chap. 16, Jesus attributes special authority to Peter, authority to bind and loose. God will back Peter up. This Petrine ministry represents a central embodiment of authority for the time when Jesus is no longer with the disciples. Matthew never mentions the papacy or Rome, but later this passage (Matt 16:17-19) became associated with the bishop of Rome where Peter was said to have been martyred, with relics to concretize the authority. But this passage is not rightly understood if it is not balanced with the next mention of church in Matthew (18:1-35, esp. vv. 1 and vv. 17-20) where the disciples form a group with decision-making authority to discipline wayward members and where they receive divine backing like Peter (v. 18), but the power of the keys is not mentioned. Mt 18:19-20 suggest the kind of meeting that resembles a church synod or council to which the divine presence is promised.

Summarizing Matthew's contribution, we may say that he proposes a balanced structure that includes both central authority and representative government. In church history, this has translated into papal and conciliar forms of government and decision-making. As the church spread and flourished, the papacy entered into conflict with the emperor of the West, later called the Holy Roman emperor or his apostolic majesty. Transposed to the civil sphere, this could amount to a central executive branch and a congressional or parliamentary branch. (In Matthew, the judicial is included in the parliamentary synod, 18:15-17). When Matthew's balanced structure is respected, it can contribute to the education of people to a constitutional, partly democratic form of government.

6. Luke-Acts

Although Luke is not as clear-cut as Matthew in ecclesiology, he certainly emphasizes apostolic authority in his Acts of the Apostles. Matthias is chosen by lot (sortition) to replace the traitor Judas. Seven helpers are chosen to minister to the Hellenists (deacons?).

Peter is highly respected, as we sense in his arrival in Caesarea to receive Cornelius. In the course of the book, Stephen and Paul become stars. Above all, there is the council in Jerusalem in chapter 15. After hearing reports from the mission field, and speeches proposing different approaches to the question of circumcision, a decision is reached and a letter is sent out, said to be approved by the Holy Spirit and the assembled leaders. This event served as a model for future councils and synods both regional and ecumenical. The book of Acts concludes with the arrival of Paul in Rome where he preaches the kingdom of God in the imperial capital. Rome's later primacy is based on its claim to possess the relics of the two great apostles, Peter and Paul.

7. The Contribution of the Dominican Constitutions and Thomistic Theology

The long winding road from the empire and the church to today's parliamentary democracies in the West cannot be traced here. We want to mention two Dominican contributions. The Christian West first had to digest the barbarian invasions and evangelize them. Then it had to work out the right relationship between the church and the Christian empire (the investiture controversy). To do this required the help of two great saints: Francis and Dominic. Francis revived the life of intense piety based on the gospels. Dominic supported this but helped with a constitutional framework and with a commitment to study. The path to the modern parliament passes through the mother of parliaments, the British parliament. Where did this model come from? One may give various answers. I will provide one from the Middle Ages promoted by the expert in classical political theory, Sir Ernest Barker. He wrote an early work entitled *The Dominican Constitutions and Convocation* (Oxford: Clarendon, 1913). His thesis was that the Dominicans came to England around 1220 with their original constitutions, which included direct elections of the prior by all the members of the priory and elections of the provincial by delegates from the priories to a provincial chapter every three years. At this time, there was a remarkable churchman named Stephen Langton (1150-1228), a master of theology in Paris and well known in Rome. He may have met the Dominicans as they were getting started on the Continent. He studied their legislation. Then in 1207 he became archbishop of Canterbury. He organized an annual meeting of the bishops of the church in England, modeled on the provincial chapters of the Dominicans. Soon there was a crisis between the king and the barons. This was settled by the document called Magna Carta fixing their rights and duties. Its first draft was in 1215 but it was frequently modified in later years. The rights of the commoners came next. With the two houses, of Lords and of the Commons, the English parliament was born. With some interruptions, this system continues to this day. For Sir Ernest Barker this system derives in part from the Dominican constitutions.[11]

In later British history there were conflicts between the Commons and the king that led to civil war and the beheading of King Charles the First (1649). In 1688, due to further tension between king and parliament, the king, James II, was driven into exile, parliament became supreme, and a new dynasty was imported to save the Protestant character of the government. This was called the Glorious Revolution of 1688; it was bloodless. To justify this event after it had happened, the philosopher John Locke wrote his *Second Essay on Civil*

---

[11] M.D. Knowles, *From Pachomius to Ignatius* (Oxford: Clarendon: 1966) surveys all the different monastic legislation up to the Jesuits, and finds the Dominican constitution the most thoroughly democratic. J.T. McNeill, in his *History and Character of Calvinism* (New York: Harper, 1954) tells how the first synod of the Reformed Church of France adopted the Dominican constitutions for the governing of their church. The Reformed tradition influenced the growth of democracy in many other countries.

Government (1690). This same essay was used a century later by the American revolutionaries to justify their revolution against George III (1776-1781), before it had happened.

The second Dominican contribution I would like to mention comes from Thomas Aquinas. When we look at Locke's system of government, we see that it was based on classical philosophy, parts of the Bible, and a standard work of Anglican theology and church government, called the *Laws of Ecclesiastical Polity* (1597), written by Richard Hooker. Hooker's work contained long quotations out of Thomas Aquinas: on popular sovereignty, natural law, equality and power sharing (see especially his *Summa theologiae* 1-2, q. 97, art. 1). These ideas then influenced Locke and the American Founding Fathers.

In the 19th Century, after the Order had been suppressed in France, it was revived by a gifted lawyer and great cathedral preacher-priest, Henri-Dominique Lacordaire. Lacordaire saw that the Order had hurt its reputation through its connection with the Inquisition. He overcame this obstacle by rediscovering the legislative genius of St. Dominic and emphasizing this liberal democratic element in the heritage, even though the Austrian chancellor Metternich was opposed.[12] Metternich saw clearly the danger posed by Lacordaire's revival of democratic government in the Order.

These Thomistic and thus Catholic roots of Locke and American democracy were carefully worked out over a long time by an American Jesuit, Fr. John Courtney Murray (1904-1967). His studies culminated in his major work: *We Hold These Truths* (1960). This work merited him a place on the cover of *Time* magazine and many invitations to dine with important politicians in Washington, D.C.

---

[12] B.T. Viviano, "The Church in the Modern World and the French Dominicans," *Freiburger Zeitschrift für Philosophie und Theologie* 50 (2003) 512-521.

His Jesuit brethren jokingly teased him. They said his middle name was not Courtney but Courthouse. His articles on religious pluralism and freedom of conscience in religious matters began in the early 1940s. The American government invited him to help draft plans for the United Nations charter and for postwar German reconstruction. The plans included the church tax going to the bishops (not to the parishes as in Switzerland). Murray's articles came to the attention of the Holy Office (Ottaviani) in Rome.[13] This led to attacks on his work beginning in 1944. The Roman censors told him to stop writing on church-state relations. Murray needed protection. This came from a fine example of Dominican-Jesuit collaboration, Archbishop John Timothy McNicholas O.P. of Cincinnati (1877-1950).

Murray's thinking became quite original and bold. He claimed that the Anglo-Saxon West had developed a fuller truth about human dignity that included religious freedom and the separation of church and state. Citizens must assume control over their beliefs and reject paternalistic states. Murray also took seriously the political effects of widespread elementary, secondary and higher education in enabling citizens to participate prudently in democratic decision-making. He even claimed that these were new dictates of natural law that provided new moral truth. In 1954 Cardinal Ottaviani told him to stop writing on these topics.

When Pope Pius XII died and Pope John XXIII convoked the Council, Murray felt it was safe to publish his synthesis and he became an expert at the Council (1962-1965). He claimed that these freedoms were an intention of nature. He helped to draft the conciliar document on religious liberty, *Dignitatis Humanae* (1965). This document was bitterly opposed by bishops from countries that were

---

[13] Ottaviani was interested in the topic because he had written on it in his own dissertation, and was professionally involved in dealings with governments.

still under fascist regimes, like Spain, Portugal and Argentina. Though the document was voted and approved by the Council, much of the natural law argumentation had been cut from the text before the vote. Murray was not satisfied but he did what he could to help the document be accepted and developed.

The Roman magisterium had not gone on record in favor of democracy clearly before the Council. Pope Leo XIII tried to move in a new direction but he was blocked by the curia mostly. Of his 86 encyclicals, several deal with various aspects of the matter. *Diuturnum* (1881) treats the origin of civil power. *Libertas Praestantissimum* (1888) deals with the nature of human liberty. *Graves de Communi Re* (1901) struggles with Christian democracy and allows the use of the term, but not the political reality. After the fall of Stalingrad (February, 1943) the Vatican knew that Hitler would not win the war. So in his Christmas radio allocution in late December 1944, Pope Pius XII conceded that under present day conditions democracy was the most normal form of government. Most bishops at the Council wanted a positive statement on democracy. Their desire was well met, in the Pastoral Constitution *Gaudium et Spes*, paragraph 75, although the opponents succeeded in getting the key word democracy deleted from the text before the final vote. Still the paragraph is excellent and should be better known.

Before Murray there were others who tried to work on a Christian theology democracy. I mention the Sicilian priest Don Luigi Sturzo, the creator of the Popular Party in Italy after the First World War. With the rise of Mussolini, he had to put his plans on hold. After the fall of Mussolini Pope Pius XII called him back to create the Christian Democratic Party that went on to govern Italy until the fall of Communism in Eastern Europe (1989).[14] Jacques Maritain, the lay

---

[14] M.P. Fogarty, *Christian Democracy in Western Europe, 1820-1953* (Notre Dame, IN: University of Notre Dame Press, 1957). Among the disciples of Don Luigi

convert philosopher, wrote several books of political philosophy, including *Man and the State*[15] and *Integral Humanism*.[16] His works has an influence particularly in Latin America.

Nowadays there is a discussion of a religious foundation for the European Union. When I speak on these topics in Europe, the audience mentions the following name: an American, now British, professor, Sir Larry Alan Siedentop CBE, has two books in which he tries to argue for the Christian roots of the European Union. They are: *Inventing the Individual: The Origins of Western Liberalism*[17] and *Democracy in Europe*.[18] He especially values the psychological perceptions of Paul (e.g., Romans 7) and Augustine, and the contributions of Alexis de Tocqueville. Although these works by Siedentop are not decisive, they argue along the same lines I have been pursuing, to show the religious and biblical roots of our societies.

8. Conclusion

We have completed a brief survey of material on a vast subject. The intention has been to provide some encouragement for further research, and to shed some light on our heritage at this time of an unusual electoral season. Neither the Old nor the New Testament provides an exclusively democratic model for the church or society, but there are abundant building blocks that can be used analogically for such a model, as we have tried to show. Neither church nor state requires an exclusively democratic model. The goal should rather be

---

were Alcide de Gasperis, Konrad Adenauer, Jean Monnet Robert Schuman and the other creators of what has come to be called the European Union.

[15] J. Maritain, *Man and the State* (Chicago: University of Chicago, 1951).

[16] J. Maritain, *Integral Humanism* (London: Geoffrey Bles, 1939), sometimes published as *True Humanism*.

[17] (London: Allen Lane, 2014).

[18] (London: Allen Lane, 2001).

a predominantly democratic polity, to enable the "ownership" of decisions, and as a check to abuse or tyranny.

The Power of Preaching Through Music
James V. Marchionda, OP

When I joined the Dominican Order over forty years ago, I never dreamed that I would spend these past eighteen years as a full-time itinerant preacher who was at the same time a music minister and composer. Through presenting diocesan and national workshops on liturgy and music and by preaching choir retreats and musical days of reflection, I have learned that music combined with the word of God is one of the surest, strongest and most fulfilling methods of preaching. Music is important for preaching today.

While attending a large music and liturgy convention early in my career, I experienced rather dramatically that music not only supports preaching but can even become the preaching. After a noted liturgist's keynote presentation, I joined the four thousand conventioneers in exiting the arena. In the midst of this hurrying crowd a tall gentleman approached and beckoned me to the side, indicating that he wanted to tell me something. The music director of a large major city parish choir, he was familiar with my setting of Psalm 139, *Draw Me to You*, with the refrain, "My God, be near me; search me and know me; save me and guide me; draw me to you." As he described teaching this piece to his choir his eyes welled with tears: he then shared his past history of deep depression and agonizing hopelessness that brought him to the brink of suicide. With tears streaming down his face at this point, he stated gently, "*Draw Me to You* saved my life!"

This experience enlightened me: music carried the psalm beyond composition and certainly beyond the initial modest intentions of the composer. The music, touched by God's Word, spoke to a broken man's heart and soul and, in his words, saved his life. Aristotle wrote: "Certain people are affected by religious melodies, and when they come under the influence of melodies which fill the soul with religious excitement they are calmed and restored as if they had undergone a medical treatment and purging."[1] This man's testimony challenged me to insure that my compositions became preachings. Music not only heightens texts; music is more powerful than words alone. With the direct support of music, God's graceful word bolstered the man's spirit. Music brought scripture and human suffering together.

1. Music in Support of Preaching

Liturgical music helps Scripture speak more effectively and helps an assembly express its faith. Songs within the liturgy present an opportunity to support the Word of God, to be connected to the scriptures and to the heart of the homily. In ideal situations, homilists and musicians have an opportunity to prepare together for weekend liturgies through mutual sharing of the Word and their own insights. Together, they can read, embrace and struggle with the meaning of the sacred texts. Then, weighing musical options, they can choose music that best reflects every moment of the liturgy, thereby availing the assembly of God's Word, spoken or sung, over and over again.

Biblical readings for the Advent season present the prophet Isaiah's depiction of the Reign of God on earth. Advent songs help to reflect Isaiah's vision in different ways. I often muse over what it might be like to include three or four different settings of the same scriptural text within the same Eucharistic celebration. An energetic processional, Proclaim the Joyful Message, can set the tone: "Soon the mountain of God will be holy, all war and destruction will cease. The earth will be filled with the wisdom of the coming Prince of Peace." At the preparation of gifts, a gentler setting of Isaiah reinforces the same theme: "From Advent to Christmas we pray for the world that

---

[1] Aristotle, cited in a compilation by Alan J. Hommerding and Diana Kodner: *A Sourcebook about Music*, (Chicago: LTP, Liturgy Training Publications, 1997) 76.

warring may cease and peace be restored. The scriptures demand it, oh, let them be heard. From Advent to Christmas, we cling to God's word." Finally, The Isaiah Song, a rousing recessional, dismisses the assembly with the commission: "They shall beat their swords into ploughshares and their spears into pruning hooks. Nation shall not lift up sword against nation. Neither shall they learn war anymore." Employing different song settings of the same text within the same liturgy is a dynamic way of using music in support of preaching.

2. Music Sometimes Saves Preaching

Good preaching is a challenge. Today's congregations are increasingly filled with well-educated women and men and with young people with forthright questions. How do preachers win and hold the attention of a broad spectrum of people with their ready access to large amounts of information through the internet and their cell phones? A public speaker realizes that connecting with the audience is of paramount importance. If the message is to be received, a preacher must first engage people at the human level. This is the challenge of liturgy in every word spoken and in every song sung.

On a recent visit to a large American city, I attended the Saturday evening vigil Mass at the cathedral. It was a grey and rainy wintry day. I gave the preacher my full attention but was soon bored. The preacher never once looked the assembly in the eye, neither at the beginning nor end of his homily. He stared at his notes, reading word-for-word in a monotonously monotone fashion. The fifteen minutes he spoke seemed like an eternity. In search of personal relief, I paid closer attention to the songs chosen for the Mass. Whoever had planned music for the liturgy was clearly tuned-in to the vocational theme of the weekend and chose beautiful, contemporary texts and music that closely reflected both the challenges and joys of following in the footsteps of Jesus. By the dismissal, my spirit was rekindled by music that refreshed my own vocation. Music restored a preaching that the preacher seemed unable to achieve. Music sometimes saves preaching.

3. Music to the Rescue

Since the first U.S. invasion of Iraq in 1993, I have attempted to include nonviolence in my preaching whenever called for by the Scriptures. This is not an easy thing to do. In his essay, "We Just Don't Get It," Robert F. Keeler states: "We still fail to apprehend one crucial element of the message of Jesus: nonviolence...We do not speak out unequivocally against violence, as the first generation of Christians did. Rather, we accept state-sponsored violence as the inevitable way of the world."[2] Even mentioning Catholic teaching on the Just War Theory (whether or not one still holds this to be valid criteria for today's wars) triggers negative reaction from no small number of Catholics: they question if a preacher should take a stance on war. Once, during a parish mission, I was preaching non-violence on a Gospel text that clearly touched on war and peace. A dozen people rose in the middle of the homily and marched out in protest. I was stunned. That drama certainly caught my attention and challenged my ability to stay on point. It is not easy for preachers who preach peace.

On another occasion, while shaking hands and greeting people on their way out of church, a gentleman waited till the end of the line to approach me, then ranted angrily about my homily. "I was forced to listen to you for fifteen minutes; now you're just going to stand there and listen to me!" At the same parish two years later the same man appeared before me, this time, with a woman on his arm. While shaking hands I recognized him and asked: "Aren't you the man who chewed my head off two years ago?" He replied in the affirmative:

---

[2] Cited in Mary Hembrow Snyder's edited Essays: *Spiritual Questions for the Twenty-First Century*, (Maryknoll, NY: Orbis Books, 2001) 96.

"Yes, and I still disagree with you. But, I have to admit, I can't stop thinking about what you preached." It was one of those moments when I realized the positive gain of remaining faithful to the gospel in preaching even if it necessarily angers some listeners.

Music can sometimes be more successful than words in preaching nonviolent themes. Several of my compositions offer nonviolent teachings direct from the scriptures. In *When Will We Learn?* – also taken from the prophet Isaiah – verse one sings: "When will we learn the meaning of the words, 'They shall beat their swords into ploughshares; and all their spears into pruning hooks; nor shall they train for war?'" A later verse employs Matthew's Jesus to ask: "When will we seek the truth behind the words: 'Go and learn the meaning of mercy?'" To that text I added, "More than our gifts, more than spoken prayer, God is revered by our love!" When I sing controversial ideas, some people seem more receptive and more passionately moved by the music than by the words. Hildegard of Bingen wrote: "A music performance softens hard hearts, leads in the atmosphere of reconciliation, and summons the Holy Spirit."[3] Texts set to music challenge the emotions as well as the minds of believers.

4. Music Within the Homily

An assembly comes alive whenever I leave the pulpit, walk into their midst, and engage them in a song that reflects the theme of the scriptures. At first, people appear surprised, but soon nod in approval. An old gospel song, *Changed My Name*, is useful for challenging all present to model our lives after the life of Jesus. I teach the people a simple three-note phrase, *"Changed my name,"* which they repeat every time I sing it throughout the verse: "I told Jesus it would be alright if he changed my name…**changed my name!**"

---

[3] Hildegard of Bingen, cited in *A Sourcebook about Music* 77.

The music is strong and engaging. Now I can preach on Baptism, Eucharist, Penance, or on what it means to be named "Christian." To support my point, I create original verses to highlight today's issues: "Jesus told me I would have to work for justice if he changed my name...**changed my name!**" Or, "Jesus told me I would have to be more peaceful if he changed my name...**changed my name!**"

This incorporates music into the homily and it brings the people right into the preaching. Because of the music, they may hum or sing the tune after Mass and remember the preaching.

5. Conclusion: Sermon and Song

Preachers like to think that members of the weekly liturgical assembly remember a good portion of their preaching. In fact, for whatever reason, sometimes they can hardly remember the main point. However, when a song reflects the theme of the preaching and speaks to the heart and soul, a person may continue to recall the tune long after the liturgy. Through this simple human act of recalling a tune, the Word of God will have another chance to impact human life. Quoting Brother Roger of Taize, "Nothing is more conducive to a communion with the living God than a meditative common prayer with, as its high point, singing that never ends and that continues in the silence of one's heart when one is alone again."[4] Music serves, supports, reinforces, even becomes, preaching. Music helps the texts themselves speak. It unveils dimensions of faith and of interior longing for God that words alone cannot yield.

---

[4] Songs *and Prayers from Taize*, published in the U.S. by GIA Publications, Inc. Cited in *A Sourcebook about Music,* 65.

Contributors

Charles W. Dahm, O.P., served in different ministries in Bolivia from 1965 to 1970. While obtaining a PhD in political science from the University of Wisconsin in Madison, he co-founded in 1974 a Catholic peace and justice center, 8th Day Center for Justice. In 1986 he became pastor of St. Pius V parish in Chicago's Mexican immigrant community where he served for 21 years. He now is the Director of the Archdiocese of Chicago Domestic Violence Outreach. He is the author of two books, *Power and Authority in the Catholic Church: Cardinal Cody in Chicago* and *Parish Ministry in a Hispanic Community*.

Jay Harrington, O.P., is Professor of New Testament and Associate Academic Dean at Aquinas Institute of Theology in St. Louis, Missouri. Author of *The Lukan Passion Narrative: The Markan Material in Luke 22,54-23,25: A Historical Survey: 1891-1997* and co-author of *The Gospel of Luke: A Cumulative Bibliography 1973-1988*, he currently serves as Regent of Studies for the Province of St. Albert the Great.

James Marchionda, O.P., is Prior Provincial of the Chicago Province of St. Albert the Great U.S.A. He remains a part-time preacher after 24 years of full-time preaching retreats and parish missions throughout the United States. He is an accomplished musician and composer whose music is published through World Library Publications, Inc, Franklin Park, Illinois and Alliance Publications, Sinsinawa, Wisconsin.

Thomas Franklin O'Meara, O.P., is a priest of the Dominican Order. He taught at Aquinas Institute of Theology (Dubuque, Iowa; now at St. Louis, MO) and then at the University of Notre Dame from 1981 to 2004. A past president of the Catholic Theological Society of America, he has written a number of books among which are *Theology of Ministry*; *Thomas Aquinas, Theologian*; *God in the World (An Introduction to Karl Rahner)*; and, *Vast Universe. Extraterrestrials and Christian Revelation.*

The late **Paul Philibert, O.P.**, served as a lecturer, professor or an administrator at several schools including Providence College; the Catholic University of America in Washington, D.C.; and Dominican School of Theology and Philosophy in Berkeley, Calif. Father Philibert served as director of the Institute for Church Life at the University of Notre Dame in South Bend, Indiana. He authored books on religious life, priestly spirituality, and the arts in worship. Further, he translated works by Marie-Dominique Chenu, O.P. (*Aquinas and His Role in Theology*), and Yves Congar, O.P. (*At the Heart of Liturgical Worship: Liturgical Essays of Yves Congar*, and *True and False Reform in the Church*). He was the third provincial of the Dominicans' Province of St. Martin de Porres (Southern). He became senior fellow at Aquinas Institute of Theology in St. Louis in 2015. He died in St. Louis on April 14, 2016.

Scott Steinkerchner, O.P., is a writer and author of two books, including *Beyond Agreement: Interreligious Dialogue amid Persistent Differences*. He also develops websites and is the editor of the online daily preaching site "The Word" (http://word.op.org). He lives in Madison, Wisconsin.

Contributors

Benedict Thomas Viviano, O.P., from St Louis, Missouri (born 1940) served as professor of New Testament and rabbinics at Aquinas Institute of Theology, the Ecole Biblique in Jerusalem, and at the University of Fribourg in Switzerland. He currently resides in Vienna, Austria. He is the author of a commentary on Matthew, *The Kingdom of God in History*, *Study as Worship*, *Trinity-Kingdom-Church*, *Matthew and His World*, *Catholic Hermeneutics Today*, *What are they saying about Q?*, and *A Short History of New Testament Studies*.

Mark E. Wedig, O.P., a Dominican friar of the Province of Martin de Porres, is Associate Dean for Graduate Studies, Professor of Theology, and chair of the Department of Theology and Philosophy in the College of Arts and Sciences at Barry University. His scholarship focuses on the intersection of culture studies, liturgical studies, and the hermeneutics of religious art. He has published in *Worship*, *Liturgical Ministry*, *Pastoral Liturgy*, *Rite*, *New Theology Review*, *Journal of Hispanic/Latino Theology*, *Chicago Studies*, and *US Catholic Historian* and recently contributed a chapter to *Transcending Architecture: Contemporary Views on Sacred Space* (The Catholic University of America Press, 2015).

Richard Woods, O.P., is Professor of Theology at Dominican University, River Forest, Illinois. Previously, he taught both undergraduate and graduate students over a 40-year career in the U.S. and England. In 2010 he was awarded the Lund-Gill Chair at Dominican University. A trustee of the Eckhart Society, he also serves as editorial advisor for Medieval Mystical Theology. He has authored 14 books and over 100 articles, mainly on theology, mysticism, and spirituality. His most recent book is *The Spirituality of the Celtic Saints*, New Priory Press (2015).

Acronyms and Abbreviations

AFL-CIO	American Federation of Labor - Congress of Industrial Organizations
AIFLD	American Institute for Free Labor Development
CBQ	Catholic Biblical Quarterly
CEBS	Comunidades Eclesiales de Base
CETRA	Centra de Estudios del Trabajo
CIA	Central Intelligence Agency
CIPCA	Centro de lnvestigación y Promoción de Campesinad
ECLA	Economic Council for Latin America
EETS	Early English Text Society
FRUC	Frente Universitario Revolunario Católico
IBC	International Bible Commentary
IBEAS	Instituto Boliviano de Estudio y Acción Social
IOC	Young Christian Workers
ISAL	Church and Society in Latin America
ISET	Institute for Theological Studies
ITQ	Irish Theological Quarterly
JEC	Juventud Estudiantil Catolica
JUC	Juventud Universitara Católica
MNR	Movimiento Nacional Revolucionario
NABRE	New American Bible (Revised Edition)
OASI	Oficina de Asistencia Social de la Iglesia
OCSHA	Hispanic-American Priestly Cooperation
RcatT	Revista catalana de teologia
RSPT	Revue des sciences philosophiques et théologiques
SPCK	Society for Promoting Christian Knowledge
SUNY	State University of New York
TDNT	Theological Dictionary of the New Testament
UNIAPAC	International Christian Union of the Business Executives
UNITAS	Unión Nacional de Instituciones para el Trabajo de Accion Sócial
USAID	United States Agency for International Development
USCCB	United States Conference of Catholic Bishops

Index

• Reference located in footnotes
* Reference located in bibliography

Neh 8, 173
Neh 8:2, 173
Lk 2:49, 162
Lk-Acts, xv, 171, 176, 178, 179, 180
Matthew, xv, 171, 178, 179, 191, 195
Mt 10:1-42, 178
Mt 16:17-19, 179
Mt 16:3, 91
Mt 18:1-35, 179
Mt 18:15-17, 179
Mt 18:19-20, 179
Mt 21, 159, 170
Acts 1:15-26, 176
Acts 4:23-31, 176
Acts 5:21, 176
Acts 15:28, 175
Acts 17:19, 22, 34, 15, 176
Rom 7, 185
Rom 12:3-8, 178
1 Cor 12-15, 178
2 Cor 8:1-9:15, 177
2 Cor 8:13-15, 178
2 Cor 8:14-15, 177
1 Thess 5:12, 173
1 Pet 4:10, 178

A School of Theology: Le Saulchoir, 76, 76•, 77-81, 81•, 82, 83, 83•, 85•, 89, 101•
Academie de la Grande Chaumière, 97
Action Française, 95
active intellect, 162
AIFLD, 137, 196
Alain de Libera, 6, 6•, 21•
Albert of Lauingen (the Great), St., xii, xvi, 1-14 passim, 15, 16, 16•, 17, 17•, 18, 20, 20•, 21, 21•, 22, 33, 36*, 41, 43•, 51•, 53, 54, 54•, 55, 55•, 70*, 71*
Albertism, 2
Albertus-Magnus-Institut, xii, 1•, 2, 2•, 4•, 6•
Allende, Salvador, 127
Altiplano, 119, 133
Alves, Rubem, 118
amicitia system, 177
anatman, 149
Angelus Silesius, 34
Antibes, 107
Anzulewicz, Henryk, 1, 2, 7, 9
Apostolic Nuncio, 116, 122
Aquinas Institute of Theology, 94, 193-195
Aquinas, St. Thomas, xii, 4, 4•, 5, 6•, 9, 9•, 17, 17•, 21, 22•, 29, 36*, 43•, 60•-62•, 67*, 70*, 77, 78, 78•, 81, 82, 85, 87-89, 124, 125, 171, 182, 194
Aristotle, xii, 4, 6, 6•, 7, 9, 9•, 78, 80, 174, 174•, 176, 177, 187, 188•
Arndt, Johann, 33
Assy, 15, 105•, 106, 108
Atelier de L'Art Sacré, 97, 97•
Audincourt, 104, 108, 108•, 109
Augustine of Hippo, St., 6, 19, 22•, 57•, 61•, 64*, 69*, 177, 185
Augustine of Dacia (of Denmark), xiii, 39-73 passim
Avicenna, 6, 6•
Avignon, 17, 18, 23
Barker, Sir Ernest, 174•, 180, 181
Bazaine, Jean, 103, 108, 109
Benedict XVI, Pope, 41, 48, 56, 56•, 57•, 62•, 65*, 70*
Bernedo, O.P., Vicente, 114

Berthold of Moosberg, 20
Besançon, 108, 110
Bishop, O.P., Jordan, 122-124, 127•, 128, 143
Blake, O.P., Vincent, 141
bodhicitta vow, 148
Boehme, Jacob, 34, 34•
Bolivia, xiv, 113-143 passim, 193
Bolivian Church, 114, 122, 133
Bonaventure, St., 22•, 49•
Book of Spiritual Poverty, 32
Boyle, O.P., Leonard, 39•, 50•, 51, 51•, 52•, 65*
Braque, Georges, 106
British House of Commons, 177
Buddha, 148, 148•, 149-151, 153, 158, 159, 163-170
buddha-nature, xv, 146, 147, 149, 153, 155-159, 162, 164, 168-170
Buddhism, 146-148, 148•, 152, 155, 165, 168, 169
  Mahayana, 148, 148•, 150, 166, 169, 170*
  Theravadan, 148•, 150, 166, 169
Buddhist scriptures, 153, 154, 165
Bulletin thomiste, 80•, 82
Burke, O.P., Jim, 119, 199•, 121, 122, 130•, 131•, 135, 136
Byrne, O.P., Damian, 20
Calacoto, 115, 122
Cappadocian Fathers, 16
Cardijn, Fr. Joseph, 116
Carroll, O.P., Br. Kevin, 119•, 122, 127•, 129, 130
Cassian, John, 39
Castro, Emilio, 118
Catholic Action, xiv, 116, 120, 124, 125, 126•, 138, 140, 141
CEBS, 117, 196
Center for Latin American Studies at the University of Pittsburgh, 134

Centro de Investigación y Promoción de Campesinad, 142, 196
CETRA, 120, 134, 136, 196
Chagall, Marc, 106
Changed My Name, 191, 192
charism, xi, 90, 139, 177, 178
charismatic
  approach, 138, 139•, 140, 141
  center, 138
  Masses, 139
  movement, 137, 138, 143
  prayer group, 137
  renewal, xiv, 130, 137-140, 143
Charles the First, 181
Chenu, O.P., Marie-Dominique, xiii, xiv, 74-94 passim, 101, 101•, 118, 194
choir retreats, 187
Chrétienté, 92, 93, 93•, 94•
Christian Democratic Party, 125, 184
Christian Family Movement, 120, 134
Church and Society in Latin America, 118, 196
CIA, 127, 135, 137
CIPCA, 142, 196
Clancy, O.P., Patrick, 115-116
Clark, James, 21•, 24•, 28•, 29•, 31, 31•-33•, 36*
Cleary, O.P., Edward, 119, 119•, 121, 122, 132, 134, 135, 138
Clock of Wisdom, 24
Cochabamba, 114, 115, 120-128, 128•, 129, 129•, 130, 132-134, 137-142
Colegio San Andres, 122
College of Cardinals, 177
Cologne, 2, 4, 9-11, 14•, 15, 18, 20, 21•, 23, 25, 51•, 54
Communists, 114
Comorapa, 115
Compendiosum breviarium theologiae, 45
Comunidades Eclesiales de Base, 117, 196

INDEX

Congar, O.P., Yves, xiii, 6•, 79•, 80, 82, 82•, 84, 87•, 90•, 93•, 95•, 99, 101, 101•, 118, 194
conquistadores, 114
Constance, 22, 23
Constantinus Africanus, 7
Constitution on the Church in the Modern World, 92
conventional truth, 149
Cordovani, Mariano, 81
Corpus Areopagiticum, 16
Couturier, Marie-Alain, xiv, 96-105, 99•-105•, 106, 107-111, 107•-111•, 112
Cristianesimo nella storia, xiii, 75•, 85
Cursillos de Cristiandad, 116, 120, 134
Dahm, O.P., Charles W., xiv, 113, 121, 125, 126, 131•, 132, 134, 135, 137, 143, 193
Dalmais, O.P., Irenée, 80
Dante, 1, 1•
Danube, 3
Das Buch Von Geistlicher Armut, 32
Davy, O.P., Thomas, 120, 120•, 121, 132, 134, 135
De bono, 7, 13•
De Lubac, Henri, 39•, 42•, 47•, 49, 49•, 50, 50•, 61•, 62•, 66*, 73*, 118
De Menil, Dominique, 99, 100, 100•
De Menil, John, 99, 100, 100•
De Santa Ana, Julio, 118
De Tocqueville, Alexis, 185
democracy, xv, 171, 173, 174, 176, 181•, 182, 184
   Athenian, xv, 171, 175, 175•, 176, 177
   Christian, xv, 125, 184
   egalitarian, 172, 177
   in Europe, xv, 185
   theology of, xv, 171
Denifle, Heinrich, 22•, 24, 32, 32•
Denis, Maurice, 96, 97, 97•
Denmark, xiii, 39•, 40, 43, 43•, 48, 57, 59, 63•, 68*

Der cherubinischer Wändersmann, 34
Desvailliéres, George, 96
Devémy, Canon, 106
DeWasseige, O.P., Eric, 141
Dietrich of Colmar, 31
Dietrich of Freiburg, 17, 20, 21
Dignitatis Humanae, 183
Dionysius the Areopagite, xii, 15, 16, 16•, 17, 17•, 21•
Diuturnum, 184
doctor universalis, xii, 1, 5, 6•, 12
Dolpopa, xiv, xv, 145-147, 155-159, 162-165, 167-169
Dominic, St., xi, xii•, xv, 10, 28, 49, 50•, 71*, 90, 106, 182
Dominican(s), xi, xiii-xvi, 3, 6, 10, 14, 14•, 17, 19, 20, 22, 22•, 23, 25, 33, 35, 37*, 39, 40•, 41•, 42, 44, 45, 45•, 46, 46•, 51, 54, 76•, 77, 78, 80, 84, 95, 97-100, 101•, 104, 112, 114-116, 118-124, 126•, 127, 128, 128•, 129-139, 139•, 140-143, 145, 168, 180-183, 194
   Bolivian, 115, 122, 128•
   brothers, 30, 120
   chapter, 23, 43
   chronicle, 18
   communities, 49, 51•, 55, 114, 128, 130, 131, 135
   constitutions, xv, 171, 180, 181, 181•
   convent, 29, 43•
   education, 39, 39•, 50, 70*
   French, 62, 95, 96, 98, 101, 120, 182
   friars, xi, xiv, 10, 40•, 48, 63, 109, 111, 115, 159, 166, 195
   German, 4, 114, 115, 115•, 116
   Initiatives, 113, 137
   Italian, 114, 115, 115•, 129
   laity/lay, 19, 23, 97•
   monastery, 30
   mystics, 23, 27
   novice, 4
   nuns, 18, 23, 26-28, 31, 43•, 106

Order, xi, 18, 19, 21•, 28, 36*, 50•, 52, 65*, 77, 78, 95, 96, 101, 171, 187, 194
priory, 4, 25, 41, 50, 64, 111
provincial, 64
school of theology, 76
sisters, 99, 129, 130
studium (house of studies), 4, 77, 81
women, 27, 29
donné révélé, 77, 89
Draw Me to You (Ps 139), 187
Dubarle brothers, 80
Ebner, Margaret, 25, 29, 3096, 30•, 31, 35*
Ebnerin, Christina, 31
Eckhart, xi-xv, 4, 4•, 15-38 passim, 145-147, 159, 159•, 160-169, 170*
Eckhart Society, 195
ECLA, 117, 196
École biblique, 40•, 55, 80, 80•, 195
École du Louvre, 96
Economic Council for Latin America, 117, 196
ekklesia, 175, 178
Elkins Park, 99
Engelbert, Abp. of Strassburg, 17, 20
England, 15, 31, 180, 181, 195
Episcopal Conference, 123
Erfurt, 17, 18, 22•
Erlandsen, Jacob, Abp., 44
Étienne Tempier, Bishop, 5
Evagrius of Pontus, 16
Éveux, 110-111
Exemplar. The Life of the Servant, 23•, 24, 24•, 36*-38*
Ex 16:18, 178
Ex 24:3-7, 172
Féret, H.M., 101, 101•
Fitzmyer, S.J, Joseph, 41•, 49•, 57, 57•, 58, 58•, 59, 60, 67*
five aggregates, 149, 150
fixed soul, 149

Fleming, Mrs. Ursula, 19
flying missions, 119
Focillon, Henri, 96
Four Noble Truths, 150
France, xiv, 5, 15, 18, 61•, 71*, 77, 90, 95, 96, 99, 102, 107, 108, 110, 111, 123, 181•, 182
Francis, Pope, 88, 88•, 94
Francis, St., 90, 180
Franck, Sebastian, 33
Frankenstein, Baron Victor, 1
Freiburg im Breisgau, 4, 58•, 67*
French Resistance, 98
Frente Universitario Revolunario Católico, 125, 196
Friend of God from the Oberland, 32
Friends of God, xii, 23, 25-27, 28•, 30-32, 35, 36*
FRUC, 125, 196
Galen, 7
Galilea, Segundo, 118
Garbha, 153
Gardeil, O.P., Ambroise, 77, 89
Garrigou-Lagrange, O.P., Reginald, 78, 79, 79•
Gaudium et Spes, 85, 91, 184
General Pinochet, 127
George III, King, 182
Gera, Lucio, 118
Geraets, O.P., Nicholas, 131, 132, 137, 138
German Teutonic Province, 115
Gilson, Etienne, 80
Glipping, Eric, King, 44
Glorious Revolution, 181
Grace, W.R., 131, 131•
Graves de Communi Re, 184
Great Decision, 9
Griego, O.P., Bro. Carlos, 129-130, 140
Groote, Gerard, 31, 32
Grosseteste, Robert, 16
Guevara, Che, 126

INDEX

Gutiérrez, Gustavo, 118
Guy of Bourogogne, 43
Gy, O.P., Pierre-Marie, 80
gzhan-stong, 146, 147, 155, 157-159, 169, 169
Hanson, Paul, 173, 173•
Harrington, O.P., Jay, xiii, xvi, 39, 193
Hartung, O.P., Martin, 132
Hebrew Bible, xv, 171, 172, 124
Heinrich of Nördlingen, 25, 27, 29, 30
Heinrich Suso, see Seuse, 22, 22•-24•, 29, 36*-38*
Heinrich Von Berg, Count, 22
Henry of Halle, 20
Hildesheim, 4, 51•
Hinnebusch, O.P., William, 21•, 22•, 24•, 28•, 31•, 36*
Hippocrates, 7
Holacheck, O.P., Terence, 121, 122, 128
Holy Office, 78, 83, 91, 183
Hooker, Richard, 182
Horologium Sapientiae, 24
Houlihan, O.P., Peter, 116, 119•, 121, 129•
Hugh of St. Victor, 16, 49•
Hughes, O.P., Edward, 115
Humani Generis, 83, 84
Humbert of Romans, 10, 11
IBEAS, 128-135, 135•, 136-138, 196
impressionism, 97
indemnification, 136
Inquisition, 182
Institute for Theological Studies, 123, 196
Instituto Boliviano de Estudio y Acción Social, 130, 196
Integral Humanism, 118, 185, 185•
Inventing the Individual: The Origins of Western Liberalism, 185
investiture controversy, 180
ISAL, 118, 196
ISET, 123, 196

isotes, 177, 178
Italy, 10, 15, 28, 62•, 65*, 122, 184
Jakobsen, Johnny Grandjean Gøgsig, 42, 43•, 44, 44•, 45•, 50•, 68*
James, Letter of, 174
Jensen, Kurt Villads, 43•, 44, 44•, 45, 45•, 68*
John of Tomback, 31
John Paul II, Pope, 20, 30
John XXIII, Pope, 84, 93•, 183
JUC, 124, 125, 127, 196
Just War Theory, 190
Justice and Peace Commission in Bolivia, 141, 142
Juventud Estudiantil Catolic (JEC), 129, 196
Juventud Universitara Católica, 124, 196
Kalamazoo, Michigan, 3, 38*
karma, 149
karmic wind, 158
Keeler, Robert F., 190
Kitchell, Jr., Kenneth F., 2, 2•
kitsch, 97, 98, 98•
Knowles, M. D., 181•
Konrad von Hochstaden, Abp., 9
Korngin, Gerard, 21, 31
Korngin, Johann, 21, 31
L'Art Sacré, xiv, 95-112 passim
La Mansión, 128, 138
La Pascana retreat house, 125
La Paz, 114-116, 119, 120, 122, 124•, 128-130, 132, 134, 135, 137, 138, 142
La Tourette, 111
Lacordaire, O.P., Henri-Dominique, 77, 90, 182
Lagrange, O.P., Marie-Joseph, 55, 55•, 78, 80, 81
Langton, Stephen, 47•, 181
Latin American Bishops Conference, 118
Laws of Ecclesiastical Polity, 182

Le Corbusier, 109-111, 109•-111•
Le Saulchoir, 76, 76•, 77-80, 81•, 82, 82•, 83, 85•, 89, 101•
Ledeur, Canon, 108
Léger, Fernand, 106, 109
Lehu, O.P. Leonard, 78
Leo XIII, Pope, 184
Les Éditions du Cerf, xiv, 95, 95•, 96, 99•, 100, 101, 112
Liberation Theology, 117
Libertas Praestantissimum, 184
Liégé, O.P., Pierre-André, 80, 123
Locke, John, 181, 182
Lotus Sutra, 150, 151, 166, 167, 169, 170, 170*
Ludwig IX of Bavaria, 9
Maastricht, 23
Macedonian military dictatorship, 176
Madagascar, xiii, 84
Magister Theologiae, 4
Magna Carta, 181
Maguy, O.P., Hyacinth, 121•, 122
Man and the State, 185, 185•
Mandonnet, O.P., Pierre, 52•, 78, 81
Marchionda, O.P., James, xv, 187, 193
Maria Medingen, 30
Maritain, Jacques, 97•, 99, 118, 184, 185•
Maritain, Raïssa, 99
Marquart of Lindau, 31
Marr, O.P., John, 122
Marx, Karl, 178
Maryknoll Fathers, 133
Maryknoll Sisters, 141
Masons, 114
Matisse, Henri, 106-108
māyā, 152, 153
McCormick, O.P., Bro. Simon, 121•, 132
McNabb, Vincent, xi
McNicholas O.P., Abp, John Timothy, 183
McNutt, Francis, 137

Medellin, 118
Meincke, Jens Peter, 5, 5•
Melloni, Alberto, 84, 84•
Mercurian, S.J., Everard, 26
Merlino, O.P., Francisco, 115•, 120, 121, 135
Mettepenningen, Jürgen, 83, 84•
Metternich, 182
Middle Ages, xi, 1, 1•, 6•, 15, 24, 28•, 36*, 39, 41•, 48, 60•-63•, 65*-70*, 78, 80, 93, 180
Míguez Bonino, José, 118
military coup in 1964, 113, 136
Mill, John Stuart, 172
Miró, Joan, 103
MNR, 113, 196
modern Catholicism, 101, 102
Montesquieu, 171
Montevideo, 120
Montpellier, 22, 52
Mosheh ben Maimon, Rabbi, 6
Mounier, Emmanuel, 118
Movimiento Nacional Revolucionario, 113, 196
Mueller, O.P., Matthias, 122, 124, 127•, 128, 141
Mulchahey, M., 39•, 45•, 46, 46•, 49•, 50•, 51, 51•, 52, 52•, 70*
Murphy, O. Carm., Roland, 59, 60•, 61•, 70*
Murray, S.J., John Courtney, 182-184
music and liturgy convention, 187
musical days of reflection, 187
Myasthenia gravis, 111
Mystical Theology, 15, 16, 17•, 22, 34, 195
National Conference of Religious, Bolivia, 121
National Seminary of San Jose, 122-123
Neoplatonic, 16, 16•, 22, 33
neo-Platonists, 6, 21•

Index

Netherlands, 15, 31, 32
Neu, O.P., Bro. Reginald, 130, 140
New Christendom, xiv, 75, 93, 118
New Pentecost, 139
Newman Center, 116
Nice, 107
Nicholas of Basel, 32
Nicholas of Lyra, 49, 49•, 56, 60•-64•
Nicholas of Strassburg, 18, 31
Nicholas von Kues (Cusa), Cardinal, 32-33
nirvana, 166, 169, 170
non-figurative abstraction, 97
Nordic-Dominican Province of Dacia, 42, 43•
Norway, 43
Notre-Dame-du-Haut, 110
Novarina, Maurice, 106
Nueva Cristiandad, 118
O'Meara, O.P., Thomas Franklin, xii, 1, 2•, 11•, 101•, 194
OASI, 142, 196
OCSHA, 123, 196
Oficina de Asistencia Social de la Iglesia, 142, 196
Opera Omnia, 2, 16•
Opus Tripartitum, 33
Order of Preachers, xi, xii, xv, 3, 28, 43, 52, 54, 70*, 77, 78•, 97•, 145•, 170*
Origen, 57
Oruro, 114, 120, 127, 127•, 128-131, 134
Osiek, RSCJ, Carolyn, 59, 60, 60•, 70*
Ottaviani, Cardinal, 183, 183•
Ottawa, 81
Ozment, Steven, 27, 33, 33•, 34•, 38*
pahuichi, 138, 139
Papal Curia, 9, 101
Paraday, O.P., Mark, 127•, 129, 138, 140
parrhesia, 176, 176•
Pastoral Commission on Youth and Vocations, 140
Paul, St., 15, 49, 87, 177

Pentateuch, 172
Perez, OFM, Lorenzo, 124
peritus, xiii, 53, 84
Peruvian Dominican Province, 114
Peter, St., 179, 180
Philibert, O.P., Paul, xiii, 75, 194
Picasso, 108
Pichard, Joseph, 95, 96, 96•, 97
Pius XII, Pope, 83, 183, 184
Plateau d'Assy, 104
Plato, 21•, 176
Pontifical Biblical Commission, 40, 40•, 57
Popper, Karl, 172
Populorum Progressio, 130
Potosi, 114
pre-Conciliar Church, 118, 119
Primitive Constitutions, xi, 52, 53, 53•, 70*
Proclaim the Joyful Message, 188
Protestants, 114, 118
Province of St. Albert the Great, xi, xiv, 115, 193
Province of Turin, 115
Pseudo-Dionysius, xii, 14•, 16, 16•, 21•
psychological counseling, 140
Quint, Josef, 21•
Ramfot, O.P., Paul, 120
rang-stong, 146, 147, 149, 155-159, 164, 169
Ratzinger, Cardinal Joseph, 20, 49•, 56, 56•, 708
Rayssiguier, L.B., 106
Rearden, O.P., Pat, 119, 119•, 122, 127, 129, 138, 140
Redmond, O.P., Kieran, 119, 119•, 122, 128
Régamey O.P., Pie-Raymond, XIV, 96, 97, 98•, 103, 105, 112
Regensburg, 4, 6•, 10-12, 51•
renovación, 138
Resnick, Irven M., 2, 2•

Revisión de Vida, 116, 125
Rhineland, xiii, 15, 22•, 27-30, 33-35, 36*
Richier, Germaine, 106
Rio Abajo, 115
Ripelin, Hugo, 17
Risley, O.P., Jack, 123, 124•, 129, 133, 138, 141, 143
Roach, O.P., Daniel, 131, 132, 138
Rogowski, O.P., Ralph, 119•, 122, 132, 134, 139•
Roger of Taize, Bro, 192
Roman Curia, 75, 101
Roman principate, 176
Ronchamp, 109, 110, 110•, 111•
Rotulus pugillaris, 39•, 41, 45, 45•, 46, 48•, 50, 51, 56, 64, 69*, 72*
Rouault, Georges, 108
Rouen, 84
RSPT, 80•, 82, 196
Rudolf von Hapsburg, 9
Sablica, O.P., Luke, 121•, 127•, 130
Sainte Marie del La Tourette, 111
Samaipata, 115
samskaras, 149
Santa Cruz, 115, 119•, 120, 121, 127, 127•, 128-131, 138, 139, 139•, 140-142
Sarracenus, John, 16
Saxonia, 28
Scheffler, Johannes, 34, 34•
Schema XIII, 85
Schillebeeckx, O.P. Edward, 80, 80•, 172
Schlumberger, Ltd., 99
School of Paris, 97, 98, 104, 112
Schultes, O.P., Reginald, 79
Schwesternbücher, 28
Scottus, John, 16
Second Essay on Civil Government, 181-182
Segundo, Juan Luis, 118
Semaines Sociales, 83
Seton Hospital, 140

Seuse (Suso), Heinrich, 17, 22, 22•, 23, 24, 24•, 25-27, 29-31, 35
shalom, 173
Shanley, O.P., Thomas, 121•, 132
Shelley, Mary, 1
Shrine of St. Jude in Chicago, 136
Siddhartha Gautama, 148•, 150
Siedentop CBE, Sir Larry Alan, 185
Siger of Brabant, 21, 21•
Siles Salinas, Dr. Luis Adolfo, 141
Sinsinawa, Wisconsin, 130, 193
Sist, O.P., Arthur, 121•, 141, 142
skandhas, 149, 152
Society of Biblical Literature, 59, 60•, 70*
Söder, Joachim, 1•, 8, 8•
Soisy-sur-Seine, 76
Sorbonne, 80, 96
Spain, 15, 28, 113, 116, 184
S. Thomas et la théologie, 81, 84
St. Martin De Porres Center, 125, 129, 139, 140
Stagel, Elsbet, 23, 24, 24•, 29, 30•, 37*, 38*
Stations of the Cross, 107
Steinkerchner, O.P., Scott, xiv, 145, 194
Strasbourg, 23•, 28, 38*
Strassburg, 4, 10, 18, 23, 25, 31
Sturzo, Don Luigi, 184
Sucre, 114, 115, 115•, 122
Sudermann, Daniel, 33
Sullivan, O.P. Timothy, 121•, 122, 124, 125, 127•
Summa theologiae, 29, 47• 182
Sweden, 43, 43•
Switzerland, 15, 23, 25, 28, 30, 40•, 126•, 172, 183, 195
synedrion, 176
Tambach, 17, 17•
Tarija, 114
tathagatagarbha, 148, 149, 153, 156, 159, 167, 169

INDEX

Tauler, Johannes, 17, 23-26, 26•, 27, 27•, 29, 30-33, 35, 37*, 38*
Teilhard de Chardin, Pierre, 118
Teutonia, 28
Teutonic Knights, 32
The Catechism of the Catholic Church, 55, 55•, 56, 66*
The Cherubic Wanderer, 34, 34•
The Divine Names, 15, 16
The Dominican Constitutions and Convocation, 180
The Interpretation of Scripture: In Defense of the Historical-Critical Method, 57, 57•, 67*
The Interpretation of the Bible in the Church, 40, 40•, 41•, 49•, 56•, 57, 58, 58•, 63•, 67*, 72*
The Little Book of Eternal Wisdom, 23, 24, 24•
The Little Book of Truth, 23, 24•
The Temple of Souls, 33
Third Reich, 98
Thomas Aquinas, St., (see Aquinas, Thomas), xii, 4, 4•, 5, 6•, 9, 9•, 17, 17•, 21, 22•, 29, 36*, 43•, 60•-62•, 67*, 70*, 77, 78, 80-82, 85, 87-89, 124, 125, 171, 182, 194
Tibetan Buddhists, xv, 145, 149
Time magazine, 182
Tridentine, 123
Trinidad, 120, 134
Troelsgård, Christian, 45•, 47•, 48, 71*
Tsongkhapa, xiv, 145-147, 149, 150•, 152, 152•, 153, 155-157, 159, 163, 165, 169, 170*
tulku, 165
Ulrich of Strassburg, 1
ultimate truth, 149, 158, 168
ultramontane spirit, 77
Une école de théologie, 76•, 77•, 81•, 87•, 88, 89•, 91, 91•, 92•
UNIAPAC, 120, 134, 196

UNITAS-Bolivia, 142, 196
Université Catholique in Lille, 123
University Center of St. Thomas Aquinas, 124
University of Fribourg, 20, 20•, 36*, 40•, 195
University of Padua, 3
University of Paris, 4, 18, 21•
University of San Andres, 116, 124, 134
Urban IV, Pope, 12
USAID,130, 196
Uzin, O.P., Oscar, 121, 123, 123•, 132, 135
V. De Wilde, O.P., V., 43•, 44•, 66*
Vaccari, Alberto, 53, 54, 54•, 55, 55•, 57•, 71*
Van Leeuwen, Jan, 32
Van Noenen, O.P., Athanasius, 115, 116, 119•
Van Ruusbroec, Jan, 31, 32
Vatican Council II, xiii, xiv, 53, 75, 76, 84, 84•, 85, 91, 93, 117-120, 133
Vence, 104, 106, 107, 107•, 108
ViaReque, O.P., Alfonso, 121, 128•, 138
Viviano, O.P., Benedict, xv, 171, 182•, 195
Walz, O.P., Angelus, 39•, 42•, 43•, 44, 44•-46•, 48•, 50•, 51•, 54•, 55•, 57•, 61•, 72*
We Hold These Truths, 182
Weber, Max, 177, 178•
Wedig, O.P., Mark E., xiv 95, 95•, 195
Weigel, Valentin, 33
Weisheipl, O.P., James A., 1•, 49, 50•, 72*
wheel of dharma, 150, 152, 155
When Will We Learn?, 191
Wilhelm of Holland, 9
Williamson, Peter, 40•, 57, 58, 72*
Woods, O.P., Richard, xii, 15, 19•, 22•, 37*, 38*, 195
Worker-Priest, 83, 90, 99-101, 141

Wrinn, O.P., Bro. Timothy, 124, 132, 139•
Yahweh, 173
Young Christian Workers, 83, 196
Zelaya, O.P., Eduardo, 121

www.ingramcontent.com/pod-product-compliance
Lightning Source LLC
Chambersburg PA
CBHW060823050426
42453CB00008B/559